THE DEVIL AND MR. CASEMENT

THE DEVIL AND
MR. CASEMENT

One Man's Battle for

Human Rights

in South America's

Heart of Darkness

JORDAN GOODMAN

Farrar, Straus and Giroux / New York

FARRAR, STRAUS AND GIROUX
18 West 18th Street, New York 10011

Library of Congress Cataloging-in-Publication Data
Goodman, Jordan.
  The devil and Mr. Casement : one man's battle for human rights in South
America's heart of darkness / Jordan Goodman.— 1st American ed.
      p.   cm.
  Includes bibliographical references and index.
  ISBN 978-0-374-13840-0 (hardcover)
  1. Putumayo River Valley—Race relations—History—20th century.
2. Casement, Roger, Sir, 1864–1916.   3. Human rights—Putumayo River
Valley—History—20th century.   4. Indians of South America—Violence against—
Putumayo River Valley—History—20th century.   5. Rubber industry workers—
Putumayo River Valley—History—20th century.   6. Atrocities—Putumayo River
Valley—History—20th century.   7. Peruvian Amazon Company—History.
8. Imperialism—Social aspects—Putumayo River Valley—History—
20th century.   9. Consuls—Great Britain—Biography.   10. Irish—Great
Britain—Biography.   I. Title.

F3451.P94G66 2010
305.898'9—dc22

                                                            2009029528

Designed by Abby Kagan

Map designed by Martin Lubikowski

www.fsgbooks.com

1   3   5   7   9   10   8   6   4   2

FOR DANNY AND BEN

CONTENTS

CONTENTS

PART III

PART IV

PART V

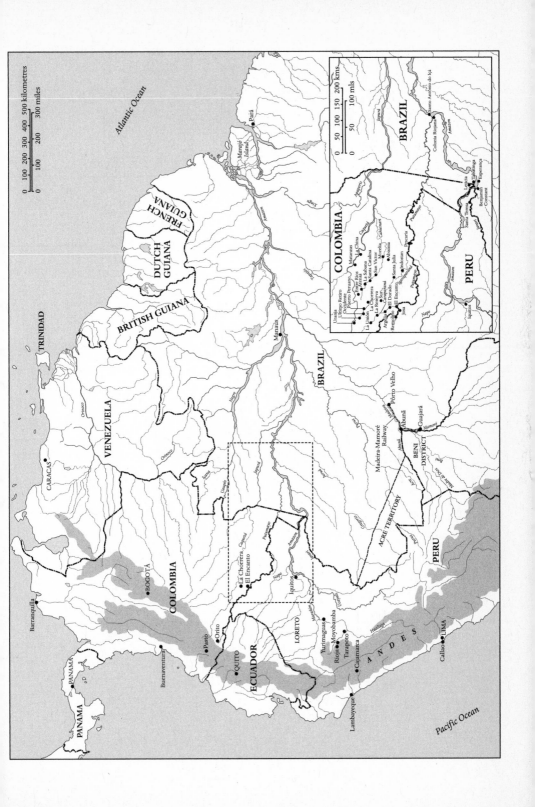

THE DEVIL AND MR. CASEMENT

INTRODUCTION

LA SELVA COMES TO LONDON

Wednesday, September 29, 1909, was a dull and rainy day in London. In the House of Commons the questioning was about to take the members of Parliament to a different and much warmer place.

Thomas Hart-Davies, the Conservative MP for the constituency of North Hackney, rose to his feet. He asked the secretary of state for foreign affairs "whether his attention has been called to the proceedings of an English company called the Peruvian Amazon Company; whether any report as to the alleged ill-treatment of British subjects from Barbados has been made by the English Consul at Iquitos; and whether he will call for a report on the doings of this company from the local English Consul at Iquitos?"

No sooner had he settled himself back on the bench than the right honorable member for Orkney and Shetland, John Cathcart Wason, a Liberal, chimed in. He asked the foreign secretary whether "his attention has been directed to the charges made against the Peruvian Amazon Rubber Company, Salisbury House, E.C.; if he has been urged by the British directors of the said company or by any of the British shareholders to inquire of His Majesty's Peruvian consul with reference to the same; and if he has acceded to their request, if any?"

The foreign secretary, Sir Edward Grey, was not in the House to answer these parliamentary questions, so the undersecretary of state for foreign affairs, Thomas McKinnon Wood, replied on his behalf. "I had not heard of the existence of the company, and have no information about it. I will ask for a report." And then followed a short exchange between McKinnon Wood and the two questioners.

MR. HART-DAVIES: Is the hon. Gentleman aware that the American Consul has already made a report to his Government on this company, and whether he can see his way to get hold of that report?

MR. MCKINNON WOOD: I was not aware of that.

MR. CATHCART WASON: Do I understand the hon. Gentleman to say that he has not received a request as to this company to inquire into the allegations?

MR. MCKINNON WOOD: That is so.

MR. CATHCART WASON: May I ask whether full publicity will be given in our dependencies in this part as to the proceedings of the inquiry?

MR. MCKINNON WOOD: I think the first step will be to obtain the report for which I have promised to ask.

What was the Peruvian Amazon Company? Where did it operate? What were Barbadians (British subjects) doing working for it? Who was ill-treating them? Why did the Americans know more about this story than did the Foreign Office?

And why these questions now?

The Foreign Office had been caught off guard by the parliamentary questions. There was really no excuse for its ignorance. When Hart-Davies alerted the Foreign Office that he was putting down a question for the parliamentary session of September 29, he enclosed in his letter a copy of the previous week's issue of a magazine called *Truth*, which contained a major article about a British rubber company, the Peruvian Amazon Company, against whom allegations were being made of unthinkable cruelty to its workforce. The article explained everything.

How the Foreign Office had missed the story is hard to explain. *Truth* was a popular and widely read muckraking magazine—its circulation often exceeded twenty thousand copies—and it scooped this story. Now in its thirty-third year, this weekly had been founded by Henry Du Pre Labouchere, heir to a banking fortune and long-standing radical Liberal MP for Northampton. Even though in his later years he handed over editorial responsibility to others, his influence remained intact: he presided over the magazine for more than thirty years, until his death in 1912. With a cover depicting a female representation of Truth holding the lamp of knowledge in her right hand and a mirror in her left, the magazine had a chatty style, providing its readers with a diet of society gossip, entertainment reviews, political commentary, and exposés of financial scandal. "People bought *Truth* with a desire to see who was 'going to get it next,' who or what institutions would be marked down for exposure," said Joseph Hatton, a well-known journalist and contemporary of Labouchere's. "City men who were shaky trembled, snobs who were chary of their supposed dignity opened the paper with nervous fingers."

Sidney Paternoster, the magazine's leading investigative journalist and assistant editor, did not disappoint his readers in the issue of September 22, for it was not just shaky City men and anxious snobs, but the whole nation that was shocked that day. A word that had become a symbol of the evil of contemporary capitalism had returned to haunt the British public. *Truth*'s readers must have blenched when they saw Paternoster's deliberately provocative headline: THE DEVIL'S PARADISE: A BRITISH-OWNED CONGO.

Only a year had passed since the country had congratulated itself on bringing to an end one of the modern world's worst atrocities, in which brutal labor regimes had spilled the blood of millions of indigenous Congolese people in a frenzy to collect as much rubber as they could for the hungry factories in Europe and the United States. And now that dreaded word "Congo" was back again.

In 1885, as a result of the Berlin Conference, at which the European powers negotiated their way to carving up Africa for themselves in the so-called Scramble for Africa, Leopold II, king of Belgium, had taken control of a large chunk of western Equatorial Africa, about the size of western Europe, and declared it as his private property. Though the wealth of the Congo Free State, as the territory was named, was at first based on ivory, by the end of the nineteenth century, rubber had become the economy's main earner and contributed significantly to world output.

During the 1890s, the first unconfirmed reports started to reach England about the atrocities being perpetrated in King Leopold's Congo Free State. The rubber regime, rumors had it, was based on a quota system, and those who did not meet their targets were systematically abused, maimed, and killed by a specialized terrorist militia, the Force Publique.

When these reports reached the Foreign Office, it was not prepared to do much more than monitor the situation. The alternative—to revisit the entire Berlin Act of 1885—was politically dangerous: it would put the partition of Africa back on the political agenda, a step that was not in the interest of any of the colonial powers.

But when these reports came to the attention of Henry Fox Bourne, the secretary of the Aborigines' Protection Society, which had been established in the 1830s in London as a pressure group to ensure the humane treatment of indigenous people throughout the world, he demanded that the Foreign Office use its influence to do something to stop the atrocities.

It was an uphill struggle. The government was loath to get involved and argued that the reports on the situation in the Congo Free State were based on unconfirmed rumors and that to the best of its knowledge, everyone there was content. Fox Bourne, however, did not accept the government's reassurance and took his concerns to the British public. It took six years of campaigning, but he managed to get a parliamentary debate on the issue, when he and his young and very committed journalist friend, Edmund Morel, provided the Liberal MP Herbert Samuel with a raft of statistics and testimonies in preparation for his opening question. The ensuing debate, in May 1903, drew support from a small group of MPs who had been similarly briefed by Fox Bourne and Morel. The politicians accused Leopold's administration not only of barbarism but also of the enslavement of the indigenous people. The House was so moved by the evidence put forth that a resolution was passed that day stating that the government of the Congo Free State had violated the guarantees—that it treat its people with humanity and that no trading monopoly should be allowed within its boundaries—it had made at the end of the Berlin Conference, which had brought this state into existence. The British government, the resolution concluded, should confer with the other colonial powers to force the Congo Free State to end its evil system.

But what were the facts of Leopold's system? So far, no one had actually been to the Upper Congo, the site of the alleged atrocities. The Foreign Office agreed to investigate the allegations of cruelty and instructed its consul in the Congo Free State, the highly experienced thirty-nine-year-old Roger Casement, to gather impartial information.

Casement was Irish by birth, the son of a devout Catholic mother and a Protestant father. The youngest of four children, he was baptized twice: once, at age one, as a Protestant, then again at age four as a Catholic. Family life was typically unsettled. The father, invalided out of the army as a captain on half pay, moved his family incessantly in search of the health that eluded him. At various times the Casements were in France, Italy, England, and St. Helier, Jersey. Then, in 1873, when Casement was nine years old, tragedy descended on the family. His mother died in childbirth, and four years later his father died, too.

Over the next few years Casement spent time near Ballymena, in what is now Northern Ireland, where his uncle owned a farm, and in Liverpool. There, in 1880, at age sixteen, after completing a standard classical education, Casement landed himself a position as a clerk in the shipping line of Elder Dempster and Company, the city's chief agents for West African shipping. Office work was, however, not to his taste, and though he stuck at it for a few years, he was always looking for a way out. His chance came in 1883, when he was posted as a purser on an Elder Dempster ship bound for the port of Boma, near the mouth of the Congo River.

Returning from that trip, Casement signed on again for two more voyages, and in 1884, with Africa firmly taking hold of him, he decided to remain working mostly in the Congo on various projects. In 1892 his life took a dramatic change when he came to the attention of the Foreign Office, which offered him a clerical post in the town of Old Calabar on the Gulf of Guinea, in what is now Nigeria. Three years later, in recognition of his skills, Casement got his first diplomatic posting, as British consul in Lourenço Marques, in Portuguese East Africa (now Moputo, the capital of Mozambique).

Casement was thirty years old and had spent a third of his life in Africa. He now found himself in a career that suited him well. The posting to Lourenço Marques lasted for five years. In October 1900 he learned that his services were now required in the Congo, on which he had become something of an expert. His new consular post, based in Léopoldville (now Kinshasa), gave him responsibility over a vast part of Equatorial Africa, including the French Congo and the Congo Free State.

En route to take up his new consular post, Casement passed through Brussels, where he had an audience with King Leopold. The two met at an afternoon meal with Leopold's family, but there was little opportunity to talk business. Leopold asked Casement to return the next day, and on that occasion the two men discussed the Congo, with Leopold doing most of the talking. Conditions in the Congo were not as good as they might be, Leopold admitted, but this was owing to a bad choice of personnel and the tropical climate. The ideals of his administration remained intact, and he intended to pursue those lofty motives. Casement was not convinced.

On June 4, 1903, after more than two and a half years as consul for the Congo region, Casement got a wire from London, telling him to get to the interior as soon as possible to gather "authentic information" about the alleged atrocities. For the next three months he traveled more than a thousand miles on the Congo River and its many tributaries, gathering information on the rubber regime. The rumors were not exaggerated. Leopold's system was brutal. In a rubber station called Bongandangu, Casement came face-to-face with the object of his investigation. "Saw Rubber 'market,'" he noted in his diary, "nothing but guns—about twenty armed men— . . . most with cap guns. The people 242 men with rubber all guarded like convicts. To call this 'trade' is the height of lying."

Casement had single-handedly created the impartial on-the-spot investigation, what he termed a "Criminal Investigation Department." Determined to avoid relying on the state for assistance, he instead used others who knew the area well and had access to transport: missionaries, mostly associated with the American Baptist Missionary

8

Union, who provided him with launches, contacts, translators, and places to stay where he could interview victims of the outrages. In a letter he wrote to the American journalist Poultney Bigelow, Casement described his investigative methods:

> There are two ways of seeing the interior of the Congo State—either blindfolded or looking for the facts . . . I chose to look for the facts. I said: he who goes to a foreign country to see the people of it and form a just conclusion of their mode of life does not confine his investigations to museums, picture galleries and public buildings, or to the barracks and reviews of soldiers or State conducted enterprises: he goes also into the villages of the people, he speaks with the peasant and the shopkeeper and enters sometimes the dwellings of the very poor . . .

Casement's findings, documented in his constant flow of dispatches back to London, appalled and angered him. The rubber-collecting system, the cornerstone of the Congo's wealth and administration, was based on coercion, violence, and cruel punishment. Collection quotas were enforced by the Force Publique, the official armed force. Those not meeting targets were beaten, flogged, shot, imprisoned, or mutilated, most commonly by having their hands cut off. Sentries ensured that villagers did not escape; women and children were kept as hostages to guarantee compliance from the men. And in the midst of all this, villages were being decimated, crops were going to ruin, and disease was rife. The system headed inexorably toward its own self-destruction, taking the indigenous people with it.

On October 20, a month or so after returning from his journey into the hell of the Upper Congo, Casement received a wire from the Foreign Office ordering him to return to London and to prepare his report. He left the Congo as soon as he could and arrived back in London on December 1, 1903. Ten days later a draft of his report, a large-scale analysis of the systematic abuse of human rights, was ready.

In February of the following year, the British government published Casement's damning description of Leopold's rubber system. Three million Congolese, he estimated, had died for rubber. This chilling report made headlines throughout the world and resulted in demands for Leopold's regime to be brought to an end. In Britain, the press did its part, as did the public meetings of the Congo Reform Association (the organization Casement helped found in 1904 to drum up support for action) in town halls up and down the country, to make the public aware of what was commonly referred to as King Leopold's reign of terror in the Congo Free State.

The disturbing history of Leopold's rubber regime had thus become widely known. For the next four years Leopold's Congo was seldom out of the news. *The Times* alone ran a "Congo" story on average every three or four days. Though readers were often spared the goriest details, they were nevertheless bombarded by graphic descriptions of one of the Force Publique's signature atrocities—the cutting off of hands and feet. In 1908, after relentless campaigns, Leopold finally caved in to public and governmental pressure and sold his property to the Belgian state.

Casement had become an international humanitarian hero and a household name. However, within him at this time began the split between his loyalty to the British government, by which he was employed and in which he still had faith, and his identification with the victims of colonialism. The more oppression and exploitation of native people he saw in the Congo, and then in the Amazon, the greater his sense of belonging to a people—the Irish—oppressed and exploited by another, the British. Even if one has a sense of this inner journey, it is hard to understand the swiftness of his public fall from humanitarian hero in 1908 to being hanged for treason in 1916. How could this have happened? Is the Putumayo the key?

As *Truth*'s readers studied Paternoster's report of the Peruvian Amazon Company, the Congo was still fresh in their minds and the parallels disturbing. There was an eerie sense of déjà vu in Paternoster's exposé, but this time it was in South America, not Africa, and it was a British company that was accused.

The company, Paternoster explained, was collecting rubber in a vast area of the Amazon Basin, where the Putumayo River, a tributary of the Amazon, flowed. The ownership of the territory of the company's operations was actually in dispute between Colombia and Peru, but the Peruvians were in effective control. Paternoster warned his readers that what they were about to learn of this company's operations made for very difficult reading. "I think it my duty," he wrote,

> to bring before the public statements which have been laid before me in regard to certain alleged atrocities in which England and Englishmen are particularly interested. They involve charges of cruelty as horrible as anything that has been reported from the Congo. They affect an English limited liability company, with English directors and English shareholders, and they have in part been made publicly without, so far as I can ascertain, any attempt at either official denial or inquiry.

The Peruvian Amazon Company, Paternoster wrote, had come into existence in the previous year, registered in London and incorporated with a capital of £1,000,000. Three of its seven directors, including its chairman, were English (Paternoster did not name them). The company's operational headquarters was in Iquitos, Peru's major Amazonian port, and all of the rubber from the forests of the Putumayo went there before being shipped down the Amazon to Europe and the United States.

Some two dozen stations, scattered over an area exceeding ten thousand square miles, with the Putumayo River as its southern boundary, organized the collection of rubber from the surrounding forest. Each station had its own manager (the chief—*jefe*), usually a Peruvian, who had a staff of salaried employees (*racionales*—who were mostly Hispanic) numbering anywhere up to twenty-five men, depending on the scale of the operations. Each station operated a quota system for its collection of rubber. The collecting was done by the Indians, mostly Huitoto people, who had to bring their quota to the station every ten days. Once the stock of rubber in the station reached the required level, it was carried by the same Indians to either El Encanto or La Chorrera, the company's main settlements in the region, whose staff included a general manager, a storekeeper, an accountant, and a medical officer. From there, the rubber was shipped by the company's steam launch to Iquitos.

Behind this apparently benign organization, Paternoster pointed out, lay a brutal system in which chiefs of rubber stations were paid on commission according to the amount of rubber they obtained from the Indians. To make his point, Paternoster provided sickening descriptions of how the Indian workers were abused, terrorized, tortured, mutilated, and murdered.

> The agents of the company force the pacific Indians of the Putumayo to work day and night at the extraction of rubber without the slightest remuneration; that they give them nothing to eat; that they rob them of their crops, their women, and their children, to satisfy the voracity, lasciviousness, and avarice of themselves and their employees, for they live on the Indians' food, keep harems of concubines, and sell these people wholesale and retail in Iquitos; that they flog them inhumanly until their bones are laid bare; that they do not give them any medical treatment, but let them linger, eaten by maggots, till they die, to serve afterwards as food for the chief's dogs; that they mutilate them, cut off their ears, fingers, arms, and legs; that they torture them by means of fire, of water, and by tying them up, crucified head down; that they burn and destroy their houses and crops; that they cut them to pieces with machetes; that they grasp children by the feet and dash out their brains against the walls and trees; that they have the old folk killed when they can work no longer; finally, that to amuse themselves, to practise shooting, or to celebrate the sábado de gloria (the Saturday following Good Friday) . . . they discharge their weapons at men, women, and children, or, in preference to this, they souse them with kerosene and set fire to them, to enjoy their desperate agony.

White people had been working in the Putumayo for only about fifteen years. When they arrived, the indigenous population was estimated to be about fifty thousand, divided into three main groups: the Andoke, the Bora, and the Huitoto, who, with a population of thirty thousand, dominated the region. Paternoster was cautious about reporting how many Indians had already given their lives to the Peruvian Amazon Company, admitting that such figures were hard to come by, but he did suggest that in the past decade or so, the population of the area had been reduced by "tens of thousands."

It is interesting that in his question to the foreign secretary, Hart-Davies referred to the alleged ill-treatment of Barbadians—British subjects—

and not to the atrocities visited upon the indigenous population, which was the subject of Paternoster's article. One may wonder where Hart-Davies got his information, for the *Truth* article did not have a word in it about Barbadians.

The most likely source was Paternoster himself. Paternoster knew that there were, or had been, Barbadians present in the Putumayo. He had also tracked down and interviewed the British consul in Iquitos, David Cazes, who was on vacation leave in London. Paternoster sought to verify the information Cazes had given him, probably through contacts at the Colonial Office in London, and concluded that the government in Barbados knew of the presence of their countrymen in the Putumayo and also knew that allegations of ill-treatment had been leveled against the Peruvian Amazon Company.

Whatever his thoughts and feelings about the suffering of the local population, Hart-Davies knew full well that no department of state had any right to interfere in the internal affairs of another country when it came to the plight of its own people; had he raised the issue of the Indians, the foreign secretary would simply have replied to this effect. But Barbadians were another matter. They were British subjects and had the right to appeal to Britain for protection. And it was the foreign secretary's responsibility to get to the bottom of the allegations.

Paternoster made no attempt to hide the fact that the story and all of the ghastly details had been previously printed in three newspapers, *La Felpa* and *La Sancion* in Iquitos, and *Jornal do Commercio* in Manaus, Brazil.

These were very obscure titles, hardly known outside of the Amazon. How did Paternoster get hold of them? How did this story ever make its way out of the Amazon and to London?

For that, Paternoster could thank a brave young American engineer named Walter Hardenburg, who had only recently arrived in London from the Amazon bearing his precious cargo of documents and the memories of his own traumatic experience at the hands of the Peruvian Amazon Company's brutal employees.

Without Hardenburg, the story of the Peruvian Amazon Company's evil empire would never have left the Amazon.

PART
ONE

1

ACROSS THE ANDES

On October 1, 1907, twenty-one-year-old Walter Hardenburg, who was working on the construction of the Colombian Pacific Railroad, and his fellow American workmate, Walter Perkins, three years his elder, set out from the construction site at Buenaventura on the Pacific coast of Colombia for the adventure of a lifetime.

Hardenburg and Perkins had been offered better positions to work on the Madeira-Mamoré Railway, an ambitious project designed to bypass the unnavigable Madeira River in the western part of the Brazilian Amazon in order to transport rubber from northern Bolivia to the Amazonian port of Manaus.

Rather than getting to the site by the normal sea and river route, Hardenburg and Perkins decided to make an adventure of their relocation by going overland across the Andes and into Amazonia. Those few Europeans who had made this journey recommended that the best way to get to the Amazon from Colombia was to travel south to Quito in Ecuador, cross the Andes there, and, once on the eastern slopes of the Andes, join the Napo River and follow its course until it met the Amazon northeast of the Peruvian town of Iquitos. Hardenburg and Perkins started to follow this recommendation, but at some point on

their way south through Colombia, for reasons that have gone unrecorded, they changed their minds and opted for the much-less-
frequented route of crossing the Andes in southern Colombia and
following the Putumayo River from its source high in the Colombian
Andes to its confluence with the Amazon more than a thousand miles
to the southeast.

It was a foolhardy and dangerous decision. The map they had with
them was large-scale and showed only the general course of the
country's main rivers, and all the advice they got should have put
them off their chosen route. In the southern Colombian town of
Pasto, the last sizable settlement in that part of the country, from
where the pair would make their final crossing of the Andes and begin
their descent into Amazonia, no one they met in their first days there
could even tell them where the Putumayo was; and the one person
they found who did know the river warned them not to go, for "if by
chance [they] escaped the cannibal Indians who inhabit its banks,
[they] would certainly fall victims to the deadly fevers which reign
there continuously." To make matters worse, Hardenburg and Perkins
also learned from General Pablo Monroy, a senior military officer
who had been there himself, that about halfway down the river's
course, where the Caraparaná, a major tributary, flowed into the Putumayo, they would be entering a kind of no-man's-land, an area whose
ownership was disputed by both Colombia and Peru. After more
than fifty years of argument and protest, General Monroy told the pair,
the two countries had recently agreed to a modus vivendi, to withdraw their garrisons and military authorities from the region to their
respective lines while negotiations about the future of the region continued. Still, the general didn't think the Peruvians were abiding by
the agreement.

But it was not all bad news, for Hardenburg and Perkins also
learned from another source that they would not need to paddle all the
way to the Amazon. About five hundred miles downriver, at a place
called El Encanto, where the Caraparaná met the Putumayo, they would
be able to catch a launch to Iquitos, from where they could continue
their journey to the railroad construction site in Brazil. It would save
them weeks of effort.

With this piece of encouragement, despite the warnings to the contrary, the intrepid pair pressed on with their decision and spent three days in Pasto buying supplies, both for themselves and to trade, that would last them two months. It was a bewildering collection of material, from hats to knives, brightly colored shirts, harmonicas, fish-hooks, and food. As Hardenburg himself put it, "When we finally got all our purchases together, we found that we had goods enough to set up a shop and our room was so crowded with them that we had hardly space enough to turn in."

Crossing the most easterly of the Andean peaks proved to be much more difficult than the whole journey until that point, and the 150 miles they traveled until they reached the first navigable point on the Putu-mayo River took them as long as it had taken them to get from Bue-naventura to Pasto. Still, they had made it so far without mishap, and on December 1, 1907, Hardenburg and Perkins, together with their provisions and now accompanied by two local boatmen, one of whom steered from the stern and the other who stood watch in the bow, set off downriver in their newly purchased canoe.

The Putumayo is navigable for most of its length—from the Colom-bian Andes until it meets the Amazon at Santo Antônio do Içá in the western part of Brazil at about three degrees south. The river has no waterfalls or rapids. It moves along placidly, meandering in long, winding curves. As the current switches from one bank to the other, the river becomes very wide in places and relatively shallow. This same action creates sand islands in the middle and on both sides. The forest teems with wildlife, both large and small—tapirs, peccaries (wild pigs), and capybaras (large rodents resembling guinea pigs) are especially nu-merous and provide excellent game—while the river is abundantly stocked with fish.

For the first few days everything went splendidly. Hardenburg and Perkins must have congratulated themselves on their decision to ven-ture onto the Putumayo River. "What a pleasant sensation it was," wrote Hardenburg, "to sit calmly in the canoe, while the swift current bore us steadily onwards, and to watch the thick, tropical vegetation, which lined the banks of the stream, swiftly recede until hidden from view by a bend of the river! How different it was from the monotonous climbing and descending of the Andes that had caused us so much toil!"

The banks of the river were alive with wild turkeys, ducks, and monkeys; flocks of parrots flew by at great speed while the forest resounded with the squeals and howls of invisible creatures. There was no shortage of fresh provisions—wild turkeys and monkeys in particular. The only problem was getting a good shot from the canoe, which wasn't easy.

But then, no more than four days into the journey downriver, the two boatmen decided that they would go no farther, and they ran away. Bad people, they warned, lived beyond.

Hardenburg and Perkins had no choice but to go it alone. So, on December 7—Perkins in the stern, perched on his high seat, and Hardenburg, eyes peeled in the bow—the two adventurers set off downriver. The next day, crossing the equator, the pair celebrated with a good stiff glass of *aguardiente*. Later the same day they stopped at a tiny settlement ("eight or ten little bamboo huts"), where the chief told them they were very brave to make the trip alone.

For the next two weeks Hardenburg and Perkins worked their way toward the Putumayo's confluence with the Caraparaná, and they experienced everything the tropics could throw at them: "suffocating heat, and not a breath of air—our thirst was astounding." They battled outbreaks of fever, ran out of fresh food, and suffered unexpected risings and fallings of river levels, which on more than one occasion left them stranded on a sandbank with nothing to do but wait for the river to rise again. They were attacked by gnats and mosquitoes whenever they weren't attempting to find shelter from bouts of torrential rain. Apart from one occasion when they ran into a band of Indians returning from a hunt, and another when they were startled by a three-man detachment of Colombian police returning to Pasto from the Caraparaná, they never saw another human being in the jungle.

On the afternoon of December 22 they spotted a house, which turned out to belong to a Colombian rubber trader, Jesús López. López alerted them to what lay ahead and told them more about the political situation.

Hardenburg and Perkins already knew, from what General Monroy had told them in Pasto, that the ownership of the area around the Caraparaná was disputed by Colombia and Peru, and that a modus vivendi was officially in place between the two countries. López warned them that the Peruvians, in clear contravention of the agreement, were harassing and violently expelling Colombian settlers. These acts, López added, were being carried out by the Peruvian military, but behind the scenes a firm calling itself the Peruvian Amazon Rubber Company was calling the shots. It was the company's intention, maintained López, to get hold of all the Colombian concessions, by whatever means possible.

Colombian rubber traders had been working their way down the Putumayo since the 1890s, and by the turn of the century they had reached the area bounded by the Igaraparaná River on the east and the Caraparaná River on the west. The farther they came downriver, the farther they found themselves from the nearest Colombian town, at the same time getting closer to Iquitos, the nearest Peruvian town, which had vastly more resources than its Colombian counterpart. At one time, there had been dozens of Colombian rubber stations in this area, but by the time Hardenburg and Perkins were on the Putumayo, only three remained, the rest having been taken over by the Peruvian Amazon Rubber Company.

López told them not to take the launch from El Encanto to Iquitos and suggested a safer, alternative route. He recommended that they aim for Remolino, five days farther down the river and the site of another Colombian post. From there they could travel overland to the Napo River farther to the south, which would take them to a point where it flowed into the Amazon just above Iquitos. There was regular traffic on the Amazon where the Napo joined it, and they would find it easy to get to Iquitos this way, which would also avoid the trouble between the Peruvian and Colombian factions on the Caraparaná.

Hardenburg and Perkins saw the sense in López's advice, and the combination of incessant rain and persistent attacks by gnats had brought to an end their initial romance with the Putumayo. At Remolino they would be able to sell their canoe, which, López promised, would be easy—Antonio Ordoñez, a Colombian who collected rubber at a place called La Unión on the Caraparaná and who used Remolino as his shipping post for Iquitos, would certainly buy it.

On December 30 Hardenburg and Perkins reached Remolino, intending to bid the Putumayo farewell and be in Iquitos shortly. But Ordoñez was away on a rubber-collecting excursion. Hardenburg left Perkins to wait with the canoe and traveled alone to La Unión, hoping to find Ordoñez. When he got there, he could not locate Ordoñez and instead pressed on to another rubber station, a place called La Reserva, where, he was told, there was another rubber trader who could help him out. This time Hardenburg was more fortunate. At La Reserva, a Colombian, David Serrano, a "short, middle-aged, coffee-coloured gentleman," agreed to help Hardenburg and Perkins by buying their canoe and any other goods they were willing to sell. Serrano sent three local guides to find Perkins and bring him and the sale goods back to La Reserva. Serrano instructed the guides to tell Perkins to make his way first to a place called Josa, Serrano's landing stage on the Putumayo near the mouth of the Caraparaná River, where he could leave the canoe and their personal baggage. The idea was a good one, for the onward route, overland to the Napo River and thence Iquitos, would pass by Josa. Luckily, Serrano needed to go to Iquitos, and he agreed to accompany the Americans to their destination. Things could not have worked out better.

While the guides were away fetching Perkins, Serrano showed Hardenburg around and also told him a harrowing story about his treatment at the hands of the Peruvian Amazon Rubber Company, which had become so powerful recently. About a month earlier, he told Hardenburg, a number of the company's employees had turned up at his place. They chained him to a tree and, before his appalled eyes, raped his wife, whom they had dragged from the house. These men then helped themselves to his stock of goods and, their business done, returned to their launch, carrying away his wife and their small son. He had not seen either since, though he had learned that his wife had been forced to be a concubine of Miguel Loayza, the manager of the Peruvian Amazon Rubber Company's station at El Encanto, and that his son was made Loayza's personal servant.

The outrage against Serrano had come to the attention of Colombian authorities, and one of them, Jesús Orjuela, the newly appointed police inspector for the region, was expected any day. Indeed, no sooner had Serrano's local guides set off to fetch Perkins than Orjuela, in company with another Colombian, arrived at Serrano's place. Orjuela expressed confidence that he could come to some agreement with the Peruvian Amazon Rubber Company, and with Miguel Loayza in particular, to make an accommodation with the Colombians in the spirit of the modus vivendi supposedly operating between the two nations.

On January 4, 1908, Perkins and the guides, carrying the sale goods, arrived at Serrano's. While Perkins dealt with the terms of the sale, Hardenburg decided to accompany Orjuela to El Dorado, another Colombian rubber station downriver, to which Loayza was to be invited for a conference concerning the future relationship between the Peruvians and the Colombians in the region.

A day later the negotiating party set off downriver for El Dorado. While Hardenburg was away, Serrano surprised Perkins by offering to sell him a "half-interest in his establishment at a very low figure—because of his fear of the Peruvians." "I accepted that offer, thinking I would be able to become friends with the authorities and that no objection could be raised. It was my intention," Perkins recalled a few months later, "to settle this matter with Serrano when we reached Iquitos. His business was in gathering wild rubber for which purpose he had about forty Indians." That business concluded, Perkins settled back to wait for Hardenburg's return.

But the peace was soon shattered. On January 12 a Peruvian gunboat, the *Iquitos*, in company with the *Liberal*, one of the Peruvian Amazon Rubber Company's steam launches, docked at La Reserva. There were hundreds of soldiers on board the boats. A party of them landed. They were looking for Serrano, but he had fled into the forest, obviously (and understandably) terrified. They ransacked the place and took away the goods in the storehouse and almost two thousand kilos of rubber. In spite of Perkins's protests, the soldiers imprisoned him on board the *Liberal*.

It transpired that Serrano's station, La Reserva, was in fact the second stop for the military operation. Previously they had stopped at La Unión, where the Peruvians had totally overwhelmed the Colombians, killing many of them. All the rubber was stolen, and La Unión itself was burned to the ground.

The gunboat and the *Liberal* continued downriver to El Encanto. Later that day, at Argelia, between La Reserva and El Dorado, the two boats intercepted the canoe carrying Orjuela and Hardenburg, who were returning to Serrano's place after a futile attempt at making peace with the Peruvians: despite several attempts to make contact with him, Loayza never turned up for the appointment in El Dorado. Orjuela and Hardenburg were promptly seized and thrown on board the *Liberal*.

Hardenburg was astonished to find Perkins already imprisoned on the boat. Perkins explained what had happened. Hardenburg now understood why Loayza had ignored invitations to talk. From Argelia, the *Liberal* and the *Iquitos* continued downriver but not before stopping at El Dorado, which was promptly destroyed.

At dusk on January 13 the *Liberal* and the *Iquitos* docked at the wharf in El Encanto. Hardenburg and Perkins were forced to spend the night on the floor of a small, unlit room. The next day, Loayza told them that they would be going to Iquitos once the *Liberal* was ready to sail. As for their baggage, still at Josa, Loayza promised to collect it and have it shipped to Iquitos.

Pretending that they were working for a large American syndicate and that any harm to them would reverberate right back to Washington, Hardenburg and Perkins managed to wrangle a concession out of Loayza. Hardenburg, it was decided, would go to Iquitos as Loayza insisted, while Perkins would remain to make sure that Loayza kept his word as far as the baggage was concerned.

On January 17, 1908, the *Liberal* was ready to go, and Orjuela and Hardenburg were escorted to the boat. Earlier that day, Hardenburg had learned that Gabriel Martínez, the Colombian *corregidor* (magistrate) for the Putumayo, had been kidnapped on December 20 farther up the Putumayo and had been a prisoner in El Encanto since then. He, too, would be going to Iquitos.

For the next fortnight the *Liberal* steamed its way toward Iquitos. After leaving El Encanto, the boat reached the mouth of the Igaraparaná, where the Peruvian Amazon Rubber Company had a number of important rubber stations, including its major settlement, La Chorrera. The boat went a short distance upriver to the shipping port of Santa Julia. There it took on firewood, turned around, and continued downriver until it met the Putumayo.

After what Hardenburg described as a tedious journey, the *Liberal* finally arrived in Iquitos on February 1. That same day, *El Oriente*, one of Iquitos's chief papers, hailed the Peruvian victory in La Unión, framing it as a fight between invading Colombians and patriotic Peruvians, with such headlines as DEFEAT AND COWARDLY FLIGHT OF THE COLOMBIANS and COURAGE AND DASH OF OUR OFFICERS AND SOLDIERS. The paper also carried a list of the boat's passengers, reserving a special paragraph for an American civil engineer, W. E. Hardenburg, who, according to the paper, "had been sent by the Colombian government to undertake studies of the area on behalf of an American syndicate."

The great adventure had turned into a harrowing experience. Hardenburg was alive, but very angry. "I hate these people and in case of a war I will return to Colombia and offer my services to you," he later wrote to Dr. Gonzalo Miranda, a Colombian official whom he and Perkins had met in Pasto. His experiences at the hands of the Peruvians preyed on his mind. Though Hardenburg himself had not witnessed any specific acts of violence against the Indians while on the Putumayo, he had seen the telltale signs of beatings and whippings, in the shape of scars on their backs—the so-called Mark of Arana.

While in the Putumayo, Hardenburg had learned that a wealthy merchant in Iquitos named Julio César Arana owned the Peruvian Amazon Rubber Company that had terrorized the Colombians and destroyed their settlements. Stumbling out of the *Liberal*'s hold and into the tropical sunshine, Hardenburg found himself in a bustling, cosmopolitan Amazonian town whose lifeblood was fed by the rubber trees that grew in the vast surrounding jungle. Soon he would be facing Arana himself.

2

IQUITOS AND RUBBER

quitos was Peru's major Amazonian settlement, but it was isolated, apart from a telegraphic link, from Lima, the capital, and the rest of the country. When asked what he knew about the town, Lucien Jerome, the British chargé d'affaires in Lima, simply stated, "[It] is in another world and [London] is nearer by mail than we are. Letters take three months and some to get to Lima from Iquitos!" Travel between Iquitos and Lima was done by ship—down the Amazon to its mouth on the Atlantic at Pará and then either catching a ship around the bottom of South America and up its western coast or across the Caribbean to the Isthmus of Panama, crossing by train and proceeding down the western coast of South America by ship. It took months. The land route, which involved crossing the Andes, was ferociously difficult, at least as difficult as Hardenburg's and Perkins's own experience in Colombia. Only the foolhardy went that way.

Isolated from Lima and the majority of the Peruvian population, who mostly lived to the west of the Andes, Iquitos's orientation was decidedly eastward, looking down the Amazon to Pará, nineteen hundred miles away, and then beyond, to Europe and the eastern United States. There wasn't much evidence of Peru in Iquitos. Almost everything was brought in via the Amazon River. Most of the town's important buildings, both private and public, were built from material imported from Europe—the stone, the iron and steel, and, especially, the vibrantly colored Portuguese tiles that adorned many private homes. In 1890 a prefabricated iron house, built and designed by Gustave Eiffel, had arrived in Iquitos from Paris.

Iquitos did not have a promising start as a commercial center. Jesuit missionaries had been spreading the word of God and converting the locals from their base in Quito, Ecuador, since the seventeenth century. By the mid-eighteenth century they had reached the Amazon, and near the site of the future town of Iquitos they founded a mission village. The process of converting the local people was difficult at first. There was resistance to conversion, and many of the missionaries died from disease, but no sooner had they begun to make a success of the mission than the Spanish king Charles III ordered all Jesuits, whom he thought too inclined to create their own state within the state, to leave Spanish America (and Spain). The mission village was abandoned, the population shrank, and the rest of the world forgot the area for the next century.

Around the middle of the nineteenth century, Iquitos, with a population of not more than two hundred people, almost all of them Indians, found itself with a new and unexpected importance. In 1851 Peru and Brazil agreed in an international treaty (grandly named the Special Convention of Commerce, Navigation and Limits) to liberalize navigation on the Amazon River. The treaty also provided for agreed upon borders between the two countries, and thereby guaranteed Peru's eastern frontier. Very soon thereafter, steamships began to ply the Amazon from Brazil to Peru.

Iquitos began to expand. Foreign shipping and capital, primarily British, were invited into the little port. There were new dockyards, ironworks, brick-making facilities, sawmills, and all the paraphernalia of an industrial infrastructure. By 1862 the population of Iquitos had increased fourfold to more than eight hundred, a quarter of whom were foreigners, mostly British. In 1864 a naval station was established with four new boats, all built in England. The population continued to grow and diversify while foreign commercial houses set up business and river traffic increased. Iquitos became the region's main port, from which panama hats and sarsaparilla, the region's chief exports, made their way to European markets. In return, Iquitos imported textiles, footwear, food, and liquor. By 1870 the value of the town's trade had increased a thousandfold since the Peruvian-Brazilian agreement of nearly twenty years earlier.

But this was nothing compared with what was to come. Iquitos was about to become a boomtown, all because of a single revolutionary material—rubber.

It's hard to imagine a world without rubber, but such a world existed until about a hundred and fifty years ago. Rubber had been known in Mexico, Central America, and the Amazon for centuries and was used to make balls, religious figurines, and torches; people in the Amazon region mostly used it to make waterproof boots.

When in 1736 the French astronomer and explorer Charles-Marie de la Condamine sent a sample of rubber to Paris from Quito, it made very little impression. It was no more than a curiosity, a material that was indeed unique—it bounced and could be stretched to many times its own length and then snap right back—but without any obvious use. A friend of La Condamine's and a fellow scientist, François Fresneau, had spent some time in French Guiana, where he saw local people making waterproof footwear using fresh latex, sticky sap that flowed in a number of wild tree species, which they had managed to extract by incising the bark. When Fresneau returned to France in 1748, he began working on the problem of how to make rubber practicable—in other words, how to make it into a liquid rather than a solid, so that its waterproofing properties could be employed in the same way as in Guiana. Fifteen years later, in what may have been the first scientific paper on rubber, Fresneau reported that turpentine, when used as a solvent, turned rubber into a liquid that could then be applied to fabric to make it waterproof.

Unfortunately, when the problem of applicability had been solved, another more serious problem was encountered. The rubber solution turned out to be chemically unstable. Its texture changed with temperature: hard and brittle in the cold and soft and sticky in the heat. Within a short time after being applied to textiles for waterproofing, the rubber would begin to flake off. Rubber boots had a short life before they started to crack and fall apart.

The solution to rubber's chemical instability came in 1839, when Charles Goodyear, in his Woburn, Massachusetts, factory, successfully stabilized rubber by mixing it with sulphur and heating the mixture: the process came to be known as vulcanization. Overnight, rubber production soared. Between 1830 and 1850 the world's rubber output increased almost tenfold, to 3.3 million pounds.

With the huge increase in production, the uses to which rubber was put multiplied enormously. As well as for waterproofing, it was employed where elasticity, rather than rigidity, was required—gaskets, hoses, belts, and buffers; gloves, syringes, and elastic bands; telegraph cables and electrical insulation; flooring; undergarments, condoms, diaphragms, and cervical caps.

But the biggest change in the use of rubber was still to come. Since the Roman period, carts and carriages had iron bands fitted to wooden wheels. Once vulcanization had solved the problem of rubber's instability, it was possible to make a rolling surface from solid rubber rather than from iron. Though solid rubber tires first appeared in the late 1840s, rubber's high price, together with low demand—from cart and carriage makers—constrained the market, and their use remained limited.

In the 1860s a new device appeared that would eventually take rubber into a new era. The first examples of the new technology, the ordinary bicycle, or penny-farthing (so called because its front and rear wheels were of different sizes), proved to be largely impractical and attracted only a small following who saw it as an expensive toy. The machine was difficult to mount and dismount; it required an immense physical effort to operate, as the wheel turned only once for each turn of the pedals; it was unreliable and uncomfortable on long journeys; and even when rubber tires were fitted to the wheels, the ride was still rough, for the rubber absorbed only a small proportion of the shock. No wonder they were called boneshakers.

Bicycle technology advanced quickly, however, and by the mid-1880s a new design emerged that solved most of the disadvantages of the previous generation's machines. The new model, called a safety bicycle, incorporated wheels of equal size and a chain drive to the rear wheel, leaving the front wheel free for direct steering. A few years later the transformation of the bicycle from an impractical curiosity to a truly effective method of transport was completed when John Boyd Dunlop, a Scottish veterinarian, successfully introduced the pneumatic, or inflatable, tire. The pneumatic tire, filled with air rather than solid rubber, absorbed the shocks of the road perfectly and gave, for the first time, a smooth ride. The sales of bicycles rocketed, and the first consumer craze was under way, with the result that rubber production more than doubled between 1890 and 1900, exceeding a hundred million pounds per annum.

By the turn of the century, all of the world's largest and best-known tire companies were in business and were making bicycle tires: Michelin in France, Pirelli in Italy, Dunlop in Britain, and B. F. Goodrich, Goodyear, and Firestone in the United States, leading firms of the so-called second industrial revolution, when science and technology were applied to industrial production. Their fortunes were about to undergo another, even more dramatic change, particularly in the United States. The late nineteenth century saw the first automobiles being made. Early automobile manufacturers, primarily Benz in Germany and Peugeot in France, owed many of their ideas and experience to the bicycle. The world's total production of automobiles stood at only 280 in 1895, all of them made in Germany and France; five years later, output had risen dramatically to 10,000 vehicles. By this time the automotive pneumatic tire, perfected by André Michelin in France, was fitted to every car. It was in the United States, however, that the car really came into its own as Americans abandoned the two-wheeled bicycle for the four-wheeled motorized device. By 1907, world output had risen to 90,000 units, the United States accounting for almost 60 percent of the total. And then, a year later, out of his factory in Detroit came the first of Henry Ford's affordable cars, the Model T, and the United States never looked back. By 1908 automobile production in the United States had doubled to 125,000 units. So enormous was the change caused by the adoption of the pneumatic tire that by 1910 about 70 percent of all the rubber produced in the world went into the automotive sector—cars, trucks, and buses. By then the world's output of rubber stood at 160 million pounds per annum, or fifty times what it had been in the middle of the nineteenth century.

Rubber production first began on the islands around Pará, at the mouth of the Amazon, but by the time of the 1890s bicycle craze, it had spread westward along the Amazon River into the Acre district of Brazil, the Beni district of Bolivia, southeastern Peru, and, most recently, the Putumayo region. The Amazon region is rich in latex-producing trees. It is the natural habitat of *Hevea brasiliensis*, the principal source of most of the world's rubber. Several species of *Hevea* grew in the Putumayo, but it was not the first tree that Europeans harvested. There was also another latex tree growing called *Castilloa*. It is a massive tree, often reaching more than one hundred feet in height. It has a lot of latex in it, but little of it can be reached by slashing the bark without damaging the tree. The most effective way of getting the *Castilloa*'s latex was to chop it down and then cut deeply into its trunk, thereby releasing all of the latex in one go. This highly wasteful method often yielded two hundred pounds of latex from a single tree. It was this tree that first attracted itinerant Colombian rubber traders, *caucheros*, as they were called, to the region in the latter part of the nineteenth century. *Caucheros* moved around the forest, identifying stands of *Castilloa*, harvesting them, moving on, and repeating the process. In only twenty years the *caucheros* had destroyed most of the *Castilloa* stands.

They then turned their attention to *Hevea*, which, although less productive than *Castilloa*—just a few pounds of latex annually—did not have to be destroyed to obtain its precious yield: it could be tapped. Shallow incisions were cut in the bark, and the latex oozed out drop by drop. Tapping saved the tree but required a different kind of labor force: one that knew the forests intimately and knew how to find the individual trees; that knew how to tap the trees properly (where to put the incisions and how frequently to collect the latex); and was available throughout the tapping season, sometimes all the year round—in other words, the indigenous people of the area.

The rubber trade in the Putumayo region was now based mostly on *Hevea*. *Hevea* grew in a dispersed pattern. About fifty trees, on average, grew in a square mile, and each Indian worker tended about one hundred trees, fifty in the process of being tapped and fifty in their resting phase. Those who organized the workforce were still called *caucheros*, though they no longer did the work of collecting rubber. The Indians of the Putumayo, mostly Huitotos and Boras, who did do the work, had their own particular way of tapping the trees and preparing the rubber. Incisions were made in the bark, and the latex was allowed to run down the trunk of the tree, where it coagulated naturally into strips of rubber. (This was in contrast to the prevailing method in most of the Amazon Basin, where the latex was collected in cups attached to the trunk.) The strips were taken to a stream, where they were washed and prepared for shipping.

South American rubber accounted for the bulk of the world's production, averaging at about 70 percent during the first decade of the twentieth century. Though Peruvian production was small in comparison with that of Brazil—the largest producer in Amazonia—at about 10 percent of the total, it was not insignificant, especially to Iquitos and Peru in general.

Iquitos grew much faster than all of the other settlements jurisdictionally controlled by the vast department of Loreto. It became increasingly clear to the Loretano politicians that keeping the regional capital in Moyobamba, a small Andean town famed for its panama hats, made no sense in this age of the Amazon rubber boom. And so in 1898 the capital of the department was officially moved to Iquitos.

Ten years later, with a population of fifteen thousand, Iquitos was not just a regional capital but a major Amazonian town of vital importance to the nation. During the first decade of the century Iquitos handled about 12 percent of total Peruvian foreign trade and provided Lima with 16 percent of its custom revenues. Militarily, too, Iquitos was crucial, for it was from this port town that the Peruvian navy plied the waters of the Amazon and the Putumayo, guaranteeing Peruvian interests in the region: the Colombians, by contrast, had no ships on the Putumayo. Aside from its importance both nationally and regionally, Iquitos was a diverse town, probably more cosmopolitan than anywhere else in Peru. Consulates from the United States and several European countries, including Great Britain, were there to represent their expatriate population and to provide the commercial and legal support to expedite the export of rubber. Great Britain was the town's chief economic partner, its importance marked by the presence of several British banks and trading firms. About half of the town's rubber exports were destined for Liverpool. Following not far behind Britain in economic importance were Germany, France, and the United States. The Booth Steamship Company of Liverpool provided Iquitos with its connection to the rest of the world. There were regular sailings to Manaus and Pará and from there to Barbados (and onward to New York), Liverpool, Le Havre, Lisbon, and Hamburg. The pound sterling was the town's unofficial currency.

3

ARANA'S WORLD

Back in Iquitos, February and March 1908 passed, and there was no sign of Perkins. While waiting for him, Hardenburg had been kicking up his heels and, thanks to the high prices in town, getting into debt.

Then came April, and there was still no word from Perkins. Hardenburg's luck, however, had taken a turn for the better. He had got himself two jobs: as a draftsman, working in the local college, and as a teacher of English to a well-heeled clientele. Saving money would be difficult in such an expensive town, but even so, he hoped to clear his debts shortly.

Then Hardenburg heard the best news yet. Perkins was alive and well, expected in Iquitos in a few weeks. On April 22 the Peruvian launch from El Encanto tied up at the wharf in Iquitos. Perkins walked off in the same clothes he was wearing when Hardenburg last saw him. He was penniless, just as Hardenburg had been.

Perkins related how, after Hardenburg's departure, he had been kept a virtual house prisoner in El Encanto. On March 20 Miguel Loayza had forced him to sign an affidavit saying that he was in El Encanto under Peruvian protection because his life would be in danger were he to remain with the Colombians, and that he was being well treated by Loayza and his subordinates. Though the document also stated that his baggage would be recovered, Perkins was never allowed to return upriver to the spot where he had hidden it, and no one from the company was sent to retrieve it. The bags were stuffed with personal belongings, engineering books and instruments, all the artifacts and geological specimens they had collected on their way downriver, technical papers, and personal diaries and journals. Aside from one diary that Hardenburg had kept with him, all the rest was lost.

Perkins gave more details of what had happened during his detention. The Peruvians had finally caught up with David Serrano. "[They] returned to Serrano's and burned his buildings, murdered him and twenty eight other Colombians who were quartered there. They took these 28 poor men, who had gathered here for mutual protection, tied their hands behind them and shot them to death. They not only shot them to death, but horribly mutilated their bodies with their machetes and threw them into the river."

While they were both in Iquitos, Hardenburg and Perkins decided to seek compensation for their losses. They blamed both Arana's company and the Peruvian military for what had happened to them. To get the compensation process under way, Hardenburg and Perkins complained directly to Guy King, the American vice-consul in Iquitos and a practicing dentist, about how they were mistreated and what they had lost. But as Perkins later told officials at the State Department, the interview was far from satisfactory. Basically, King told them not to bother. Iquitos was a lawless place, and interested parties would do whatever they could to discredit their case. As they all knew, King's livelihood was dependent on these same people, and he didn't want his lucrative business to suffer owing to unprovable accusations and complaints.

Disappointed with King's response, the only logical thing seemed to be to take their complaint directly to Arana.

By a stroke of luck, Arana happened to be in Iquitos at the time when Hardenburg and Perkins went to lodge their complaint at his door. He had just returned from London, where he had intended to float his new concern, the Peruvian Amazon Rubber Company, with vast capital reserves. Poor trading conditions, however, had forced him to postpone the flotation, and he was now back in Iquitos waiting for things to improve.

The rise of Julio César Arana's fortune and power was rapid and entirely the result of the Amazonian rubber boom and Iquitos's position in it. Arana was born on April 12, 1864, in the town of Rioja in northern Peru, situated between the cordillera rising high behind it and the lush valleys of the Amazonian forests below. The Arana line hailed from the town of Cajamarca, in the Andean highlands to the southwest of Rioja, and from there the men of the family had spread out in all directions seeking their fortunes and finding different fates. Martín Arana, Julio César's father, ended up in the respectable straw-hat trade in Rioja.

Julio César entered his father's business at age nine, and during the next few years he hawked his father's goods over an increasingly large area. When Julio was fifteen, Martín Arana, rather than see his son enlist in the war against Chile, sent him to Cajamarca, where he learned bookkeeping and general business administration.

Two years later Arana knew enough about business to begin to take advantage of the new economic opportunities that the rubber boom was bringing to the Peruvian Amazon. Instead of working out of Rioja and the Andean hinterland, he decided on the town of Yurimaguas on the Huallaga River, a tributary of the Amazon, as the base of his operations. He would now be able to sell his father's panama hats throughout the Amazon Basin, venturing into Brazil and Colombia as well as northeastern Peru.

Soon, however, Arana realized that much more money could be made out of rubber than out of panama hats. But he needed more cash to invest, and it came by way of a very convenient marriage. At the age of twenty-three, after a six-year courtship, Julio César Arana married Eleanora Zumaeta, a childhood sweetheart from a well-heeled Rioja family. He could now put the pieces in place for a profitable commercial venture. In 1888, the year after his marriage, Arana invited his new brother-in-law, Pablo Zumaeta, to join him in business. Together the partners opened a trading post in the nearby town of

Tarapoto, in a rich rubber-growing district. The following year they moved deeper into the trade by buying a part of a rubber forest near Yurimaguas. Arana and Zumaeta then set off for the Ceará, the northeastern Brazilian dust bowl, to hire cheap labor, possibly some of the cheapest in the world. The Ceará had recently experienced a devastating drought in which half a million people had lost their lives; those who survived were desperate for work. Arana and Zumaeta found twenty men who would sell themselves for practically nothing to get out of their hell.

Debt peonage, where an individual bound himself or herself to and worked for a creditor until the debt was cleared, was a fundamental part of the Peruvian labor system. The debt could take any form, such as the creditor paying for the cost of getting the person to the workplace, or paying for provisions, or simply an advance on wages. Slavery had been abolished in Peru in 1854, but debt peonage, which was perfectly legal, was widely regarded as a way of keeping wages down and making such Peruvian primary products as minerals, sugar, and rubber cheaper than they would otherwise be and competitive on the international market.

And so, with their Brazilian peons working the rubber trees, Arana invited Abel Alarco, another brother-in-law, to join him and Pablo in the rubber trade, and in 1889 the three men set up business in the boomtown that was Iquitos.

Through his involvement in the rubber trade, Arana rose rapidly to a position of great importance and power. In 1902 his was one of a handful of small to medium rubber-exporting firms in Iquitos. At the time, his firm accounted for about 8 percent of Iquitos's rubber exports and about 5 percent of its total imports. But he was well on his way to leaving the competition behind, and it was the Putumayo that proved the key to his eventual dominance of the trade. He was already doing enough business in the Putumayo with the Colombian traders to ensure that most of them were on his books: the Colombians had to sell their rubber in Iquitos, and it was there, because their own supply lines were so distant and difficult to access, that they also purchased their supplies and negotiated credit. Arana arranged everything for them.

However, being a mere provider, a facilitator, was not enough for him. He wanted greater involvement in the rubber trade and decided that his best strategy was to enter into partnership with the leading Colombian traders in the Putumayo. The decision couldn't have been wiser. His first partner, Benjamin Larrañaga, one of the pioneers of the Putumayo rubber business, sold out to Arana in 1903, and later that year another Colombian, Gregorio Calderón, did the same. Arana had become a rubber trader, and he set up his new company, J. C. Arana y Hermanos, with headquarters in Iquitos. As partners he took on his two brothers-in-law, Pablo Zumaeta and Abel Alarco, and his own brother Lizardo. Very soon after its creation, Arana opened a branch office of the company in Manaus, where Lizardo directed operations.

Arana was now in a powerful position. He was cash rich and could easily have extended trade credit and mortgages to the remaining Colombian rubber traders in the Putumayo area. Instead, he decided that he wanted their concerns for himself, and he offered them partnerships in the way he had done to Larrañaga and Calderón. Arana's financial reserves were substantial. From 1904 onward he annexed valuable rubber properties on both the Caraparaná and the Igaraparaná rivers, amounting to more than forty settlements.

At this point Arana recruited Barbadians to work for him. Besides being on the regular steamer route from Manaus to Europe and the United States, Barbados had become a source of cheap labor, and the island's government strongly encouraged emigration to solve its economic problems. The island's sugar-based economy was in serious trouble, and a significant proportion of Barbadian men had no employment. A large number had already gone to work on the Panama Canal project. Arana sent his brother-in-law Abel Alarco to take advantage of the economic crisis to recruit a cheap labor force. Over nine months some two hundred Barbadian men became indentured, initially for a period of two years, to Arana's company. The Barbadians expected to be employed as laborers, but Arana had other plans for them. By using foreigners with no ties to the locality or the people, he was able to initiate a more ruthless regime. It was extremely difficult for the Barbadians to disobey orders; as foreigners, they could hardly melt away into the surroundings even if they wanted to escape. In this remote part of the Amazon Basin, there was really no one and nowhere to turn to if they needed help.

By 1907 Arana was the only Peruvian rubber trader in the Putumayo region. His steam launches alone visited the area; the Colombians had mostly disappeared, and the small handful who refused to sell out to him were at his mercy deep in the remote jungle.

While Arana was turning the Putumayo region into his personal fiefdom, he was also entrenching his position as a rubber trader. His exports soared from a level of 35,000 pounds in 1900 to 1.4 million pounds in 1906, by which time he had become Iquitos's leading rubber exporter, shipping about a third of the town's rubber downriver to the bustling ports of Liverpool, Le Havre, Hamburg, and New York. He had also become politically powerful in Iquitos, in Loreto, and across the Andes in Lima. His presence in the Putumayo gave Peru important leverage in its argument with Colombia over the boundary issue. At the same time, being in the area also meant that he could provide Lima with intelligence about any encroachments by Colombians. It was a cozy and mutually reinforcing relationship. Arana, the powerful merchant and staunch patriot, had forged a formidable economic and political foundation for himself.

His ascendancy was not yet complete. Rubber was an international commodity, and Arana's sights went far beyond the Amazon and his business premises in Iquitos and Manaus. Europe, after all, was within easier reach than Lima. In contrast to the other merchants in town, many of whom flaunted their wealth and position by having their dwellings decorated with the most beautiful and lavish imported tiles, Arana's house was modest. He did not really see himself as a resident of Iquitos: he wanted to make his mark as a man of the world. By 1906 he knew Paris, Bordeaux, and Biarritz as well as he did the Amazonian towns. In 1907 he moved his family to Biarritz, and the middle of that year found him shuttling between Biarritz and Paris.

But it was the City of London, the financial center of the world, that was uppermost in Arana's mind. His plan was quite simple. Having become the main supplier of rubber from the Peruvian Amazon, he was going to London to incorporate his enterprise. On September 6, 1907, he created a company called the Peruvian Rubber Company, which purchased the business and properties of J. C. Arana y Hermanos. Later on that month, the company's name was changed, and it began trading as the Peruvian Amazon Rubber Company. Its flotation, with a nominal capital of £1,000,000, was ready.

But despite the publicity and the tastefully produced prospectus, the flotation ran into problems as the world price of rubber collapsed. Late 1907 witnessed a bank panic in the United States, followed by a stock market crash: the ripples were felt throughout the world as prices and output fell sharply. Arana was advised to hold back until conditions improved, and he returned to Iquitos.

In May 1908, listening to Hardenburg and Perkins make a case for their losses in the Putumayo, Arana was polite but unhelpful. As Perkins later recounted, "We laid the matter before J.C. Arana who was in Iquitos at the time of my arrival there. We did this, simply stating what our luggage was composed of, and that we thought we should be paid for it. He promised 'to see about it.'"

But they heard no more from Arana. His silence, together with Dr. King's reluctance to do anything, forced Perkins and Hardenburg to change their tactics.

Meanwhile, economic conditions began to improve, and rubber prices began to rise. It was time for Arana to return to London and resume the flotation of his great company.

Before doing so, he made two significant changes. The word "rubber" was dropped from the firm's name, and it was restyled as the Peruvian Amazon Company. It had also assembled an impressive board of British directors. The first was Henry Manuel Read, an old South American hand, having been at various times manager of the London Bank of Mexico and South America; a director of the Peruvian Corporation, a sprawling company based in London, with controlling interests in Peruvian railways, steamers, mines, and guano deposits; and a director of Lima Light, Power and Tramways Company. Read had twenty years of experience in Peru but had never ventured beyond the coast. The other board members were John Russell Gubbins, a businessman with forty years of experience in Peru; and Sir John Lister-Kaye, an impeccably reared aristocrat with royal connections—lieutenant in the Royal Horse Guards and groom-in-waiting to Edward VII. Lister-Kaye was easily the most distinguished member of the board and one of its most socially respected. He and his wife were highly sought-after society people on both sides of the Atlantic, moving easily between London and the country, New York and Newport. The British board gave the company the kind of stature and importance that would win it respect in the City of London and from all those whose financial dealings took them there.

The Peruvian Amazon Company was successfully floated on December 8, 1908. Three hundred thousand shares at £1 each were offered to the public, and the remaining £700,000 ordinary shares stayed within the Arana family, giving them control over the new company. The board of directors and the registered headquarters were in London. Organizing the day-to-day activities of the company were two offices: one in Iquitos, where Pablo Zumaeta was the general manager, with direct responsibility for operations in the Putumayo, and the other in Manaus, where Lizardo Arana was in charge of commercial transactions in this hub of the Amazonian rubber trade.

Arana was on top of the world. He was in complete control of a vast rubber-producing territory—more than ten thousand square miles— the largest of its kind in South America, into which no one could venture without his knowledge and permission.

4

SALDAÑA ROCCA'S WORLD

Desperate to air their grievances and to make a successful claim for compensation from the Peruvian government, Hardenburg and Perkins decided that Iquitos was a dead end. A more promising route, they thought, would be to seek compensation by pressing their claim in the United States through the State Department. As Perkins came from a family with political connections, he decided to take their case to Washington while Hardenburg remained in Iquitos.

By the end of May 1908 Perkins was on his way by steamer to Manaus. By a strange irony, on board at the same time and also bound for Manaus was Julio César Arana. Stranger still, he made Perkins a business offer.

> During the voyage we conversed about the rubber industry and when we reached Manaos [sic], where he has an office, he had a letter written, making me a business proposition intended for Hardenburg and myself jointly. Nothing had been said about why he should do this, more than that he said the Peruvian employees he had on those lands offered to us, were very inefficient. I have no reason to think that he made us this liberal proposition to deter us from making a claim for

damages. It was a plain business proposition, open for our acceptance or rejection.

Once Perkins was safely back in the United States, he immediately started pestering the State Department about their losses and seeking compensation. The State Department reacted by dragging its feet for months, most of the time ignoring Perkins. When it did contact him, it was to announce that the department was only willing to consider a claim for $5,000, as opposed to $20,000. And then things got worse. It turned out that the State Department had informally approached the Peruvian government, which had agreed, as a special favor, to compensate the two men's losses to the tune of $2,500, an eighth of what Hardenburg and Perkins had originally demanded. This was a big blow. They had both hoped for much more. Perkins lost interest in the matter and turned his attention to making a new life for himself in his home country. He and Hardenburg would never see each other again.

Ever since Hardenburg was a boy, growing up on his parents' farms, first in Galena, Illinois, and then in Youngsville, New York, near the Catskill Mountains, he had dreamed of seeing the Amazon. But working in Iquitos was probably not how he had imagined he would be spending his time on that great river.

And then one day in June 1908, about four months into his stay in the town, Hardenburg's life took a dramatic turn. A young lad appeared at the door of the building on Iquitos's main street where Hardenburg had borrowed office space for his English lessons. Hardenburg had never seen the lad before and was therefore surprised when he said he had come especially to speak to him, but not about taking classes.

The boy's name was Miguel Galvez. He explained that he was the son of Benjamin Saldaña Rocca, a maverick newspaper owner who had recently been forced out of town and was now working in Lima.

The forty-three-year-old Saldaña Rocca had distinguished himself as a soldier, but some time earlier had decided to settle in Iquitos. In a foretaste of things to come, on August 9, 1907, while Arana was in Europe, Saldaña Rocca had petitioned the judge of the criminal court in Iquitos to proceed with charges against eighteen employees of J. C.

Arana y Hermanos. The petition provided brief details of horrible acts of violence and barbarism against the Indians who collected rubber for the company in the Putumayo region. One incident, perpetrated at the Ultimo Retiro section (a company station to which rubber was brought), involved two Barbadians. Saldaña Rocca described the sickening scene:

> The sub-manager, Argaluza, ordered the death of an Indian woman called Simona, because he thought she had relations with a young man whose name was also Simon. The death of this unhappy woman was most terrible. Argaluza ordered the Barbadian negroes Stanley Lewis and Ernesto Siobers, known by the nickname Frailecito (= little monk), to administer 155 stripes to the woman, and when her thighs were cut to pieces he locked her up in a room and left her until she was worm eaten; then the brave Argaluza ordered one of his employees to kill her. The latter refusing to kill Simona, Argaluza took his rifle and said: "If you don't kill her, I will kill you," thus forcing the ignorant employee to become an unwilling criminal.

Saldaña Rocca urged the judge to move quickly, "as the bones of thousands of Indians who have been murdered lie scattered round the houses of the sections such as Matanzas, Ultimo Retiro, Sabana, Santa Catalina, San Victor and all the other dependencies of El Encanto and La Chorrera . . . a visit of inspection [should] be undertaken as soon as possible, before the bones of the victims can be made to disappear."

But all Saldaña Rocca got from the court was silence.

Two weeks later he tried a different and more daring approach—he made public his attack on Arana in the first issue of his own newspaper, *La Sancion*, on August 22, 1907. The paper's name, best translated as "The Castigation," gave a clue that this was no ordinary publication.

Saldaña Rocca, editor and proprietor, was on a crusade. He was going to tell the truth about what was really going on in Iquitos behind the veneer of prosperity and progress. Iquitos was a dangerous place, especially for those on the wrong side, he told his readers. "Enough of mysteries and cover-ups," he declared; "enough of derision, abuse, prevarication, thefts, assassinations, embezzlements and fraud. In such a noble and worthwhile task nothing nor anyone can stop me: I will fight undaunted and without respite, scorning the switchblade of the assassin and the pistol of the thug."

The paper contained a variety of articles and notices covering local news, court reports, port movements, poems, and small literary pieces; hard-hitting swipes at his competition, the newspaper *El Oriente*, which did not share Saldaña Rocca's view of the Iquitos establishment; snippets of news from Lima and overseas papers; and, as he promised, the uncovering and hounding of those committing crimes against the people.

The main architect of this wave of criminality, Saldaña Rocca maintained, was Julio César Arana. In almost every issue of the paper, Saldaña Rocca published damning revelations about his prime target. This took various forms: sometimes just an editorial comment; sometimes a lengthy attack, as when, over a three-week period, he published the contents of his unsuccessful criminal petition; and, from the start, the printing of eyewitness accounts by past employees of Arana's company of how Arana was running his operations in the Putumayo as a coercive and violent system—about the torture, maiming, and murder of the indigenous people.

The first issue of *La Sancion* set the tone for the paper. It contained a letter from Julio Muriedas, who had worked for Arana in La Chorrera—one of the regional headquarters of the company in the Putumayo—for three months. Muriedas described what he had witnessed in the Matanzas section, whose chief, Armando Normand (of whom a great deal more would be learned over the coming years), operated a reign of terror. "The chief," Muriedas wrote,

> Armando Normand, applies 200 or more lashes, which are given with rough scourges of crude leather, to the unhappy Indians, when they— to their misfortune—do not deliver punctually the number of rolls of rubber of the weight desired; other times, when the Indian, fearful of not being able to deliver the required amount of rubber, flees, they take his children, suspend them by their hands and feet, and, in this position, apply fire, so that with the cruel pains produced by this torture, they will tell where their fathers are hidden.

La Sancion, with its motto "To defend the interests of the people," seemed to have been popular. Though originally planned to appear twice a week, within a few months of its first appearance *La Sancion* became a daily. By then it had been joined by another Saldaña Rocca publication, *La Felpa*, which was launched on August 31, 1907. *La Felpa*, which translates as "The Scolding," was quite different from its sister paper. It was shorter in length, only four pages, appeared fortnightly, and used various features, including a political cartoon as its center spread, to make its point.

In case Saldaña Rocca's readers had any doubts about what was going on in Arana's empire, the very first issue of *La Felpa* carried a series of four graphic tableaux titled "The Crimes of the Putumayo: FLAGELLATIONS, MUTILATIONS, TORTURES, and TARGET PRACTICE," showing how the Indian workers were being horribly maltreated.

Over the coming months, Arana's Putumayo operations would continue to make *La Felpa*'s center spread; and sometimes so did Arana himself, always appearing perfectly turned out as a proper Edwardian gentleman, with a sharp, neatly trimmed beard and a smart, well-fitting suit adding to his distinction, but never as a man with clean hands. On more than one occasion Saldaña Rocca had him portrayed as a devil; on most occasions Arana and his men were surrounded by skulls.

The last issue of Benjamin Saldaña Rocca's newspaper had come out on February 22, 1908, three weeks after Hardenburg's arrival in Iquitos.

Miguel Galvez told Hardenburg that his father had been tipped off that the police were on their way to escort him out of Iquitos. It was no coincidence that Arana had just returned from London. Before Saldaña Rocca fled, he had had just enough time to gather all his documents, which he left with Galvez's mother, who kept a pension on the waterfront. Galvez heard from his father in Lima, urging him to pass the package of documents on to someone who would make good use of them to continue the crusade against Arana. Hardenburg was the person he chose, though we do not know why. Perhaps it was because he was an American, an outsider in Iquitos.

At any rate, Hardenburg accepted the package. The material, most of which has survived, contained the revealing letters written by ex-employees of Arana to Saldaña Rocca, many of which had already been printed in *La Sancion,* together with back issues of both of Saldaña Rocca's titles. Reading the graphic testimonies that Galvez handed him, Hardenburg finally understood what lay behind the scars—the Mark of Arana—he had seen on Indian bodies in the Putumayo: the abusive violence, the maiming and killings that were part and parcel of collecting rubber in Arana's Putumayo.

Saldaña Rocca's material galvanized Hardenburg's desire to expose Arana, and over the next twelve months Hardenburg collected his own evidence. While on Arana's company launch traveling to Iquitos, he had met two Colombians, and he now called on their personal contacts in Iquitos—sympathetic Colombians and Peruvians similarly disaffected with Arana—to testify in writing to what they had witnessed or experienced in the Putumayo. In his search for corroborating evidence, Hardenburg received unsolicited letters as well as responses to detailed questions he sent out to specific individuals. Hardenburg was highly organized and asked pertinent questions: Who extracts the latex from the trees? How are these people paid? How does the company treat its workers? Is it true that the bosses treat the Indians barbarously, that they beat and maim them? Is it true that they cut off their arms, legs, and heads? Is it true that they shoot them for fun? He received answers in long testimonials, all of them sworn in front of a notary in Iquitos. They made disturbing reading.

Hardenburg had managed to collect testimonials from twenty people willing to recount their experiences of Arana's empire. The evidence was palpable: the abuses were unimaginable. At the same time, Hardenburg became increasingly aware that it was unsafe for him to stay in Iquitos, although, in his account of his time there, he didn't say whether he actually received threats. He suspected, however, that his extracurricular activities were known. He told his English students some weeks before his actual departure that he would be suspending the classes. By then he had decided to use the material he had collected and his own experiences in the Putumayo to write a book exposing the atrocities committed by Arana and his men.

At the beginning of June 1909, Hardenburg bundled together his book manuscript, the depositions made to him, and those he had inherited from Saldaña Rocca, and made his way to the Booth Steamship Company wharf, where he boarded a ship bound for Pará and eventually Liverpool.

PART
TWO

5

OVER TO THE FOREIGN OFFICE

Hardenburg was on a mission. From Liverpool he made his way to London, where he found lodgings near St. Pancras train station. Early in August 1909 he went to the offices of the Anti-Slavery and Aborigines' Protection Society in Vauxhall, South London.

The society had a fearsome and well-deserved reputation for rooting out and pursuing perpetrators of what we would now call human rights abuses. The society was in fact quite recent, having been formed in June of that year as an amalgamation of two older societies—the British and Foreign Anti-Slavery Society and the Aborigines' Protection Society. Both were originally formed in the 1830s to ensure that the Emancipation Act of 1833, which outlawed slavery in Britain and its possessions, would also act as an inducement and an example for other nations to abolish slavery in their respective countries and possessions. The newly amalgamated Anti-Slavery and Aborigines' Protection Society had a broad agenda to protect the welfare of indigenous people everywhere. The society had large worldwide networks of correspondents who reported on local cases of abuse; they lobbied members of Parliament and the Colonial and Foreign offices; and through their magazines, they kept their members up to date with the progress of campaigns.

Hardenburg had a meeting with John Harris, the society's organizing secretary. Explaining who he was and what he had come about, Hardenburg presented Harris with the material he had brought out of the Amazon. Harris later recalled how moved he had been by the testimonials, especially so since he was, at the time, helping to organize the work of the Congo Reform Association. He had no doubt that the testimonials were telling the truth: the echoes of the Congo were unmissable. Harris immediately prepared letters of introduction for Hardenburg to various prominent members of the society, but he insisted, when Hardenburg returned two days later, that he should waste no time in taking the story to Sidney Paternoster at *Truth*. From his own experiences with the Congo campaign, Harris had learned how important it was to get public sympathy on board as soon as possible. *Truth* was the most effective way of achieving quick results.

Paternoster certainly stirred it up. On September 27, the week after publishing "The Devil's Paradise: A British-owned Congo," Robert Bennett, *Truth*'s editor, received a letter from the Peruvian Amazon Company's headquarters in London Wall, in the City of London, dated just a couple of days earlier. It was fairly short and to the point.

"The Directors have no reason to believe that the atrocities referred to have in fact taken place, and indeed have grounds for considering that they have been purposely mis-stated for indirect objects. Whatever the facts, however, may be, the Board of this Company are *under no responsibility for them, as they were not in office at the times of the alleged occurrences*" (my emphasis).

The letter was printed in the following week's issue of the magazine (September 29, 1909), in which Paternoster continued to provide the reading public with further eyewitness accounts of conditions in the Putumayo. This time Paternoster raised the temperature further. He startlingly revealed, through a testimonial by an ex-employee of Arana's called Celestino Lopez, that at the rubber station of Santa Julia it was a "negro" who had "flogged most barbarously" three Indian women. Later in the same article, Paternoster provided further evidence, in the shape of a testimonial from a Colombian trader that had appeared originally in the *Jornal do Commercio* of September 14, 1907, that some Barbadians in Arana's employ were as much the perpetrators of abuses as victims of them.

Paternoster ended his commentary on the criminal acts of the company by repeating his challenge: "I trust that the directors of the Peruvian and Amazon Company [*sic*] will be the first to admit that the case as it stands demands their earnest attention, and that they will, after fully investigating all the circumstances, take effectual steps to remove all ground for unfavourable criticism of their business in future."

Paternoster had surely ruffled the Peruvian Amazon Company's feathers, but the Peruvian government had also taken offense at what he had reported in the September 22 issue of *Truth*. In a letter to Bennett, Eduardo Lembcke, the chargé d'affaires at the Peruvian legation in London, expressed deep concern at the allegations leveled at the Peruvian Amazon Company. Lembcke began by categorically denying the allegations. It would be impossible, he remarked, for his government not to have known about any such acts on the Putumayo, for the area was well served by state officials and had a strong military garrison. The Putumayo was not, he added, "a sort of no-man's-land"; it is "in direct communication by steamer and other rapid routes with Iquitos: and Iquitos "is connected by telegraphic and wireless installations with Lima and the whole of the Republic." In short, "it is impossible to admit that acts of the nature described could have been committed without the guilty parties being promptly and severely punished by the authorities." As for *La Felpa* and *La Sancion*, they

> should not be given the least credit, as both these papers were started by the same editor for dishonest purposes, and for that reason were so shortlived. The said papers published fantastic crimes alleged to have been committed by the employees of the firm of J. C. Arana and Hnos., and when the employees of this old and well-known house commenced proceedings for libel against the said editor, he disappeared in order to evade the grave responsibility he had incurred.

Lembcke ended this robust letter by upholding the honor of the Peruvian military. "I must therefore repudiate in the most deliberate manner the accusation contained in the said article and based on the malicious information supplied to you, and I protest most emphatically against references therein made that soldiers of the Peruvian Army could be capable of committing the acts of inhumanity described by Mr. Hardenburg."

Sidney Paternoster did not, of course, let Eduardo Lembcke have the last word. Refuting the chargé d'affaires, he again used Hardenburg's firsthand knowledge, emphasizing that Saldaña Rocca was never prosecuted and that after leaving Iquitos, he was openly working for a newspaper in Lima; that it was Saldaña Rocca who denounced the company and not the other way around; and that the Peruvian government had agreed to compensate Hardenburg and Perkins. With clear reference to the Congo, Paternoster pointed out that soldiers or civilians in out-of-the-way parts of the world are quite capable of acts of cruelty and oppression toward indigenous people.

From here on, events snowballed. Allegations and counters to those allegations peppered the pages of the British press. But ultimately *Truth* could only expose and embarrass the British-listed Peruvian Amazon Company. Only the British government could take the matter further. It was up to the Foreign Office, at whose door the problem was laid by the parliamentary questions, to get at the truth.

The attention of the Foreign Office, and its secretary of state, Sir Edward Grey, was mostly focused on continental European affairs, particularly Germany's naval buildup, which in a decade had seen the size of the country's navy increase until it was second only to that of Britain. Grey had been in the post since 1905 and was considered a success: he had already scored a significant diplomatic achievement with the Anglo-Russian accord of 1907, which led directly to the Triple Entente between Russia, France, and Britain.

But although the Amazon was a world away from that of Great Power politics, the Foreign Office could hardly pretend that it had had nothing to do with the Putumayo: after all, British subjects were living and working there, and Britain had a responsibility to protect their welfare. To help the Foreign Office get to the bottom of the story, Thomas Hart-Davies mentioned that David Cazes, the British consul in Iquitos, happened to be in London. The Foreign Office should lose no time in contacting him.

On October 1 Francis Campbell, the assistant undersecretary of state at the Foreign Office, wrote to Cazes at his London address asking him to provide Sir Edward Grey with a response to the allegations contained in the September 22 issue of *Truth* and the subsequent parliamentary questions. Cazes responded promptly, saying that the allegations were, on the whole, unfounded. The two Iquitos papers that were used by *Truth* had "little standing or reliance"; the Barbadians—most of whom had gone home, he said—had complained to him in the past of being ill-treated, but many of the complaints were unjustified; from what he had seen of the Putumayo Indians, they were well treated; and as for Arana, he and his company were, Cazes insisted, "very attentive to the complaints."

Cazes's letter did not, however, find much favor back in the Foreign Office. He was an unpaid servant (as were many consular officials), and the Foreign Office suspected that he was involved in the rubber trade. Moreover, as one clerk acutely pointed out, "Cazes letter is not really to the point. The question is are the atrocities alleged by *Truth* to be perpetrated in the name of a British Co., or on its behalf, true or not." Cazes's response appeared ambiguous at best. The one conclusion that could be drawn from Cazes, however, was that there were probably no Barbadians left in the Putumayo, and even if there were, as one clerk put it with the full weight of the racism and prejudice of the time behind him, "their evidence would be worth little all West Indians being liars."

Several days after his letter had arrived at the Foreign Office, Cazes appeared in person to clarify and correct some of his written statements. The Barbadians had first been imported four years earlier, he said, but they could not adapt to the climate. Most left, and the few who did remain were free to come and go as they pleased. Cazes was sure that the reports of cruelty to the Indians were exaggerated and that the stories had originated with the Colombian government, which had much to gain from embarrassing the Peruvians. He also thought that the American consul in Iquitos had visited the Putumayo and submitted a report to Washington, though he did not know the substance of it.

Meanwhile, the Foreign Office had also contacted Charles des Graz, the resident British minister at the Lima legation, and Victor Huckin, the British consul in Bogotá, for any information they had. Graz wrote back that he had little to say, as the Putumayo was so far from Iquitos, and Iquitos was even farther from Lima. Huckin confirmed that he had heard that Colombians had been harassed by the Peruvians in the Putumayo, but he had no further details at hand.

As for the report on conditions in the Putumayo prepared by the American consul in Iquitos and referred to in Hart-Davies's parliamentary question, the Foreign Office contacted James Bryce, the British ambassador in Washington, who passed on the request to the State Department.

The acting U.S. secretary of state, Huntington Wilson, wrote back to Bryce a fortnight later that his department had no such report, contradicting what Cazes had said in his interview at the Foreign Office.

But the State Department was wrong. Two reports had in fact been received. Had they simply been mislaid, or did the State Department have some reason to withhold the reports at this time?

An American consulate had been opened in Iquitos in 1906, reflecting the growing importance of Peruvian Amazon trade to the United States. Once Kansas-born Charles Eberhardt had settled in his new post as consul, he began sending dispatches, giving his State Department superiors, and potential American investors, a picture of Iquitos and its surrounding region.

During 1907 Eberhardt had met and befriended Georg von Hassel, a German civil engineer and explorer who had spent the better part of fifteen years in South America, mostly in Peru, working for the Peruvian government on land surveys. Hassel's 1903 map of the Peruvian Amazon was, according to Eberhardt, "the most reliable and authentic one, and, though published some four years ago, it is still, in the main, accurate." Eberhardt was convinced, as were many American and European anthropologists, that indigenous cultures were on the brink of extinction. Even in the short time since the publication of von Hassel's map, Eberhardt was certain that "some of the smaller tribes may have ceased to exist." Eberhardt was in a unique position to shed some light on the little that was known of the culture of these people. He submitted his ethnographic information to the State Department in a report of November 30, 1907.

The report was typical of ethnographic accounts of the time, with sections on customs, religion, material existence, and cannibalism and a few photographs used to illustrate particular points. Toward the end of the report, however, Eberhardt stepped onto more controversial terrain, in a small section on slavery.

It was clear that he had been deeply disturbed by what he witnessed on his trip. He likened the prevailing labor system of debt peonage to slavery—Peruvians, he commented, would resent his saying so. It was not peonage that worried him so much as instances of the sale of Indian slaves, normally to households in Iquitos, who would use loopholes in the law to camouflage their purchases. Eberhardt described the process but felt it should not be made public—at least not with his name attached.

Apart from the enslavement of Indians in Iquitos households, Eberhardt observed another disturbing practice:

> That there is considerable maltreatment of the Indians of certain districts, there can be little doubt. In fact, they are often most cruelly treated and tortured, in a manner similar to the reports we read from the Congo, and I myself have seen some very inhuman acts regarding which I shall deal more fully in a separate, confidential report later on, touching general conditions in the territory in dispute between Peru and Colombia.

That promised report was written on December 3, 1907. Its innocuous-sounding title, "General Conditions in the Putumayo River District of Peru," gave little hint of the allegations contained within. Eberhardt had spent six weeks with Hassel in the Putumayo River area and on its two main tributaries, the Igaraparaná and the Caraparaná. Though he excused himself for having not spent enough time to have a thorough knowledge of what was going on in the area, he felt that he had seen enough of the conditions "which a promoting company would probably not make public, and which the department, at least, might be interested in knowing."

Eberhardt told of a tract of rubber land, approximately twelve thousand square miles, bounded by the Caquetá, Igaraparaná, and Putumayo rivers, where the indigenous people were experiencing the most horrible conditions. Eberhardt estimated that ten thousand Indians were involved, their lives totally controlled for the purpose of collecting rubber by a group of foremen and their assistants, all armed, numbering about two hundred. "In the vicinity of La Chorrera," he wrote, "considerable land has been cleared . . . and it is a sad sight to see these Indians—once the owners of this vast region—men, women, and children alike, filing along in the distance over this clearing, heavily laden with rubber from their rubber forests, which they lay at the feet of their conquerors." Eberhardt recounted stories of brutality, of violence, of murder and terror inflicted on the Indians as they were forced to collect rubber for which the foremen received a percentage. The foremen drove the Indians to the point of death, many of them, including children, being mutilated and brutally beaten as a lesson to the others. Those who tried to escape were rounded up at gunpoint. "When the Indians flee to the forests, expeditions headed by armed whites and made up of Indians of neighboring tribes toward whom the runaways have always been hostile go in pursuit, and so, hunted by the whites and surrounded on all sides by hostiles of their own race, they are eventually killed or brought back captives to work as slaves of the whites."

Eberhardt remarked that in the past two years Barbadians had been recruited to the positions of armed overseers. From them he had learned quite a lot about what was going on in the area.

Eberhardt's report betrayed his frustration at being unable to bring any pressure to bear on the Peruvian government. He was, as he put it, "consul of another Government." And he added, tellingly, "Nor as a plain American citizen could I have had anything to say on the subject, when I remembered our own treatment of the North American Indian, whom we killed because he would not stand by submissively while we took away his lands." His superiors in Washington were not pleased with that comment.

What was going on in the Putumayo, Eberhardt explained, could only be likened to what had been exposed in the Congo several years earlier. The criminal acts he witnessed and heard of were being committed, he told the department, by employees of a private company based in Iquitos: J. C. Arana y Hermanos.

Eberhardt's report reached Washington early in February 1908, but he wanted his authorship to be concealed. If, he wrote, the conditions he described should be exposed, "I should prefer that it come from some other sources, for I was treated with the utmost kindness and consideration by the representatives of the company during the entire trip, as will be the case with anybody visiting that district from Iquitos, from the fact that they must depend entirely upon the company for transportation and accommodations in general."

Not long after, Eberhardt left Iquitos and went home on leave. He quit the Iquitos consulate early in 1908 and moved on to the less politically sensitive posting of Barranquilla, Colombia.

Eberhardt's observations were extremely insightful and would have been very useful to the Foreign Office, but their existence was denied, and for the moment, the Foreign Office was left with Cazes. It had to look elsewhere to confirm or deny the allegations.

Fortunately, when Charles des Graz telegraphed to say that he could not be of much help, he added that a Captain Whiffen had made a lengthy visit to the Putumayo in the previous year and was now back in England. Graz was certain he would be of use.

The Whiffen lead was a godsend because until this point the Foreign Office had had to rely entirely on Hardenburg's evidence. True, he did provide documentation to support his allegations against the Peruvian Amazon Company, but there was no independent way of assessing his "facts." Moreover, Hardenburg wasn't a British subject. What the Foreign Office really needed was corroborating evidence from a source that they could assess to their own particular satisfaction. Who better than an officer in His Majesty's army?

6

AN OFFICER AND A GENTLEMAN

Captain Thomas William Whiffen would prove to be a key figure in investigating the conditions in the Putumayo. He had visited the area and had met with Julio César Arana. He was also involved in one of the Amazon's most enduring and controversial mysteries—the disappearance in the forests of the Putumayo of the French explorer Eugène Robuchon.

Though no one at the Foreign Office seemed to remember, Captain Thomas Whiffen had in fact come to the department's attention a few months earlier. In early July 1909 they had received a letter from the British consul in Pará stating that a month before, Whiffen had walked into the consulate, long after his reported murder "by uncivilised Indian tribes in the Caquetá region of the Amazon whilst prosecuting a journey of exploration from Iquitos to Manaõs [sic]." Ambrose Pogson, the British consul, thought that for a man who had been missing for almost half a year, he was "in comparatively good health."

Whiffen was thirty years old at the time. He came from a wealthy family. His grandfather, Thomas Whiffen, founded the pharmaceutical firm that bore the family name, and his father, Thomas Joseph Whiffen, carried on the business. But chemical formulas, figures, and stocks were of little interest to Thomas William. Instead, he was attracted to military life and travel. Serving in the Boer War with the Royal Inniskilling Fusiliers, he was wounded in December 1899 in the Battle of Colenso. For several years he appears to have drifted inside the military, alternatively fit and unfit for active service. He was promoted to captain in 1904, and in 1905 he joined the 14th Hussars. About a year later he went on half pay, with no duties in the service. He was free to travel, and the Amazon beckoned him.

Whiffen wanted to solve the mystery of the French explorer Eugène Robuchon, who had disappeared late in 1905 in the Putumayo region while under contract to the Peruvian government to survey Arana's territory. Robuchon's disappearance had shocked European and American geographical and anthropological societies, who had become complacent about the dangers that awaited European explorers in the wild.

Eugène Robuchon had arrived in Iquitos in July 1903, and he had planned to get to an area of northeastern Bolivia that he wished to explore in depth. He brought his wife and his dog along, hoping to make important ethnographic, zoological, and botanical collections and to produce a travel narrative replete with photographs and phonographic recordings.

Robuchon was a professional explorer. Since his youth in the Vendée region of France, helping his father, Jules, a professional photographer, he had been fascinated by South America, especially its geography and natural history.

This was his second trip there. On the previous one he had met a young Indian woman, whom he baptized and named Hortensia. They were married on their return to France and were now returning to visit her family in northeastern Bolivia. Robuchon wanted to take the opportunity to make a thorough exploration of this relatively unknown area.

While the couple were in Iquitos outfitting for their journey farther up the Amazon toward Bolivia, they met Julio César Arana. Robuchon's credentials and his zeal for exploration impressed Arana so much that he invited the couple to visit the Putumayo. Robuchon remarked in a letter to his father that Arana had "shown great kindness" to them. Toward the end of September, Eugène, Hortensia, and Othelo (his Great Dane), after boarding one of Arana's steamers in Iquitos, found themselves in La Chorrera rather than northeastern Bolivia.

For the next two weeks Robuchon and a party of guides and carriers from La Chorrera went exploring and traversed a significant part of Arana's territory. During this period Eugène tried to see and experience as much as he could of the indigenous people, and he seemed to be satisfied with the results. He collected many artifacts, including a few skulls, witnessed a strange tobacco rite and a cannibalistic feast, took many photographs, and captured on wax cylinders the dialects he heard. He was energized by the jungle, despite being lost for several days on end. He found the Huitoto and the Bora people cordial to him, though the fear of being eaten by them preyed on his mind. He appreciated having his dog and his guns with him while he stayed with them.

Meanwhile, Robuchon's activities had come to the attention of the Peruvian government. Hoping to legitimize its claims to the Putumayo region, the government instructed Arana to ask Robuchon to make a complete survey of Arana's property. A contract to that effect was drawn up and signed in September 1904.

Robuchon was given precise instructions on the route he was to follow, taking in the entire region bounded by the Igaraparaná, Caraparaná, and Putumayo rivers. He was also to record the area's natural history and ethnography and to produce a photographic record of his exploration, paying especial attention to landscape, the indigenous people, and the rubber stations.

In August 1905 Robuchon sent Hortensia back to his family in France and embarked on his trip. A few months later, on November 14, he was in the small rubber post of Urania, on a tributary of the Igaraparaná near the northern extremity of Arana's territory. Here he took the opportunity to write to his father again. This would be his last chance, as his work would take him to parts of the region from where communication with the outside world would be impossible. Robuchon was embarking on a sweeping exploration along the boundary of Arana's land, starting with a long overland track to the Caquetá River.

Once there, he planned to journey by canoe until he reached the Cahuinari and from there back to the Igaraparaná. He knew that this part of the trip was "excessively dangerous," but he was confident that should anything happen to him, "his friend Monsieur Arana would not forget Hortensia."

Nothing more was seen of Robuchon. He had just turned thirty-three.

Arana wrote to Hortensia—who was living in Poitiers with her in-laws since her return to France—on several occasions during 1906, hoping that one day he might be able to send her news that her husband had returned from the forest. Such things did happen, he assured her, but in the summer of 1907 Arana wrote saying that they had given up all hope that her husband was still alive. Arana said that what he was able to find out for sure was that Robuchon had last gone into the forest with two Indian guides at the end of December 1905, and he was not heard of again. The guides had vanished as well. The best guess was that he had disappeared in the environs of the rubber station of El Retiro by the banks of the Putumayo. A part of his baggage had been retrieved and a "few written lines indicating the direction he was going to take but which, because of the action of the humidity, were now illegible."

Despite the fact that Arana had promised Robuchon that if anything happened to him, he would look after Hortensia, she never heard from Arana again.

In April 1908 Whiffen set off from London for the northwest Amazon. The standard account of Robuchon's fate, first given by representatives of Arana's company, was that he had been killed by local people—and possibly eaten. Whiffen, on the other hand, had heard a story that Robuchon was alive, and was being held as a prisoner by a band of Indians.

Whiffen arrived in Iquitos via Manaus in the second week of June. While there, he met and subsequently hired a Montserratian named John Brown, who had been working in the Putumayo for Arana's company for several years. Brown knew the Putumayo and Huitoto, one of the dominant language groups of the region, well. Cazes arranged for Whiffen to get a passage on one of the Peruvian Amazon Rubber Company's launches going to El Encanto, which he reached in mid-August. Several days later Whiffen, Brown, and more than twenty Indians, many of them armed, headed out into the jungle in the direction of the Igaraparaná, their destination being the rubber station of La Chorrera.

On August 22 the party reached La Chorrera, and from there Whiffen's route took them cross-country toward the Cahuinari and the Caquetá rivers, which they reached almost one month later. This was the area where Robuchon was last seen alive.

By the end of October 1908 Whiffen and his party had reached the point where the Cahuinari meets the Caquetá. In the clearing, they found evidence of a deserted shelter, which Brown confirmed was Robuchon's last camp; and soon thereafter Whiffen unearthed "eight broken photograph plates in a packet, and the eye-piece of a sextant."

And that was about it. Nothing more of interest came to light, though various paths from the clearing were carefully examined. Believing that Robuchon would have chosen to escape from his predicament by working his way farther down the Caquetá, Whiffen decided to follow his hunch all the way downriver until a point not far short of where the Caquetá meets the Apaporis River. When nothing turned up, Whiffen reversed his course to explore the other side of the river. There he came across the wreck of a raft, which Brown confirmed was Robuchon's. But it held no clues.

For the next two months Whiffen and his party headed northward through the jungle toward the Apaporis River, hoping that the Indians living in this area would have some information, but nothing came of his inquiries.

Whiffen and his party made it back to La Chorrera on February 22, 1909. He had seen a fair bit of the land beyond the Putumayo, but he had not solved the mystery of Robuchon's disappearance. Whiffen's best guess was that Robuchon was "located by a band of visiting Indians, captured, and either murdered or carried away in captivity to their haunts in the north bank of the Caquetá." According to Whiffen, Robuchon probably died in March or April 1906.

Back in Iquitos, rumors abounded that Robuchon had been disposed of by Arana's men, as he had taken incriminating photographs of the horrible crimes they had committed. These rumors were illustrated by Saldaña Rocca who, in *La Felpa*, printed two cartoons on the topic, one showing Robuchon's death on Arana's conscience, the other a sketch of an Indian being flogged, based on a photograph of Robuchon's (the original of which survives). Both Hardenburg and a visiting Colombian poet, Cornelio Hispano, claimed to have seen prints of Robuchon's photographs of atrocities circulating in Iquitos.

It didn't take long for the Foreign Office to track Whiffen down to a hotel in Harrogate, where he was recuperating after his grueling Amazonian experiences. On October 18, 1909, he telegrammed to say that he was happy to help with a report; three days later his report arrived in Whitehall. Detailed and running on for thirteen pages, it took the form of a set of responses to particular statements made in the issues of *Truth* for September 22 and 29 and October 6 and 13, 1909.

It was fortunate for the Foreign Office that Whiffen was not off adventuring somewhere, for he turned out to be as helpful as Cazes was not. Whiffen explained that he had passed through the Putumayo region on two occasions in the past year or so. Though he, personally, had not seen any evidence of atrocities, he was absolutely certain that they were taking place. When he was in the area on his first visit, his movements were known in advance, and he guessed that company representatives had carefully removed any evidence of abuses: "prisoners were liberated, flogging ceased, and outwardly affairs assumed a peaceful and a humane aspect." On his second visit, however, he did discover, hidden in the forest beyond the houses, stocks and whipping posts. It was then that the stories he had picked up in Iquitos began to make sense—horrifying accounts that were very similar to the ones Hardenburg had collected.

In his Foreign Office report Whiffen produced evidence from John Brown, his guide in the Putumayo and, according to Whiffen, a reliable witness. Brown's account was at least as appalling as the ones reproduced in *Truth*. He related to Whiffen how in 1906 or 1907, [two section chiefs] had in custody the Chief of a tribe from the vicinity of Morelia, who was accused of conspiracy against them. After a drunken orgy the man was tied to a tree in the compound. The two section heads proceeded to have a shooting match; the man who excised the Indian's penis by means of a bullet to be declared the winner. The native was afterwards despatched according to the ordinary method.

Whiffen spoke about the system of collecting rubber as "absolutely that of forced labour with its necessary and attendant evils." He was particularly struck by the demoralization he found prevalent among the Hispanic chiefs of the rubber stations, a characteristic "inseparable from the placing of practically absolute power in the hands of such men." Whiffen went on to relate a conversation he had had with Abelardo Agüero, the chief of the Abisinia rubber station: "Agüero confided to me one day that he did not treat his Indians in the same brutal fashion as was customary amongst other Chiefs of Sections. If a man refused to work or failed to bring in his quota of rubber, he gave him three chances: the first time he warned him, the second he beat him, and as to the third—well, he took care that the man did not have a fourth chance."

These chilling descriptions fully supported what had appeared in *Truth*. But Whiffen also provided vital information on the standing of the Putumayo with respect to Peruvian interests in the region. He was absolutely certain that the "territory, some hundreds of square miles in extent, is administered by the Company itself, there being no effective administration or occupation by the Peruvian Government. The Commissario of the Central Government at Lima makes an occasional voyage to the district, returning to Iquitos in the same launch after a few days stay . . . he, together with the few soldiers in the territory, is a secretly paid servant of the Company."

Another piece of information Whiffen provided was that many of the instances of atrocity were actually performed by Indians on Indians, under command of employees of the company. He explained that the company would take on (and arm) young Indian men of a tribe hostile to that being dealt with, "thus putting them perhaps at the mercy of their hereditary enemies," who were also in fear of losing their own lives if they didn't carry out instructions. Finally, Whiffen told the foreign secretary that he had met Arana in Manaus in June and confronted him with what he had learned in the Putumayo. "Explaining the situation," Whiffen wrote, "I received promises from him that the Chief of the Putumayo district, Macedo, should be immediately recalled, and that searching reforms should be inaugurated, together with a complete change of personnel. I have no means of knowing whether these promises have been kept."

Whiffen's report dealt squarely with the allegations of atrocities committed by the Peruvian Amazon Company. It thoroughly supported Hardenburg's assertions. The Foreign Office was able to accept Whiffen's report as true not only because he was an officer and a gentleman but because the War Office, too, was prepared to attest to his character. "He was," they said, "a sensible kind of fellow" and "what he says is to be credited." Just the guarantee they could understand and accept.

Full and truthful as Whiffen's report was, it had been about a month since Hart-Davies's parliamentary question, and still the Foreign Office had learned nothing more about the Barbadians, their main concern at this point. Just a few days after the parliamentary questions were asked, the Colonial Office told the Foreign Office that they had no information on the subject from the government of Barbados. This was untrue, as Paternoster himself had discovered and as Cazes's letter to the Foreign Office made clear. The Foreign Office kept pestering the Colonial Office about what they knew. At the end of October the Earl of Crewe, secretary of state for the colonies, gave in to pressure, telegraphed the Barbados governor Gilbert Carter in Bridgetown, and asked him straight out "whether negroes were illtreated, [and] whether they still work for the Company."

A day later the Colonial Office had its answer. Carter telegraphed back:

> On several occasions Barbadians have complained of ill-treatment whilst employed [in] Peru in the service of Arana Hermanos. British Consul Iquitos obtained dismissal of Ramon Sanchez Commercial Agent Putumayo in consequence of complaints received from Barbadians

against him. No Barbadians working for Company now, emigrants to Peru have ceased for 3 or 4 years.

If this was true, the Foreign Office had nothing further to do. The complaints were well in the past. "It seems that we have at present no grounds of complaint against the Co.: a propos of Barbadians so the enquiry is perhaps scarcely necessary," wrote an official.

But then everything changed. Louis Mallet, an assistant under-secretary of state at the Foreign Office, with more than twenty years' experience at the department, had an interview with Captain Whiffen on November 10. Silent about the Barbadians in his written report, Whiffen now presented new facts. First of all, he said, there were two hundred or three hundred Barbadians and other British West Indians in the service of the company when he was in the area just a year ear-lier. And then he added the most serious charge: "Some of them," he said, "are practically slaves as they are in debt to the Company and have to work out their debt in service—others are well paid. They and Peruvian half castes are the slave drivers of the Indians and are used to inflict the punishments described in *Truth*."

This was totally at odds with the information that came from the Colonial Office and from Cazes. The Foreign Office pressed the Co-lonial Office for more information. They wanted a report from the governor of Barbados responding to Whiffen's very serious revelations. To move things along, the Foreign Office repeated two other facts it had learned from Whiffen: one, that John Brown, his guide in the Putumayo, could now be contacted in Montserrat; and two, that Whiffen had already written to the governor of Barbados telling him about what he knew of the Barbadians and their circumstances.

Despite the urgency, the machinery of colonial government moved sluggishly, and the answers, when they came, were insubstantial. By the end of November, almost a full month after the interview with Whiffen, all that the Foreign Office had heard from Barbados was what they already knew. The key questions—Were there Barbadians still in the Putumayo? And what were their circumstances?—had still not been answered from within government circles.

Amid the silence, however, the Colonial Office did make the sug-gestion that "it is worth considering whether a consular officer should be sent to make inquiries on the spot and that if Sir E. Grey decides to send an officer, it might be well if he could be accompanied by some Barbadian official." The Colonial Office's suggestion fell on deaf ears at the Foreign Office. Louis Mallet responded in a cool, logical, and ultimately dismissive manner: "It would be useless, *if it were possible*, to send a Consul. He would be allowed to see nothing—the country is almost impassable, and without the goodwill of the Company, it is not possible to live in the Putumayo." "Captain Whiffen," Mallet added, "laughed at the idea when I suggested it."

Truth, meanwhile, continued its own campaign against the Peruvian Amazon Company and continued to publish on the subject throughout October and the first half of November 1909.

The main thrust of Paternoster's attack on the company now was that they were ducking out of the allegations by repeating that they had no responsibility for what may or may not have happened in the past. Paternoster insisted, however, that they, at the very least, had a responsibility for finding out whether the allegations were true. The public, he claimed, demanded it.

There is no evidence to suggest that *Truth* had heard anything from the directors of the company. While there was silence from the London board, its supporters in Peru weighed in with counteraccusations. One set of these appeared in a letter first printed in the Lima newspaper *El Comercio*, a copy of which came into Paternoster's possession from a shareholder of the Peruvian Amazon Company. Juan Tizon, who identified himself as being closely associated with the Peruvian Amazon Company and having recently been prefect of Loreto, wrote the letter from Iquitos. Hardenburg, he said, was a blackmailer.

The truth about Hardenburg was this, Tizon stated: along with other engineers, Hardenburg had been working for the Colombian government on a railway project not far from the Putumayo, but he had fallen out with his superiors. He decided to try his luck in Peru but got no farther than La Unión, where, unfortunately, he became caught up in an attack on the launch *Liberal* by Colombians with the intent of taking its valuable cargo of rubber. The Peruvian naval vessel *Iquitos*, which happened to be in the area, came to the assistance of the *Liberal* and successfully repulsed the Colombian attack, but in the ensuing confusion Hardenburg became separated from his baggage. Hardenburg was offered and accepted passage on the *Liberal* on its return trip to Iquitos. Tizon explained that Hardenburg's baggage was most likely stolen from him during the skirmish by Indians, but Hardenburg, when he got to Iquitos, insisted that Arana's company was responsible for its loss and demanded compensation to the tune of £7,000. Hardenburg threatened that if he didn't receive this money, he would "publish a book in which he would depict the imaginary horrors, which, according to him, were being committed in Putumayo. When I left Iquitos Hardenburg was still there earning a living as a teacher of English, but . . . he has recently left for Europe where he has carried his threat into effect."

In the October 27, 1909, issue of *Truth*, Paternoster had repudiated every single statement of Tizon's letter. Still, engaging in accusation and counteraccusation was not going to help the cause. The directors of the Peruvian Amazon Company had to act—but who could make them?

Arana, meanwhile, had entered the picture. Cazes let Sir Charles Hardinge, the permanent secretary at the Foreign Office, know that Arana had written to him at his private London address asking him what he had said about how the Barbadians had been treated in the Putumayo. The Foreign Office forbade Cazes to answer him.

Arana's writing to Cazes at his private address suggested an improperly close relationship between them; that Cazes consulted the Foreign Office about it implied that he might be willing to switch sides.

The time had come to review the situation. Near the end of November, Louis Mallet, who had interviewed Whiffen and knew more about the state of affairs in the Putumayo than anyone else in government, undertook to write a memo summarizing what was known about what he was now calling the "Peruvian Amazon Atrocities." Because of its high profile, Mallet's memo would determine what the Foreign Office should do next.

The memo captured the dilemma facing the Foreign Office. Mallet felt that the allegations that the Peruvian Amazon Company had horribly abused its Indian labor force were essentially true, but he could not see what the British government could do about it. As he put it, "Even if the Company, if gently approached, promised to make reforms, how could we see them carried out? If we were aggressive the Company would register itself in another country. We could not send an expedition to Peru, to this remote and savage spot. We could not ask the Consul at Iquitos to go there—and it would be useless if he did for all trace of cruelty would disappear as he advanced." "Arana," Mallet continued, "promised reforms, asked to see Captain Whiffen in Paris a few months ago, and told him that the reforms were progressing and again confirmed this in London a few weeks ago. But Captain Whiffen is convinced that nothing is being done at all and there can be no proof if anything is done."

Mallet also did not doubt Hardenburg's integrity. He had learned from James Bryce, the British ambassador in Washington, that the U.S. government knew about Hardenburg's and Perkins's misadventures and their witnessing of the murder and other outrages committed on the Colombians and had no reason to doubt that the pair were telling the truth. The Peruvian government, he added, had more or less accepted their claims by agreeing to compensate the two men for their losses.

On the basis of everything before him, Mallet recommended that the time had come for the Foreign Office to initiate a more direct approach. He advised that the Foreign Office should take the unprecedented step of writing directly to the Peruvian Amazon Company at their headquarters in the City of London.

"Proceed accordingly," Grey noted in his characteristic bright red ink at the end of Mallet's memo. "It is a most horrible story."

7

OUR MAN IN THE PUTUMAYO

On November 24, 1909, a letter went to the secretary of the Peruvian Amazon Company at Salisbury House, London Wall, the company's registered address in the City of London. The letter began by saying that Sir Edward Grey, after studying independent reports, was fully convinced of the truth of the state of affairs in the Putumayo as stated in several issues of *Truth*.

There followed a point-by-point indictment of the company's procedures, including the following facts as they were understood by the Foreign Office: that the Peruvian government's representative and the soldiers in the area were in the company's pay; that the Indians were compelled to work under a system of forced labor; that the company employees who directed the Indians were paid by result, not by salary; that "organised tyranny accompanied by gross abuses must almost necessarily ensue when such a system is introduced"; that the instances of "ill-treatment, rape, mutilation and murder" were true; that the Colombians were massacred and Serrano brutally murdered; and that Julio César Arana, the owner and one of the directors of the company, had known what was going on and was therefore complicit in the atrocities.

The letter ended with a request for assurances from the company's directors that they had already taken, or were now prepared to take, measures to reform the company's procedures and administration, including changing its personnel, for, as the letter continued, "it is clearly highly discreditable, as your Board will doubtless admit, that a British Company should be in any way responsible for the present disgraceful state of affairs, the existence of which there is unfortunately no reason to doubt."

Two days later, on November 26, 1909, the Peruvian Amazon Company acknowledged the receipt of the Foreign Office's letter, but it would be more than a month before they responded in full.

The Foreign Office was now inextricably involved in the Putumayo. It had taken a bold step in writing directly to the Peruvian Amazon Company: this was not something the Foreign Office did lightly. While it waited for an answer, there were some loose ends to tie up.

One of these concerned the United States. On the same day the Foreign Office received the acknowledgment from the Peruvian Amazon Company, it dispatched a letter to James Bryce, the British ambassador in Washington, bringing him up to date on all the events surrounding the Putumayo issue. Included with the letter were copies of several issues of *Truth*, a copy of Whiffen's report, and a copy of the letter to the Peruvian Amazon Company. These inserts were for Bryce's attention, but Bryce was to go one step further, a step that had to be taken carefully, whose outcome was by no means a foregone conclusion. Grey wanted Bryce to share these with the State Department, "to enquire whether the United States Government would in the circumstances be prepared to join with His Majesty's Government in calling the attention of the Peruvian Government to the matter."

Bryce had been made British ambassador in 1907 during President Theodore Roosevelt's second term, and he knew and liked the United States: Charles Hardinge, the permanent undersecretary under Grey, remarked that Bryce knew more about American history and the country's Constitution than did most Americans.

At the core of U.S.–Latin American relations lay the Monroe Doctrine, first articulated by the U.S. Congress in 1823. This rationale came directly out of the Latin American wars of independence during the first two decades of the nineteenth century. The United States, itself born of revolution, was the first country to extend diplomatic relations to the newly formed South American republics. As administrations came and went, the interpretation of the Monroe Doctrine changed, but its basic tenets remained the same as far as American policy makers were concerned: to exclude European influence from the continent and to expand U.S. trade and investment and foster peace and stability in order to do so.

For most of the nineteenth century the United States' chief concern was its own continental development, and the Monroe Doctrine remained largely in the background. But as the century drew to a close, the United States, now one of the world's major economies, began to involve itself in the imperial struggle with the Great European Powers and Japan. At the same time, it embarked on a more aggressive policy toward its Hispanic neighbors.

In December 1904 President Roosevelt articulated an important reassessment of the Monroe Doctrine when he spelled out to Congress what came to be called the Roosevelt Corollary: namely, to add to the authority of the Monroe Doctrine the right of the United States to intervene in Latin America, especially to ward off any growing European interests, and to be able to coerce the republics in case they went astray, in American eyes.

While President William Howard Taft, who had been elected in 1908 following Roosevelt's two terms in office, adhered to the principle that the United States had a right to intervene in Latin America, he advocated using dollars, in the form of substantial loans to Latin American regimes, rather than bullets, to bring about closer ties. In its ideal form, Taft's dollar diplomacy was an economic rather than a military policy; in fact, U.S. troops were ready and sometimes employed to shore up tottering regimes.

This was the background to the relationship between Britain and the United States when it came to Latin American affairs. In practice, it meant that Britain would defer to America's overwhelming interest in the region and not do anything to antagonize the country's leaders. As Foreign Secretary Sir Edward Grey commented on the accommodation between the two countries as regards the Central American republics, "[They] must succumb to some greater and better influence and it can only be that of the U.S.A." That same comment could be taken to apply to all of Latin America.

Now, in late 1909, Bryce was being asked by Sir Edward Grey to get the Americans involved in the Peruvian Amazon Company affair. Bryce accordingly wrote to Philander Knox, the secretary of state, on December 11, 1909. The request for the assistance of the American government was gingerly placed within the body of the letter, suggesting that representations to the Peruvian government "will come with greater force if made jointly by the two Powers whose citizens have been witnesses." All Bryce could do now was wait for a reply.

Meanwhile, John Cathcart Wason, the Liberal MP who had asked one of the first parliamentary questions about the Putumayo back in late September, now returned to questioning the Foreign Office. He wanted to know what claims were being made against the Peruvian Amazon Company with regard to their ill-treatment of the Barbadian workers.

Mallet confirmed that complaints of Barbadians being ill-treated had reached the Colonial Office in the past, but no current claims, to his knowledge, were being made against the company. Mallet also had more information about the scale of the Barbadian presence in the Putumayo. Between September 1904 and June 1905, more than two hundred Barbadian men had been recruited to work in the Putumayo on two-year contracts, and a certain Abel Alarco, an agent of Arana's company, had seen to all of the arrangements. As to the present situation, Mallet could add nothing. The Colonial Office had still not established whether any Barbadians were actually in the area working for Arana.

At about this same time, the Foreign Office was told by Travers Buxton, the secretary of the Anti-Slavery and Aborigines' Protection Society, that his society had been disturbed by the articles in *Truth* of "the systematically cruel treatment of native Indians employed by the Peruvian Amazon Company," and that they had been writing to the company since early October asking the directors to receive a small delegation from the society, which wished to discuss the allegations and ask for a full investigation of them. The company had, so far, not agreed to a meeting.

The Foreign Office viewed the society's involvement as problematic. "It is very tiresome," Mallet wrote to his colleagues, "that this society should interfere and we must be careful not to be dragged into another Congo affair and not to be forced into a hostile attitude to Peru." By this Mallet meant that when it came to Latin America, the British government had to move cautiously and always with the full support of the American government. He warned his colleagues that the Foreign Office must not let itself be pressured by the Anti-Slavery and Aborigines' Protection Society to act impulsively.

While the Foreign Office's deliberations on whom to contact for corroborative information were kept firmly within the department's four walls, the Anti-Slavery and Aborigines' Protection Society had been keeping the issue in the public eye by informing leading British newspapers, such as *The Times* and the *Manchester Guardian*, of their own dealings with the Peruvian Amazon Company.

The Peruvian Amazon Company replied to the Foreign Office in a letter on December 30, 1909. The directors of the company, it said, knew nothing of the allegations until they read them in *Truth*; if such atrocities took place, they happened before the board was constituted, and the directors could not be held responsible for past events. The letter added that Hardenburg and Whiffen were, in any event, blackmailers and their statements were consequently worthless, and the company denied all the other allegations that were printed, including the crucial one that the Indians were made to work under a system of forced labor.

Included in the company's letter was a printed circular addressed to its shareholders and signed by Julio César Arana. He categorically denied that any atrocities had occurred, and he turned the burden of proof onto *Truth*, which had described, in his words, "deeds so vile that it seems incredible that such an important newspaper should have given them prominence without a fuller inquiry." In support of this, Arana made the following pledge: "I absolutely deny that lawlessness has of late existed in the Putumayo Region, for neither the Peruvian Authorities, who efficiently fulfil their duties of maintaining order and administering justice, nor I myself would have allowed such a state of things to exist."

Arana then launched into an attack on Hardenburg, accusing him of blackmail, citing in evidence a telegram from Arana's lawyer in Iquitos that spoke of Hardenburg demanding £7,000 to stop him from publishing in London a "defamatory book against the firm in the Putumayo." Arana continued this line of argument by informing his shareholders that Captain Whiffen, too, sought to blackmail him. He described how in early October, after returning home from his travels in the Putumayo, he had met Captain Whiffen in Paris. Whiffen told him that he had been contacted by *Truth* for a statement about the allegations, which he knew to be false, and he would be saying so. Knowing that Arana was on his way to London, Whiffen told him to meet him there, at his club. After dining at the Café Royal, the pair went on to the Alhambra Music Hall in Leicester Square before adjourning to the Royal Automobile Club in Pall Mall. There, recounted Arana, Whiffen demanded the sum of £1,000 to tell *Truth* what Arana wanted told. Arana said that he took the offer to the board, which promptly refused to accede to Whiffen's proposal. The following day, Whiffen called on Arana at his hotel, hoping for money. When it was not forthcoming, Whiffen prepared that "most untruthful report" for the Foreign Office.

The rest of the circular lauded the company's achievements, assuring its shareholders that everything had been and was being done to ensure that the agents and employees of the company behaved properly. Its ending was upbeat: "I can only assure the Shareholders that . . . every care will be taken so that [the management] may be conducted . . . in such a manner that they will be proud to be connected with this great enterprise, which is at present passing through initial difficulties, but for which a most satisfactory and brilliant future can safely be predicted."

Once the company's letter and Arana's circular were passed around the department for comment, Mallet again took charge of how the Foreign Office should handle its response. There was no point, he argued, in going over the same ground as before, because the company would simply answer with counteraccusations, including charges of blackmail against Hardenburg and Whiffen. Both *Truth* and the Anti-Slavery and Aborigines' Protection Society through its members had ensured that the public wanted answers, not counteraccusations. What was needed, Mallet urged, was pressure on the board to find out what was going on in the Putumayo—to "satisfy public opinion in this country by instituting a thorough and impartial investigation into the state of affairs . . . with the object of devising a system of reforms in the administration which will put a stop to the present abuses and prevent their recurrence in the future." He recommended that the Foreign Office suggest that the company dispatch an impartial commission to do the required investigating.

Sir Edward Grey agreed to this approach. Mallet was now also thinking of attaching a British consular official to the proposed commission, but according to him, the time was not yet ripe to suggest it to the company. On February 8, 1910, the Foreign Office wrote to the Peruvian Amazon Company suggesting the way forward. If the company was still "obdurate," as the Foreign Office put it, then it would call in Sir John Lister-Kaye, one of the company's directors, for a chat.

February passed, and there was only silence from the company. Little, indeed, was progressing in the Putumayo story in London apart from a further communication from the Colonial Office, which finally came up with an exact figure, 196, for the number of Barbadians who had emigrated to Peru to work for Arana. This was a useful piece of information, but the more important question of whether any Barbadians were still in the Putumayo remained unanswered.

And then, on March 8, 1910, that issue was put smartly aside when a letter arrived at the Foreign Office from the Peruvian Amazon Company. The company had a new secretary, Henry Gielgud, who had previously worked for the accounting firm of Deloitte, Plender, Griffiths and Company. He had spent late May, June, and July 1909 in the Putumayo auditing the company's books and visiting rubber stations around La Chorrera and El Encanto. When he returned to England, he made a report to the board on November 24, 1909, of his visit to the company's Putumayo properties, which, according to the company's then secretary, was highly complimentary. Conditions there were described as excellent. From the company's point of view, therefore, he was an excellent choice for secretary: he had been to the Putumayo and would toe the company line.

Orme Garton Sargent, one of the Foreign Office's junior clerks, was the first to react to the letter: "The tone of the letter," he remarked, "is somewhat truculent and does not hold out much prospect of the Co. being ready to listen to reason. They bring forward no new facts but merely deny once more in toto the allegations basing themselves on Arana's statement enclosed in their previous letter and on the Peruvian Chargé d'Affaires letter to *Truth*." He advised that nothing could now be gained by going over the same ground again and that the Foreign Office should answer the letter by repeating that the company should undertake an investigation on the spot to find out who was right—Hardenburg and Whiffen or Arana.

Louis Mallet agreed wholeheartedly with Sargent's analysis, but he felt that a more psychological approach at this point might be better. The response should simply say that the company's letter made it perfectly clear that they had no intention of investigating the allegations, and leave it at that. Mallet, as usual, got his way, and with approval from Grey, the corresponding letter carrying this short, abrupt point was sent on March 31 to the company headquarters.

A fortnight earlier, an unexpected letter had arrived at the Foreign Office by way of the Colonial Office. It was from Montserrat, and it contained a statement by John Brown, Captain Whiffen's guide during his visit to the Putumayo.

Brown's statement went straight to the point: "I will tell you everything I know about the ill-treatment of the English subjects who live in Peru." He continued:

> They beat us with swords, they put us in guns (hands tied across knees with guns underneath knees), and did us all manner of wickedness. We cried for help but there was none. We tried to escape, but there was no means of doing so—only one small steamer which belonged to the same company and they would not take us away. They still continued beating and ill-treating us English subjects, and they treated the Indians in the same way. The cruelties practised in that place are shameful. They (the Spaniards) would take a man, tie his

hands together behind his back with chains and hang him up, and then beat him with sticks or swords.

Brown recounted that he had arrived in the Putumayo in April 1905 in a party of fifty West Indians, most of them from Barbados. Though their contracts ran for only two years, they found it impossible to leave after their time had expired. The West Indians were hired, he said, to go into the forest to look for Indians and kill them. If they refused, they were beaten.

In June 1908 Brown had managed to get away from the Putumayo on the company launch on the grounds that he wanted to remit money home from Iquitos. It was then that he met Captain Whiffen and told him all he had seen in the Putumayo. He accepted Whiffen's invitation to join him on the expedition to the Putumayo to search for Robuchon.

Brown also said that he had told Cazes about the cases of ill-treatment, but nothing had come of it. Indeed, Brown was convinced that Cazes "seemed to me to be in league with the Peruvians." The statement ended with a plea: "The other British subjects cannot get out, they are slaves. They are in need of help and there is no help they can get."

The Foreign Office now had its first real confirmation that Barbadians had still been working for the company in the Putumayo in 1908. Yet prejudices at the Foreign Office almost dismissed Brown's testimony when Sir Charles Hardinge, the permanent undersecretary, cast doubt on the reliability of the evidence, arguing that the writer would have needed a diary of events in order to recall dates and names so precisely, the implication being that black people didn't keep such things.

Armed with John Brown's supporting statement, the Foreign Office was more certain than ever that Barbadians were still working for Arana and that the abuses were continuing. The presence of the Barbadians in the Putumayo was the Foreign Office's only entry point into a matter that, politically, was predominantly a Peruvian one. Only a British consul and an official of the Barbadian government, who could talk directly to the Barbadians, could assess once and for all whether the abusive system persisted. At the same time, the Foreign Office wanted to involve the Peruvian government, but to do that, it needed American support, and it was still waiting to hear from the American administration as to whether it was willing to make a joint representation with the British.

On April 11, 1910, James Bryce in Washington indicated that the United States probably wouldn't be going along with Britain, certainly not at that time. Although he had still not heard from the secretary of state officially, Bryce had learned that the American government was trying to broker a deal between Ecuador and Peru concerning disagreements about their common border, and pursuing the Peruvian Amazon Company case would endanger these talks.

Bryce was right. After arguing over their borders since independence more than eighty years earlier, Ecuador and Peru had finally agreed to let the king of Spain arbitrate on their respective cases. The king's decision was due in June 1909, but when the Ecuadorians learned by way of a leak that it was not going to be favorable to them, they withdrew completely from the negotiations and put their country on a war footing. The Peruvians responded in like manner. In both countries, nationalistic demonstrations were held and hostile public opinion stoked. By April 1910, with thousands of troops amassed on both sides, war seemed inevitable. U.S. secretary of state Philander Knox, who had previously proposed U.S. arbitration between the two countries, sought the help of Brazil and Argentina to get Peru and Ecuador to the negotiating table.

According to Bryce, Knox's hands were tied: the moment was far too sensitive for him to approach the Peruvians on any matter other than their dispute with the Ecuadorians; even answering Bryce's letter might be construed as implicit agreement with the British position. Although it had no official confirmation of this from Knox, the Foreign Office was not hopeful.

Away from Whitehall, the Anti-Slavery and Aborigines' Protection Society was upping the pressure on the government and on the company. The Foreign Office received a string of letters from the society, pushing for an answer from the company and insisting that the company send a commission to the Putumayo with a British consul attached. The society also reminded the Foreign Office that "in many of its features the system of enforced rubber collection closely resembles that of the Congo State; moreover, [we do] not hesitate to say that nothing reported from the Congo has equalled in horror some of the acts alleged in detail against this rubber Syndicate. The nature of the evidence is indeed too revolting to permit of full publicity." As if this were not enough, the society also (to the annoyance of the Foreign Office) coordinated a petition among its affiliated, mostly Christian, organizations, demanding of the Foreign Office that "British representatives should be appointed on such Commission, and that in any enquiry which may be held a British Official should be present during the proceedings to watch British interests." The society passed to the press its correspondence with the Foreign Office and reprinted these letters in its own magazine, the *Anti-Slavery Reporter and Aborigines' Friend*. The society also sent a stream of letters to the Peruvian Amazon Company itself, reminding it of the serious allegations of cruelty and worse in the Putumayo.

There was further pressure on the government in Parliament, where questions continued to be asked about the Peruvian Amazon Company. British MPs kept the Putumayo issue in the public eye while pressing the government for action.

It was to be a combination of the society's efforts and a groundswell of public opinion through Parliament, more than the Foreign Office, that forced the Peruvian Amazon Company to bow to an investigation. On June 8, 1910, the company wrote to the Foreign Office, informing it that the company was arranging for a commission of investigation to go to the Putumayo "to report on the possibilities of commercial development of the properties of the Company and also to enquire into the present relations between the native employees and the Agents of the Company." Henry Gielgud, the company secretary, would be one of its members, as would Colonel Reginald Bertie of the Royal Welsh Fusiliers. Bertie was known to the Foreign Office as the younger brother of Sir Francis Bertie, the British ambassador in Paris. The Foreign Office hoped that Colonel Bertie would be impartial, but they weren't sure that he didn't have a connection with the company. Other members had yet to be appointed.

Junior clerk Orme Sargent welcomed the company's positive attitude. "They have I suppose at length realised that they had better take some action with a view to vindicating themselves in the eye of the British public." We can only imagine what conversations took place around the board table as they discussed the Foreign Office's recommendations. The directors probably decided that holding out against public opinion could hurt the company more than giving in. Making a stand against the Foreign Office might antagonize the company's shareholders, who would not want the publicity. At least one of the directors, Sir John Lister-Kaye, whose identity had so far not been made public, would not have wanted to draw attention to himself, as his several directorships in the City depended on his good name.

The company agreed to send a commission. It was a big step forward, and the moment had come to persuade the company to allow government officials to accompany the commission. Parliamentary questions and letters from the Anti-Slavery and Aborigines' Protection Society to the Foreign Office ensured that the pressure was not relaxed. In mid-June, Sir Edward Grey announced to the House of Commons that he was going to suggest to the company that a consul and a Barbadian official should accompany the commission.

A week later came the disappointing confirmation from Washington that Knox and the State Department were indeed too involved in the border dispute between Peru and Ecuador to make a case of the serious allegations made against the Peruvian Amazon Company. The State Department was happy to let the British government proceed with its own investigation, since the company was British.

A setback for sure, but better news was on its way. On July 13, 1910, the Peruvian Amazon Company stated that it had no objection to Grey's suggestion of attaching government officials to the commission—so long as the Peruvian government agreed to the idea. The commission's composition, the company announced, was now set. Gielgud and Bertie would be going as planned, and they would be joined by three others: Walter Fox, a botanist with a special interest in rubber trees and onetime superintendent of the Botanic Gardens in Penang, British Malaya (now part of Malaysia); Louis Barnes, a former tropical farmer with experience in sugar plantations in South America and Africa; and Seymour Bell, a merchant. The commission, the company reiterated, would be looking only into current conditions and would not inquire into past relations between the Indians and the agents of the company. Arana repeated this in a letter he wrote to Cazes on July 25. The commission had only a commercial purpose. Investigating "crimes said to have been committed in the past years" was the business of the Peruvian government alone. It was Sir Edward Grey, Arana noted, who was calling it a "Commission of Investigation" only to satisfy those MPs who kept asking questions in the House of Commons. Colonel Bertie confirmed the specific limited nature of the company's commission in an interview he had with the Foreign Office.

A few days later came word from Lima that the Peruvian government had no objection to a British consul visiting the Putumayo. The company, though, had the upper hand. The Putumayo properties were closed to the outside world; access was possible only on company launches; and the company's agents would be able to stage-manage the investigation and show only the benign side of the operations. Whiffen had experienced this. As to having a consul attached, the directors were probably hoping for someone in the Cazes mold, who would be vulnerable to the company's influence.

Several names of likely consular candidates had been put forth in the Foreign Office. One was Lucien Jerome, the British chargé d'affaires in Callao, Lima's port city, who was temporarily running the consul in La Paz, Bolivia. A preferred alternative was the permanent British consul in La Paz, Cecil Gosling, who was on leave in England at the time. While these names were being discussed, however, full diplomatic relations between Bolivia and Britain, suspended fifty years earlier, were restored. Gosling returned to La Paz, and Jerome to Callao. David Cazes had already ruled himself out because of his close ties with Arana. No other names seem to have surfaced. The idea of sending a Barbadian official was dropped because the Barbadian legislature was unwilling to cover the costs.

Behind the scenes, however, the Anti-Slavery and Aborigines' Protection Society continued to influence events and worked strenuously to ensure that their candidate for impartial observer was chosen. After several meetings with Sir Edward Grey, beginning in early June, they got their way. The society's preferred candidate was none other than Roger Casement, whose report of conditions in the rubber-growing area of the Congo Free State had been instrumental in bringing Leopold's evil regime to an end.

If the Peruvian Amazon Company thought it would be able to hoodwink the Foreign Office's appointment to the commission, they couldn't have been more mistaken. This was no David Cazes. Roger Casement was the most experienced and most universally lauded investigator of human rights abuses of his day. He was an absolutely committed humanitarian and would stop at nothing to get to the truth.

8

EYES OF ANOTHER RACE

In late June 1905 Roger Casement had been awarded the Companion of Saint Michael and Saint George for his work in the Congo, an order reserved for those who distinguished themselves in the country's foreign service. On two occasions, however, Casement had avoided presenting himself at Buckingham Palace, on the grounds of ill health. He wanted to turn the award down, but his friends convinced him that it would be unwise to burn his bridges at this point. Reluctantly he accepted their advice. He was torn between being an Irish nationalist and a servant of the British state. He feared that his award would be frowned upon in Ireland. In a sign of things to come, Casement explained in a letter to Edward Clarke, an assistant clerk at the Foreign Office, "You know I am a confirmed Home Ruler . . . and I shall now be regarded askance in every respectable quarter of Ireland."

Wherever he went and whomever he met, Roger Casement rarely failed to make a deep, lasting, and highly favorable impression. Edmund Morel, who spearheaded the Congo Reform Association and became a close friend, described Casement, then age thirty-nine, at their first encounter in late 1903, only days after he arrived in London from the Congo.

> It was one of those rare incidents in life which leave behind them an imperishable impression. I saw before me a man, my own height, very lithe and sinewy, chest thrown out, head held high—black hair and beard covering cheeks hollowed by the tropical sun. Strongly marked features. A dark blue penetrating eye sunken in the socket. A long lean, swarthy Vandyke type of face, graven with power and withal of great gentleness. An extraordinarily handsome and arresting face.

The politician and writer Stephen Gwynn, who was Casement's exact contemporary, provided a similar picture of the man when they were both attending a Gaelic festival in County Antrim (now in Northern Ireland) in June 1904. "Knight errant he was; clear-sighted, cool-headed, knowing as well as any that ever lived how to strengthen his case by temperate statement, yet always charged with passion." Behind those fine, unforgettable looks was also a rare speaking voice. "Casement doesn't talk to you—He purrs at you," said a consular colleague.

Despite the praise he received from the government and the public, Casement had become uncertain whether he was really cut out for the consular service. His relationship with the Foreign Office had become strained over his Congo report. Though it had been published promptly, the decision was taken that the report would omit all personal names and even place-names, substituting instead letters and symbols, arguing that it was the system and not individuals that was on trial. Casement was furious, but his protests fell on deaf ears. He even thought of resigning from the consular service in protest. He went on leave without pay.

By mid-1905 he was in financial trouble. Whatever he felt about his superiors in the Foreign Office, he had to get paid work in the consular service. He began to search for a position in September of that year, writing directly to the foreign secretary Lord Lansdowne.

For many months Casement received no reply. He was getting desperate. "My plans are not of my own making," he wrote in March 1906 to his cousin Gertrude Bannister, "and my movements do not altogether depend on my own wishes." And so it dragged on until finally, at the end of July, Casement heard that he was about to be offered a post. Bilbao was indicated initially, but when the offer came, it had been changed to the Brazilian town of Santos, São Paolo's port.

Casement arrived in Santos on October 9, 1906. He hated it as soon as he landed. By late June 1907 he was back in London and once more considering leaving the service for good, turning down a posting in East Africa. Continuing to vacillate over his Foreign Office career, he learned that a vacancy had opened in Haiti and that the job was his from the end of December. He was interested, but when he visited the Foreign Office in November, the offer had mysteriously metamorphosed into another Brazilian posting, this time at the Amazonian port of Pará (present-day Belém).

Casement hemmed and hawed, but the Foreign Office was firm: it was Pará or nothing. And so, once again, Casement packed his bags to cross the Atlantic to Brazil. Although he knew little of Santos before he got there, Pará was another matter: the previous consul, William Algernon Churchill, had stayed for almost ten years and had already briefed him on what he should expect. The city was large, with a population exceeding 120,000 people; the rainy season, lasting from January to June, was disagreeable; and the cost of living was high. On the other hand, there wasn't much to do, only writing and sending trade reports back to London.

Casement left England on January 18, 1908, and traveled to Paris to visit friends. He then headed north to Le Havre, where he boarded the Booth steamer RMS *Anselm* for Madeira and spent a couple weeks on the island before boarding the SS *Clement*, another Booth steamer, bound for Pará.

By coincidence, traveling to Pará on the same steamer was Julio César Arana, returning to Iquitos following the temporary suspension of his company's flotation in London. Exchanging pleasantries at the captain's table as they crossed the Atlantic, the Peruvian and the Irishman, in their own ways highly distinguished-looking, had no inkling that in eighteen months' time one would be accusing and exposing the atrocities perpetrated by the other.

Disembarking at Pará on February 21, Casement took formal charge of the consulate on March 1. No sooner had he done so than he started complaining to Lord Dufferin, a clerk at the Foreign Office, about the state of his office, especially the cavalier treatment of its confidential archives, the fact that prostitutes were using the building to solicit for business, and the extortionate cost of living. Not for the first time he threatened to resign.

Casement could not shake off his dislike of Pará. In late April and early May he left the city to travel up the Amazon to Manaus as a guest of the Booths, who owned and ran most of the steamships on the river, including those to Iquitos. From Manaus he went to the building site that was the Madeira-Mamoré Railway. In July he fell ill and went to Barbados to recuperate, but it afforded him only a temporary respite. In early November he wrote to the British chargé d'affaires in Brazil that he had had enough: "The Doctor," he wrote, "says I must get away or I shall break down . . . I presume F.O. will permit me to go away— or I fear a complete breakdown here. The place is not fit for a dog—& to be losing a great deal of money as well as one's strength and health is not good enough . . . It is a loathsome place—and people." On December 4 he was in Liverpool, just off the boat from Pará and on his way to Dublin: "I am much better for getting away," he commented with relief to Morel.

He may have hated Brazil, but he couldn't escape for long. Shortly after arriving back in England, he learned that he had a new posting and a promotion. He had been selected to be the British consul general in Rio de Janeiro. He accepted immediately: it was the most senior post he had ever been offered, and for the moment at least, his misgivings and criticisms of the Foreign Office were put aside.

Casement extended his leave of absence as long as he could, but by early March he was on his way to Rio, officially taking charge of the consulate on March 22, 1909. Predictably enough, he hated Rio, too, as he kept telling Morel on every occasion that offered. After five months' residence it was already a "long nightmare." His reaction to Rio was the same as it had been to Pará. The only saving grace about Rio was that he was in a senior position and that he spent a great deal of time in Petrópolis, forty miles directly north, originally the summer residence of the Brazilian emperors, but now the home of the foreign diplomatic corps.

Casement's lively correspondence with Edmund Morel gives us a rare glimpse into his unfolding political consciousness, something he naturally withheld from his superiors at the Foreign Office. Indeed, the Foreign Office—especially the foreign secretary, Sir Edward Grey—was a particular target of Casement's invective. Casement was robust in his criticism. As far as he was concerned, Grey was a failure. He was duplicitous, saying one thing, doing another; weak and without policy; and mistaken in his choice of friends and foes, particularly siding with the French over the Germans. Casement cited Grey's treatment of Ireland; his inaction over the Congo; his part in the Denshawai massacre in Egypt of 1906; and his abandonment of Dinuzulu, the Zulu chief, who was tried for treason in 1908 (he protested his innocence and was released after two years in prison to live out the rest of his life on a farm in the Transvaal). Although Grey was the specific target of his ire, Casement was contemptuous of the Foreign Office in general, saying on one occasion, "If the F.O. were to blow up tomorrow, save for the loss of historic records, it would be a great blessing for the country to be left for six months without such an institution."

Casement also had contempt for Americans, particularly Teddy Roosevelt, whom he thought duplicitous as well. When Roosevelt, in his famous Guildhall Speech of May 1910, told the British to either rule Egypt or get out, Casement had had enough. "It is impudent in the extreme for this man to go round Europe haranguing people on their duties to civilization when his own country presents one of the most lawless aspects of modern life the whole world affords." When Morel tried to tell Casement that England and the United States were the two "great humanitarian powers," Casement responded by saying that "England more than America perhaps—but both are materialistic first and humanitarian only a century after."

Not surprisingly, given that these letters were written to Morel, the Congo was still the main topic under discussion. In a revealing passage, Casement seemed to accept African colonialism as a fait accompli, but for Africans, he argued, it had come with a terrible price. "What has civilization itself been to them?" he asked Morel rhetorically. "A thing of horror—of smoking rifles and pillaged homes—of murdered fathers, violated mothers and enslaved children." The solution to the continent's troubles could come only if the European powers included Africans as partners in a humane political process—"the stream of gentler humanity," as he put it.

Though most of their correspondence concerned the Congo, Casement began to talk increasingly about Ireland and his own sense of Irishness. In April 1907 he had revealed to his friend and colleague, the political activist and intellectual Alice Stopford Green, that it was during the time he was investigating Leopold's evildoing that he first confronted his own sense of being Irish. "When up in those lonely Congo forests where I found Leopold—I found also myself—the incorrigible Irishman," he wrote. It was then he understood clearly that he was not only observing gross abuses of humanity but he was seeing the plight of the Congolese through the eyes of a people, the Irish, who had suffered similarly under British rule. "I realized then," he explained, "that I was looking at this tragedy with the eyes of another race—of a people once hunted themselves, whose hearts were based on affection as the root principle of contact with their fellow men and whose estimate of life was not of something eternally to be appraised at its market 'price.'" He admitted that before seeing conditions in the Congo, he had convinced himself that imperialism was good: "British rule was to be extended at all costs, because it was the best for everyone under the sun, and those who opposed that extension ought rightly to be 'smashed.' I was on the high road to being a regular Imperialist jingo." He was now over that phase of his life. He ended the letter to Alice Stopford Green with the following prophetic words: "And I said to myself then, far up the Lulanga river, that I would do my part as an Irishman, wherever it might lead me personally."

Now, at the end of June 1909, writing to Morel from Brazil, his attitude to British rule in Ireland had hardened further. "It is not British honour appeals to me so much as Congo men and women. British honour, so far as I am concerned, disappeared from our horizon in Ireland more than a century ago—and I am chiefly concerned in endeavouring to recover our own Irish honour."

Casement gave whatever money he could spare to Irish causes, such as the Irish Language Colleges in Cork, and promised financial support for several publications. Ireland consumed his mind as it did his bank balance. He knew, however, that power was not in the hands of the politicians who held public office. Whether he was beginning to think about a militant form of Irish nationalism is not clear, but he knew that any struggle would be hard. The world was not as it seemed.

"Our rulers," he reminded Morel, "are not necessarily a few cabinet ministers—but the great financial, territorial, commercial and a host of other interests . . . great, greedy strongholds of worldwide power."

After almost a year in Rio, Casement asked for and received a leave of absence. On March 1, 1910, he left Rio and headed to Buenos Aires. Three weeks later he was in Bahia, from where he crossed the Atlantic back to Europe, eventually landing in Liverpool on May 1. As it turned out, although he would never return to Rio, he was still not entirely done with Brazil.

He spent the first half of May in London before leaving for Dublin and Belfast. He then headed toward the Casement family seat of Magherintemple, Ballycastle, in County Antrim.

For two weeks Casement busied himself with family social occasions. But on June 17, a letter arrived for him that brought the festivities to a halt. Casement's life was about to take a new turn.

The letter was from the Reverend John Harris at the Anti-Slavery and Aborigines' Protection Society in London. Harris had been speaking to the Foreign Office for a few weeks about whom to send to the Putumayo, and Harris's letter to Casement told him unofficially that Sir Edward Grey had agreed that he should be the choice. Harris wanted to see him at the society's offices in London and also wanted him to meet several MPs who wanted to talk to him about the Putumayo. At once Casement wired back to say that he would be in London in a week's time.

On June 23 he met both Harris and Travers Buxton, the secretary, at the offices of the society. After they had shared their Putumayo material with him, Casement went to the House of Commons, where he met several MPs, including Sir Charles Dilke, the veteran of the Congo episode, Noel Buxton, and Josiah Wedgwood, both of whom had long antislavery associations.

The next three weeks were taken up with meetings and social events in London, and Casement saw Edmund Morel, Arthur Conan Doyle, whom he had met a few years earlier, and Alice Stopford Green, among others. On July 13, the day the Foreign Office learned that the Peruvian Amazon Company had agreed to a consular official accompanying the commission, Casement called on William Tyrrell, Sir Edward Grey's private secretary, who told Casement that he would be going to the Putumayo. He was then sent to Grey's office for a private meeting.

During their meeting that day, Casement and Grey spoke about the difficulties that lay ahead. They both agreed that arriving "at a wholly independent opinion of the facts connected with the recent charges against the Company's officials" would not be easy, but Grey was not dictating how Casement should go about his work. Casement's official brief was to look at allegations of ill-treatment of British subjects by a British company—a legitimate issue for a British official to investigate on foreign soil. And that is what was publicly said about Casement's functions. Privately, though, Grey told Casement that he should find "the facts connected with the general rubber regime in the country visited," but he should do so as discreetly as possible. Other than that, Casement was given carte blanche, including freedom of travel to the Putumayo by some other means than with the commission, should the opportunity present itself.

The departure of the Peruvian Amazon Company Commission was imminent. Casement spent the preceding week in a frenzy of activity: two days at the Foreign Office poring over documents; dinners with family members and friends; a quick trip to Ireland; another day at the Foreign Office; meetings at the House of Commons. On Saturday, July 23, he boarded a train for Southampton. The sailing of the *Edinburgh Castle* for Madeira was scheduled for later that day.

What was going through Casement's mind as he boarded the *Edinburgh Castle*? When Harris contacted him in Ballycastle, Casement had jumped at the chance. It was as though he had been waiting for this moment, for—as he once put it to Morel concerning Leopold—he was a "tiger who knew . . . where to sniff his prey." He clearly relished the possibility of repeating his Congo success. He had already tackled one of the greatest rivers in the world to reveal horrendous atrocities; now he had the chance to travel up another of the world's great rivers to expose more horrors. Even before Harris's letter, Casement knew something of what had been going on in the Putumayo. He had read the early issues of *Truth* when in Rio de Janeiro. He had, moreover, alerted the Foreign Office to trouble in the Putumayo between Peruvians and Colombians in June 1908, just a few months after he took charge of the Pará consulate. On that occasion, an article had appeared in *A Provincia do Pará*, the city's leading daily, with the headline BLOODY VIOLENT CRIME: HORRIBLE ATROCITIES. The article accused the Peruvian Amazon Rubber Company of the attack on the Colombians (and Serrano's horrible murder) at La Unión and La Reserva. At about the same time, Casement had a visit from Captain R. G. Williamson of the *Clement*, which had brought him and Arana to Pará a few months earlier. Williamson told Casement then that he, too, had heard about trouble in the Upper Amazon and in particular in the Putumayo, the property of Julio César Arana. Casement later recalled that he had no authority to investigate and report on the trouble, as it was not in his consular jurisdiction.

For diplomatic reasons Casement was confined to investigating the condition of the Barbadians he hoped to meet in the Putumayo. The Indians, the real witnesses and victims, were probably beyond his reach, but he must have been wondering how he might get closer to them.

As he made his way to Madeira on the first leg of his voyage, he had plenty of time to reflect on these past events and how he was going to get to the bottom of the allegations. His Congo experience would come in handy. Casement and the commission members arrived in Madeira on July 27. Four days later they were all on board the SS *Hilary*, of the Booth Steamship Company, heading across the Atlantic for Pará.

Casement knew that he had been given a tough assignment. He was surrounded by a group of men who had a very different agenda from his. They were going to make an assessment of the current commercial situation in the Putumayo and make recommendations for further improvement. Theirs was an economic and financial mission.

Casement was obliged to travel as a guest of the commission— "from start to finish I shall be doing everything 'by your leave'"—not only because those were the terms of his engagement but also because it was impossible to get to Arana's territory without using one of the company's launches. It was a closed shop. Worse still, he was not convinced that much would come of the investigation. "We shall be fairly well hood-winked," he confided to Morel.

Casement had learned that the commission members knew little of the charges that had been made in London against the company. Casement did all he could to inform them of these issues. Before he left England, he had been shown all the material that both the Foreign Office and the Anti-Slavery and Aborigines' Protection Society had amassed. Among it was Hardenburg's book manuscript, which included the affidavits he had collected in Iquitos testifying to Arana's violent regime. Casement took a typed copy of this document with him. Four other books—Henry Bates's *The Naturalist on the River Amazon*, Alfred Wallace's *A Narrative of Travels on the Amazon and Rio Negro*, William Herndon and Lardner Gibbon's *Exploration of the Valley of the Amazon*, and Reginald Enock's *The Andes and the Amazon*—would provide him with rich descriptions of the region. But most important of all was his copy of Eugène Robuchon's posthumously published travel account *En el Putumayo y sus afluentes*, edited and translated by Arana's close friend and the Peruvian consul in Manaus, Carlos Rey de Castro, and hurriedly published in Lima in 1907, with the words *"Edicion Oficial"* (Official Publication) emblazoned on the cover page, in time for the planned flotation in London of the Peruvian Amazon Rubber Company. Through his careful (and selective) editing of Robuchon's journal, Rey de Castro succeeded in portraying the company as a civilizing force for good, changing the Indians from their "wild and cannibalistic primitive state to useful commercial subjects." Because Arana intended to use Robuchon's account as the company's prospectus, the book had information that appeared nowhere else: it contained a detailed description, including many photographs and a map, of the area Casement was going to visit as well as a full list of the rubber stations and the names of their managers.

Casement showed the commission members both Hardenburg's manuscript and Robuchon's book so that they would have some context for understanding the testimonials he was hoping to get and they were going to hear.

They arrived in Pará on August 8. Casement found the city unchanged, and he couldn't wait to leave. But the *Hilary* remained in the port for four days, during which Casement spent time with the British and the American consuls. On August 13 the ship was ready to depart for its next and final port of call, Manaus.

A day before they were due to dock, Casement learned that Colonel Bertie, the commission's leader, had been advised by the ship's doctor that proceeding any farther up the Amazon would be detrimental to his health and that he should return home. Though Casement was aware in Pará that Bertie had not been feeling well, it came as a blow that he would be abandoning the trip. Bertie, Casement believed, would have provided the kind of objective, impartial leadership that the commission needed; when the Foreign Office learned of Bertie's return, they, too, shared Casement's dismay. The new leader would be Louis Barnes, the commission's expert on tropical agriculture and the member with the most extensive experience working in primary production.

On arrival in Manaus on August 16 the commission and Casement went their separate ways upriver to Iquitos. The commission boarded the *Urimaguas*, a Peruvian Amazon Company launch, and Casement, wishing to rely as little as possible on the company's hospitality (following the strategy he had adopted in the Congo), continued his journey aboard the *Huayna*, a smaller ship belonging to the Booth line. Casement hated Manaus, and the intense heat certainly didn't help. As for his floating home for the next several days, it was, he wrote irritably, a "beastly ship."

Leaving Manaus on August 17, the *Huayna* passed the mouth of the Putumayo River six days later, and the mosquito-infested waters got shallower and murkier. The going was tough and erratic, with lots of time at anchor. Casement expected the *Urimaguas* to have caught up with his boat by then, but there was no sign of it. Later, after what seemed interminably slow progress, the *Huayna* reached the Brazilian-Peruvian border, completing formalities first in Tabatinga and then in Leticia, the first Peruvian settlement on the Amazon (it is now in Colombia). Restless at the little ship's lack of progress, Casement found some comfort in conversation with the captain, who, on one occasion, confirmed somewhat matter-of-factly that Indians were the victims of forced labor and that their children were sold into slavery in Iquitos and elsewhere farther up the Amazon.

Fortunately, on August 29 the *Urimaguas* caught up with the *Huayna*, and Casement took his chance to change to the faster ship. He was now back with the commission members, playing bridge with his hosts.

Next day, they passed the mouth of the Napo River and twenty-four hours later reached Iquitos, their final destination, docking at eight in the morning.

Now the real work would begin.

PART
THREE

9

THE UTTERMOST PARTS OF THE EARTH

aoutchouc was first called 'india rubber,'" Casement jotted down in the notes he was making while in Leticia, four days before disembarking in Iquitos, "because it came from the Indies, and the earliest European use of it was to rub out or erase. It is now called India rubber because it rubs out or erases the Indians."

Casement was disappointed by Iquitos, as he had been by every city he had been posted to in Brazil. It was, he thought, well situated—that is, it had a broad expanse of river on its doorstep—but it was far too hot and had too many mosquitoes for his liking. As for the look of the town itself, Casement had only critical things to say. "[H]orribly neglected & dirty. The 'streets' atrocious, the homes poor. Hundreds of soldiers in blue dungarees." But as Casement would discover, Iquitos, like the Amazon itself, was full of news, rumor, and general deceptiveness. Gossip was very hard to conceal, but truth was hard to find.

Casement's first day there gave him a good taste of what was to come. After being whisked off to Cazes's home, where he had been invited to stay while in Iquitos, Casement met with the prefect of

Loreto, Dr. Alayza Paz Soldan, with Cazes present as interpreter. Casement found Soldan, who had only recently taken over as prefect, to be straightforward and honest—unlike the previous incumbent who, according to Hardenburg, had been in the pay of the Peruvian Amazon Company. But Soldan seemed unaware of what was going on in the Putumayo, saying only that Arana's company was contributing immensely to the prestige of Peru. When, toward the end of their two-hour talk, Casement asked Soldan to whom he should refer his concerns should he find the condition of the British subjects wanting, Soldan suggested any one of three company agents. When pressed for the name of a Peruvian government official, Soldan suggested the *comisario*, Señor Amadeo Burga—the brother-in-law of Pablo Zumaeta, Arana's brother-in-law. Casement now had a pretty good idea of what he was getting himself into. Arana had stretched an impenetrable web of influence over the Peruvian Amazon, and there was no way of avoiding one of his family, one of his associates, or one of his friends.

The next day, September 1, was Casement's forty-sixth birthday. Finding an interpreter, someone who knew the local Indian languages plus Spanish or, ideally, English, was his first job. He understood very well that an interpreter would be key to the commission's work. While on board the *Edinburgh Castle*, about midway between Southampton and Madeira, he had written to Gerald Spicer at the Foreign Office to try to get John Brown, Whiffen's Putumayo guide, to meet him in Iquitos. Brown was married to a Huitoto woman and knew the language of her people: there could not have been a better choice. But when Casement arrived in Manaus, he learned from the Foreign Office that Brown was ill in Montserrat.

This was a major setback, and it was looking as though the commission would have to rely on interpreters provided by the company at the individual rubber stations. Such interpreters were bound to be loyal agents of Arana's; they would doubtless report everything that happened back to their boss.

Few in Iquitos seemed to know the Huitoto and Bora languages, the two major linguistic groups in Arana's territory. But then a ray of light appeared when Casement heard of an Indian who was able to speak Spanish as well as seven other Indian languages. This man was at the moment working on the Napo River, about two hundred miles from Iquitos, and Casement wasted no time in chartering a launch to bring him to the town. Five or six days, Casement reckoned, and he would have the perfect interpreter.

Meanwhile, he did not know for certain whether there were any Barbadians left working for the company (he had only the Foreign Office's best assessment that some were probably still there) and, if there were, where they might be found. The question tormented him because he had no right as a foreign official to question anyone other than British subjects. If all the Barbadians had left, the trip, the whole enterprise, would have been in vain.

Cazes in London had told the Foreign Office very little of what he must have known about the situation in the Putumayo—probably in the hope that if there were no Barbadians in the picture, there would be no inquiry. However, once the investigation was under way Cazes, as British consul, had to appear cooperative. He had invited Casement to stay at his home and helped him make the necessary contacts. He even informed Carlton Morris, jokingly known as the Barbadian consul and the unofficial voice of the Barbadian community in Iquitos, that Casement was on his way. Morris was in the confidence of many of the Barbadians and was eager to meet and talk with Casement.

Casement was about to strike gold, and for the first time since the revelations had appeared in *Truth*, there would be a positive answer to the big question—were there still Barbadians working for Arana? In the afternoon, two Barbadians came to see Casement at Cazes's residence. They had arrived from the Putumayo on the Peruvian Amazon Company's launch *Liberal* a few days before, and Carlton Morris had seen to it that they visited Casement as soon as possible.

The first man Casement interviewed was twenty-nine-year-old Frederick Bishop. He had been contracted in Barbados for work in the Putumayo in March 1905 and had traveled to Peru with a batch of men, which included John Brown. Not long after he arrived at the Putumayo, he had been assigned to Eugène Robuchon as a guard on Robuchon's second and fatal journey into the forest. When Robuchon knew he was in trouble, he had sent Bishop and a number of Indians back to Morelia, the closest rubber station, to get help. Bishop almost died getting back to Morelia, but he managed to get a relief party organized to return to Robuchon. But when, after some time, the relief party found Robuchon's last camp, he had vanished.

Bishop had worked for Arana for more than five years in the area around La Chorrera, the Peruvian Amazon Company's main settlement on the Igaraparaná River. During this time he had learned the Huitoto language and knew many of the agents employed by Arana.

Bishop answered questions put to him by Casement and occasionally by Louis Barnes, the commission's leader, who was also present, and his answers confirmed what Whiffen and Brown had said in their separate statements about the abuses committed. Bishop's job was to go into the forests, armed, to bring in Indians who had failed to collect the requisite amount of rubber. The recalcitrant Indians were rounded up at the point of a gun and marched to the rubber station, where they were flogged on their bare buttocks. The bleeding cuts were washed with vinegar or salt, and then the Indians were sent back to the forest for the next collection cycle. Punishments meted out for not delivering rubber in sufficient quantities included being put into chains or into the stocks. In Casement's words, Bishop

> declared that Indians were entirely enslaved, that they were hunted, flogged, chained and murdered, and that he himself had been up to the very date of his departure, actively employed in flogging and otherwise coercing the Indians, to compel them to work rubber or supply the other wants of the Company's agents. He made categoric statements as to murders of Indians occurring within his knowledge, of gross and constant immorality indulged in by many of the principal agents, and of a system of robbery and oppression of the Indians quite as black as anything alleged by Hardenburg.

Horrors aside, Bishop provided other information, which amplified certain points made by Hardenburg and Robuchon. For example, the Indians received no regular payment for the rubber. Sometimes, if they brought in even more rubber than they were supposed to, they were given such items as gowns, knives, and axes. They received no food to take with them into the forest for the next collection—though they were fed, to an extent, in the stations themselves. They were "half-starved"; their own vegetable and fruit plots were neglected because they had no time to tend them, so great was the pressure to bring in rubber. The Indians got weaker, and the weaker they got, the less rubber they could collect and the more they were punished.

The rubber collections were run with the help of the Barbadians and an armed force of Indians and half-castes called the *muchachos de confianza*, as well as those Indian chiefs who made their people work for the company. "The system was not trade at all; it was a lie to call it so—the Indians were slaves, and had to do what they were ordered," declared Bishop.

Bishop had a lot more to say, and Casement recognized that he was invaluable: he could speak Huitoto, knew the Putumayo and its evil system right up to the present time, and was prepared to talk. Promising him protection, Casement asked him to work as his personal servant and interpreter on the trip to the Putumayo. Bishop accepted.

Over the next few days Bishop elaborated on many of the points he had made during his first interview, naming names and citing many instances of brutality on the part of the company's agents. He also emphasized that when Gielgud and Whiffen had separately visited Arana's territory, everything was cleaned up and evidence of evildoing hidden: the recalcitrant Indians were marched into the forest and kept there until the visitors departed. It was only because of the presence of John Brown that Whiffen had learned anything about what was going on.

The next Barbadian that Casement interviewed was a man named Nellice Walker, age twenty-seven, who had been recruited a little before Bishop. Unlike Bishop, Walker ended up in El Encanto, the company's station headquarters on the Caraparaná. His account was totally different from Bishop's. He had not witnessed any ill-treatment toward either fellow Barbadians or Indians and had heard of none. It seemed to him that this sort of abuse happened at La Chorrera rather than at El Encanto, where Miguel Loayza, who seemed to be a decent person, was in charge.

But although Walker offered nothing new about abuse, he did give Casement what he wanted more than anything else. The Foreign Office's hunch was right. Walker confirmed without doubt that there were still a number of Barbadians working up in La Chorrera—perhaps nine or more—but only one other at El Encanto. Casement now had the informers he would need to make a proper investigation of conditions. Would he find them, and more important, would they talk?

The weather in Iquitos took a turn for the worse—it rained heavily for several days. During this time Casement hosted a dinner for the commission members, David Cazes and his wife, and two others—Pablo Zumaeta, a senior official of the Peruvian Amazon Company and Arana's brother-in-law; and Lizardo Arana, Arana's brother and partner. Lizardo knew the commission and Casement quite well, as they had all traveled together to Iquitos from Southampton.

Casement was keeping his enemies close. He confided in William Tyrrell, Sir Edward Grey's private secretary, that inviting "two of the principal criminals" was a wise move. "We are all of us acting with great caution," Casement wrote, "and secrecy even (as if we were the criminals) for it is clear the rascals are very suspicious—especially of me. I . . . drank their health in Iquitos champagne and said nice things! The dinner cost me £12—but I fancy the toast will cost me dearer some day . . . Putumayo is a 'sealed book' even in Iquitos—it is amazing how everyone nearly is either afraid or 'in the swim.'"

On September 9 Casement received four more Barbadians. The first three men had little to say. They had worked on the company's launches in different positions—one a fireman, one a mechanic, and the other a steward. None had done any shore work and so knew nothing about conditions in the rubber stations. But the fourth man had quite a story to tell.

Joseph Labadie, who wasn't entirely sure how old he was but guessed he was twenty-two, had been in the area for the past five and a half years. His first assignment was in the Iquitos area, working as a steward on one of the boats used by the Iquitos Trading Company, in which Cazes had a stake. After a few months he got work as a cook on one of Arana's company launches and soon ended up in El Encanto in the same role. He then moved over to La Chorrera, where he was given a gun and told to "work with the Indians" at the rubber station called Sur, a few hours' walk to the southwest of La Chorrera. It was there, at Sur, that Labadie witnessed a dreadful murder.

He recounted that one day about two years earlier, Carlos Miranda, the chief of the station, ordered one of his *muchachos de confianza* to go into the forest and bring back a woman. Soon thereafter, the "boy" returned with the woman, who was chained around the neck. Miranda then ordered another "boy" to take her into the bushes and shoot her. She got two shots, said Labadie, who witnessed the gruesome episode. He continued. "They cut off her head, after shooting her, and it was brought in to them all and shown to the Indians, and they were told if they 'did bad' they would be treated the same way." Then they burned the body. Labadie had never seen the woman before that day, nor did he know what she had done wrong.

Labadie had left the company's employ about a year previously. He concluded the interview by repeating that "in the sections [rubber stations] the men in charge did just as they pleased; they flogged Indians, and killed them and burnt them, without anyone stopping them."

Casement retired to bed early, comforted by a good dose of quinine. In the night, the rains lashed Iquitos with thunder and lightning.

With Labadie interviewed, Casement thought he had seen all the Barbadians in Iquitos who were willing to talk to him.

As the scheduled day of departure for the Putumayo approached, Casement's plans hit a setback. The launch he had sent up the Napo returned to Iquitos without the interpreter. The Indian man, it was reported, had gone farther up the Napo and was probably in Ecuador by now. It was not worth the expense, Casement thought, to send a launch that far upriver to find him. But in the meantime, while the launch was away, Marius Vatan, a French trader and onetime French consular agent in Iquitos, had recommended a trustworthy Peruvian, named Viacara, who knew the Huitoto and Bora languages and whom Arana had at one time employed. Viacara had left the company after refusing to shoot two Indian chiefs. This alone made him a potentially more reliable interpreter than any the company would supply. With the help of Viacara and Bishop (and his knowledge of Huitoto), Casement felt they would get by.

The launch that would take the commission and Casement to the first major stop, La Chorrera, was the *Liberal*, which had arrived from the Putumayo on September 10, the day after Casement had spoken to Labadie and the others. Casement learned from them that four Barbadians were on the launch, but when he asked to meet them, they refused. One in particular provoked Casement's interest: Stanley Lewis had appeared in Hardenburg's account on more than one occasion.

The time had come to wind things up in Iquitos. Casement was in a hurry to send his first letter to Gerald Spicer at the Foreign Office, together with the depositions he had taken from the Barbadians. He wanted this early draft report to get to the Foreign Office before he left for the Putumayo. He feared that anything could happen to him up there. La Chorrera was more than a thousand miles from Iquitos. As Casement put it in his covering letter, "It is only sent to you in case I might get lost or disappear or something up there, or die of fever, and my papers might be overhauled long before they reached Iquitos, or they would be at the mercy of the people, who are in dread of our visit. I am viewed with grave suspicion already, I think, but as I have got the commission with me we are all right."

The first ship to depart Iquitos was the *Urimaguas*, the launch that had brought the commission members to Iquitos from Manaus, but Casement, suspicious of Arana and his agents, would not entrust his material to it. Casement had learned that Arana was actually traveling to Manaus on it. Instead, he entrusted the package to the *Huayna*, which was leaving Iquitos the same day as he and the commission.

As Casement was busily preparing the material for the Foreign Office, he received a visit from Adolfus Gibbs, one of the four Barbadians who had arrived in Iquitos on the *Liberal* the day before. They had initially refused to talk, but evidently one of their number had changed his mind in the meantime.

The twenty-four-year-old Gibbs had been contracted in April 1905 along with ninety fellow Barbadians. After working in and around Iquitos, he ended up at La Chorrera and from there transferred to the rubber station of Abisinia, a five-day hike southeast through the forest. He often went out on commissions to round up Indians. On one occasion, while operating out of Morelia, a station under the jurisdiction of Abisinia, Gibbs witnessed a decapitation of a sick and emaciated Indian, who, when released from the stocks, had tried to run away while still wearing his chains. The murder was carried out by one of the *muchachos*, a young man of eighteen. He chased the man, dragged him back to the station, and chopped his head off with a machete. A few minutes later this same *muchacho* decapitated another young man, also because he had tried to escape.

Gibbs told this story to Casement in the presence of Louis Barnes, the head of the commission. He was willing to tell more, but since he was working as a fireman on the *Liberal*, the rest of his deposition could wait. As evening drew in, Casement strolled over to the offices of Booth Steamships and entrusted his bulky letter to their safekeeping and delivery.

Clearly, as the members of the commission realized, these Barbadians were confirming everything that Hardenburg and Whiffen had alleged. Except, that is, for one point Whiffen had stressed: the Barbadians, he contended, were often used to mete out punishments, and so far, with the exception of Bishop, all of the men Casement interviewed had denied any part in the violence and murders. They were witnesses only, they maintained. Stanley Lewis's reluctance to talk to Casement might have been because he was not so innocent.

On September 14 the *Liberal* was ready to depart for the Putumayo. Casement, Frederick Bishop, Viacara—the Peruvian interpreter—and the commission members all joined the ship. Casement expected Gibbs to be on board and intended to interview him again, but was disappointed to hear that he had deserted. On the other hand, Stanley Lewis was working on the ship as a steward and would be trapped on board for a week or more with his would-be interrogator.

10

LA CHORRERA

Casement found it hard to get comfortable on board the *Liberal*. During the day it was blisteringly hot, and at night it was cold. The mosquitoes, "like drops of fiery poison," continued their assault even on the broad expanse of the Amazon River. For three days the *Liberal* steamed downriver, at one point almost capsizing because of a violent hurricane, and narrowly avoiding a tornado in midstream, until, just before midnight on September 16, the ship turned in at the mouth of the Putumayo River for its long ascent toward La Chorrera.

During the voyage Casement slept feverishly. His demeanor improved eventually when he realized that the vicious mosquitoes had departed and that the sand flies, which he had been warned were worse, were actually not so bad. A day later the *Liberal* passed through the Brazilian military post and customs and entered the disputed territories claimed by both Peru and Colombia. Herons, small green parrots, and several species of palms were a welcome sight.

It was now September 18, and still Stanley Lewis had not approached Casement, even though the captain told Lewis that his presence was required. Then, two mornings later, when the ship was about ten hours from the mouth of the Igaraparaná, Lewis appeared and submitted himself to Casement's scrutiny.

Like the other Barbadians, Lewis had come to the Peruvian Amazon in 1905, though, age fifteen at the time, he was considerably younger than most of his countrymen and fellow workers. Lewis couldn't remember everything that had happened since his arrival in the Amazon, but he did recall that he had worked in several places under the overall control of La Chorrera, including La Sabana and Santa Catalina to the east and Ultimo Retiro to the north. Although he had moved around a bit, his responsibilities were always the same: to round up Indians to bring their rubber to the station. As in the other cases Casement had heard about, the chief of the section or his underlings gave orders to flog those Indians who had not done what was required of them.

At this point in the questioning, Casement surprised Lewis by asking him about the instance when he had allegedly flogged an Indian woman. Lewis admitted that he had done this, along with another man known as El Frailecito (the little monk), whose name was Ernest Seales. The station's subordinate chief had ordered the two Barbadians to flog a woman named Simona. After the flogging, Simona was taken out into the forest and shot by a man. This man, who would not identify himself other than by the initials M.G., had written about this incident in a letter to Saldaña Rocca on July 16, 1907, that formed a part of Hardenburg's depositions.

Lewis said that he had never punished any more Indians after that time, and that he was tortured for his intransigence by José Fonseca, the chief of the Ultimo Retiro station. Lewis was lucky, he admitted, that he'd gotten away from Ultimo Retiro (and Fonseca) and found work on the company launches.

The details, Casement wrote, were "revolting" but convincing. The ship stopped at Pescaria, a small fishing village belonging to the company, and Casement saw several Huitoto women who, he concluded, were in sexual servitude. The next day, September 21, the *Liberal* was making good time up the Igaraparaná. It was no more than a hundred yards wide, a deep, slowly moving river, clearer than it looked—"more like pea soup or lentil broth." It wound its way northwest through overhanging bush, the "canal in the woods," as Casement romantically termed it. In the morning the *Liberal* docked at another company post. It was called Indostan (Hindustan), one of the many somewhat absurd names given to these remote places. Consisting of little but a single-dwelling house and a large clearing, Indostan existed to provide cassava, rice, sugar, and other foodstuffs for the personnel at La Chorrera, farther up the Igaraparaná. According to Casement, some fifteen to twenty Indian boys and girls worked on this plantation, all showing signs of malnutrition or worse. "Several of them were sick with fever and three little girls, quite children, were in a half-starved condition, and yet busily employed. The only well-fed persons were the white man Zumaran [the manager] and his Indian mistress." Casement would see a lot more situations like this in the weeks to come. At Indostan he also saw his first example of the appalling punishment handed out to Indians. "Found prisoner in heavy chain ('Bolivar,' a Boras boy), crime trying to escape. It was round him from the neck to the waist and then padlocked to one of his ankles." Casement did not believe Zumaran's assertion that Bolivar had tried to escape. The commission members agreed and had Bolivar released to be taken with them to La Chorrera.

Casement had now seen for himself, in just one company outpost, and not even a rubber station at that, all the telltale signs that everything he had read had prepared him for—malnutrition and disease, slavery, and abusive and illegal punishment.

As the *Liberal* worked its way up the Igaraparaná, the land got higher and the air clearer. Casement spoke again to Lewis, who provided more gruesome details of José Fonseca's regime at Ultimo Retiro: "murders of girls beheadings of Indians and shooting of them after they had rotted from flogging"—"disgraceful statements," Casement recorded.

About twenty hours after leaving Indostan, the *Liberal* reached La Chorrera.

La Chorrera, literally a spout or gulley, was sited just below a steep cataract of the Igaraparaná. The settlement had been built high up on the banks of the river. As soon as the *Liberal* tied up, four Peruvian Amazon Company dignitaries boarded and welcomed their guests.

The delegation's head was Juan Tizon, who had been with the company only a few months, having previously been a bureaucrat in Iquitos and, for a short time, acting prefect of Loreto. His name would have been familiar to Casement because Sidney Paternoster had reprinted a letter of Tizon's, refuting all charges made against the company, in *Truth* on October 27 of the previous year. A surviving photograph of him shows a kindly-looking man, and this is precisely how he struck Casement: the acceptable face of the company's operations. Here in La Chorrera, Tizon represented the administration of the company and was overseeing the work of the managers of El Encanto and La Chorrera. He would be with Casement most of the time. Next below Tizon in the company hierarchy was Victor Macedo, the manager of La Chorrera, followed by Dr. José Rodriguez, the medical officer, and Francisco Ponce, the accountant.

With sweeping views, fast-running water, and relatively fresh air, La Chorrera certainly had its physical charms. The human scene, however, replicated the wretchedness Casement had seen at Indostan. One of the first sights to greet him as he stepped off the launch was three Bora Indians showing "broad scars on their bare buttocks—some of them 1½" or 2" broad. Weals for life. This is their wealfare, their daily wealfare. All slaves."

Casement wasted no time in getting down to business. The next day, September 23, he asked Tizon and Macedo to bring to him five Barbadians he had caught sight of the previous day. As he waited for the men, Casement brooded on his situation and the likely outcome of his investigations. Sir Edward Grey, it is true, had given him a free hand, but his instructions were disturbingly vague in their purpose. Here he was, a representative of the British government in a foreign country, asking British subjects about how they had been and were being treated by servants of a company that was registered in London and was at the same time Peruvian. He was here as a guest of the company and with the permission of the Peruvian government. But where would the investigation lead him? What was its greater purpose? Should he content himself with "a perfunctory enquiry, as to whether they are happy, well treated or in distress etc."?

Casement was in a real dilemma. He wanted to know the truth, and only the Barbadians could give him the facts he sought. To get them to talk, possibly to incriminate themselves, he needed to offer them protection, effectively to take them out of the Putumayo with him. He had to make sure, at the same time, that Tizon, upon hearing the Barbadians' evidence, did not take it upon himself to alert the authorities in Iquitos.

Casement feared that once the Peruvian authorities in Iquitos got their hands on the Barbadians, they would be made scapegoats and the real criminals would get away scot-free: "The Barbadians will be nobbled and terrorized into denying everything," he remarked. Casement, in the Putumayo, felt himself in the middle of a criminal net, and he couldn't imagine that it would be any different in Iquitos. He was being hosted by a murderer and waited on by his henchmen. How could he feel safe anywhere? Casement's best hope was that Tizon would be so convinced by the Barbadians' evidence that he would take the matter straight to the company's management in Iquitos to insist on far-reaching reforms. That, after all, was the real purpose of the investigation. Involving the judicial authorities in Iquitos would only bring the investigation to a halt. It was a risky strategy, but there was really nothing else he could do.

Casement decided he would actively engage Tizon and make sure that he attended the interviews along with Louis Barnes, the head of the commission. The interviews began in the early evening. Victor Macedo was clearly anxious about the proceedings. He planted himself near the door that opened up onto the building's veranda, nervously awaiting the Barbadians. Casement did not invite him in. After all the anticipation, this first meeting did not start off well. Casement was certain that Donald Francis, the first man to be interviewed, was lying (he later admitted it to Casement); the next two men, who were employed in La Chorrera, knew nothing about life outside the settlement. However, the fourth man, James Chase, was ready to talk. Chase was twenty-three years old and had been in the company's employ since 1904. For a few years he had worked in La Chorrera and Ultimo Retiro, but he had gone to Iquitos to get medical treatment. When in April 1908 he returned to the Putumayo, he was sent to Abisinia, the rubber station run by Abelardo Agüero, a man first mentioned in Whiffen's Foreign Office report of the previous year. Chase's job, like so many of the other Barbadians, was to go out on the so-called commissions to round up the Indians and their rubber. He had witnessed floggings and killings until quite recently. Chase was not comfortable talking. He gave his evidence "under a sense of fear; his agitation was plainly marked, and he was greatly disconcerted." Tizon interrupted Chase's accounts on several occasions, trying to assure Casement that the killings were exceptional and that the floggings were a thing of the past, but Chase kept to his story. "This man's interrogation," Casement remarked, "constituted for him a trying ordeal."

Tizon was on the defensive, and this was not good for Casement's plan. The next witness, however, was completely convincing. Stanley Sealy was twenty-one years old when he first arrived in La Chorrera. Between 1905, when he was recruited in Barbados, and May 1908, when he went up to the Putumayo, he had worked in various jobs, mostly in Iquitos. The promise of a decent salary attracted him to the Putumayo.

In the little time he had been in Arana's territory, he had witnessed some horrible scenes and had, he admitted, participated in some. Casement was moved by his testimony. "Sealy," he wrote, "spoke like a man throughout and my heart warmed to the ugly black face, shifting from side to side, his fingers clasping and unclasping but the grim truth coming out of his lips. Says he had flogged Indians himself— many times—very many times." Sealy spoke of flogging men, women, and children. The chief of the station ordered the floggings, the number of lashes—sometimes as many as twenty-five—depending on how short they were of the quota of rubber. The Indians just lay down and took it, he said.

Tizon reacted at last, saying that only sweeping reforms would do.

As they were winding up this first day's business, Frederick Bishop, Casement's guide and interpreter, told him that another Barbadian had just shown up. He wanted to speak to Casement, and he had come especially for this purpose from his job working on the company's launches that plied the upper part of the Igaraparaná, above the falls.

Early the next morning, September 24, Joshua Dyall appeared. Casement did not warm to Dyall: "The man is a brute," he concluded, "but has been employed by greater brutes." Dyall, who had been brought over from Barbados at about the same time as the others, spoke about the early days in Arana's employ and mentioned by name a whole slew of Barbadians whom he knew. Many had left, but a few were still around. This was excellent information because until that moment Casement had not known precisely which rubber stations he needed to visit. Ultimo Retiro, Matanzas, Abisinia, and La Sabana (sometimes referred to as Savana), he now learned, would be worth visiting. Dyall thought that there were no more than ten Barbadians out there.

During the course of his testimony Dyall confessed to the murder of five Indians: two he had shot, two he had beaten to death, and one he had flogged to death. He did not do this, he said, of his own volition, but under orders from the station chiefs for whom he was working. Casement knew these names well from Hardenburg's manuscript and Robuchon's book: José Fonseca, now at La Sabana, Alfredo Montt at Ultimo Retiro, and Armando Normand at Matanzas.

Sealy's and Dyall's chilling and compelling evidence had convincingly won Tizon over to Casement's argument that the Barbadian evidence could stand just as it was and that Tizon could and should act on it alone. He confided to Casement that he now understood the system to be one of slavery, that it had to change, and that the station chiefs were criminals who were capable of anything. What he feared most was that if these allegations led to the company's being shut down, a far worse system might take its place, in which the individual station chiefs, with their armed gangs and local power, might inflict even greater harm on the Indian population. Casement fully agreed. "If the Company were to disappear," Casement remarked, "the fate of these unhappy Indians would be far worse."

After a five-day stay during which they interviewed six Barbadians, Casement, the commission, and Tizon left La Chorrera on September 27 to go upriver to visit the rubber station of Ultimo Retiro. With them were several Barbadians—Frederick Bishop, plus Sealy and Chase, who had been recruited to act as servants, guides, and interpreters for the commission members.

The next morning, they arrived at the small rubber station of Occidente. There were no Barbadians there, but the commission had chosen to stop because it was the first opportunity to observe how the Indians drew the latex from the trees, one of the objectives of the commercial investigation.

Occidente was typical of many rubber stations. About every fort-night the Indians who lived in the surrounding forest were required to bring their quota of rubber, called a *puesta*, to the station. Weighing up to fifty pounds, each *puesta* consisted of slabs of rubber in the shape of sausages—called *chorizos*—about one yard long. The *chorizo* was made by first coagulating the latex tapped from the rubber trees, succes-sively washing the resulting mass with cold and hot water, and finally beating it into shape with a wooden pestle. Once each Indian had delivered four or five *puestas* to the station, the collection cycle was complete, and the shipment, the *fabrico*, was ready to be moved by the Indians to La Chorrera.

The station consisted of two buildings. One, a large house, pro-vided accommodation for the staff and acted as a storehouse for the *fabrico* until it was ready to be moved. On the veranda stood the in-strument that played the key part in the system of terror—the *cepo*, or stocks. It was there to punish Indians who did not deliver their quota of rubber. Casement described it thus:

> [It consists] of two long and very heavy blocks of wood, hinged to-gether at one end and opening at the other, with a padlock to close upon a staple. Leg-blocks so small as just fit the ankle of an Indian are cut in the wood. The top beam is lifted on the hinge, the legs of the victim are inserted in two of these holes, and is then closed down and padlocked at the other end. Thus imprisoned by the ankles, which are often stretched several feet apart, the victim, lying upon his back, or possibly being turned face downwards, remains sometime for hours, sometimes for days, often for weeks, and sometimes for months in this painful confinement.

The *cepo* at Occidente was more than thirteen feet long and seven feet high. The diameter of the leg holes, of which there were two dozen, was a mere 3¼ inches.

The other building on site was the *maloca*, a communal house, covered with a thatch of palm leaves. The *maloca* was the Indian com-munity's ancestral and sacred space.

Casement and the commission had come to Occidente at just the right time: the next day, in celebration of the ending of the present *fabrico*, the Indians, perhaps as many as a thousand, were expected to attend a dance. It would be the first time that the visitors could see so many Indians in one place.

The following day, as they watched the spectacle, Bishop told Casement that although the festivities were routine—there were about four each year, corresponding to the number of *fabricos*—this dance seemed to him quite different. It was being staged for the benefit of the visitors. Normally, Bishop revealed, the "Indians were cuffed and kicked, and at night . . . the *blancos* [would] go out, excited with drink, and commit abominable orgies with the women and girls by force—even raping prisoners in the *cepo* [the stock]." The Spanish word *blanco* was often used generally to refer to white people, but as Bishop and others used it, *blanco* also connoted power over indigenous people.

The staging could not, however, disguise the evidence of abuse. The Mark of Arana was visible everywhere. "One small boy, a child, quite recent red weals unhealed & many other small boys show marks of flogging," noted Casement. "I never saw anything more pathetic than these people. They move one to profound pity."

Casement could only observe the Indians, he had no right to question them, but he knew that everything in the place depended on them—"They paid for it all." Casement turned on Tizon when Tizon welcomed Casement as his guest to the celebration of the *fabrico*. "The food we eat, and the wine we drank, the houses we dwelt in, and the launch that conveys us up river—all came from their emaciated and half-starved, and well flagellated bodies."

Casement wanted to persuade all the commission members, as well as Tizon, to think as he did about the Indians. He worked on them individually and as a group. Louis Barnes and Seymour Bell (Bell spoke perfect Spanish), Casement believed, would agree with him eventually. He was less concerned about Walter Fox, since Fox had little to do with the company per se; and Henry Gielgud, in his position as company secretary, might prove to be a major stumbling block.

A few days into their stay in Occidente, Casement had a conversation with Louis Barnes on his return from one of the commission's botanical and commercial forays into the forest. Their exchange showed clearly the distance between Casement and the commission members in understanding the situation they had all come to examine. As Casement recounted,

> The Commission returned about 1 o'clock [p.m.]. They had found two Indians, rubber tappers only, and had seen, Fox said, only three rubber trees. They seemed quite surprised. I said to Barnes I was surprised at his surprise. I asked Barnes had he not yet grasped that this story of Indian labourers was a lie. There were no labourers— there was no industry on the Putumayo. It was simply a wild forest inhabited by wild Indians, who were hunted like wild animals and made to bring in rubber by hook or by crook, and murdered and flogged if they didn't. That was the system.

Barnes seemed surprised that none of the white employees knew where the rubber trees were located or where the Indians were working. Casement, almost rebuking him, pointed out that trees were of no concern to the employees. All they cared about was that the Indians did not escape. The company was forcing Indians to bring in more and more rubber and to search over ever larger areas for trees. "The system was one of sheer piracy and terrorization," Casement reiterated, "and if you lifted the lash you stopped the supply of rubber."

All the time in Occidente, Casement became more and more frustrated with the commission members. One moment he believed he had succeeded in making them see the system for what it was, a moment later they seemed to fall back into thinking of it as an ordinary commercial operation. Casement was beginning to think that it might be better for the commission to proceed without him. He had already heard and seen enough to make up his own mind.

As it turned out, however, the present *fabrico* had been delayed, and the *Liberal*, which would be taking the rubber down to Iquitos, was now not expected in La Chorrera until early November. Casement had no option but to continue with the commission to the rubber stations they intended to visit. But before they did so, he arranged with Tizon to have all the remaining Barbadians assemble at La Chorrera to await his return. He would interview them all there.

On October 6 the party of visitors and the Barbadians in their entourage continued their trip up to Ultimo Retiro, which they reached the next day. As its name—the Last Retreat—suggests, this rubber station was the farthest from La Chorrera. At this point the Igaraparaná was very narrow—a mere thirty yards wide—and not practically navigable beyond. The station house, as Casement described it, stood "like a fortress stoutly stockaded on the apex of the rising ground some 50 or 60 feet above the water. The house [was] built like a ship, with its bows facing the river." The Indian *maloca* was small. There were women and children around but no men. Casement concluded that the women were concubines of the station staff.

Here Casement found just one Barbadian, a man called Edward Crichlow, who had been in the employ of the company since late 1904. Crichlow fed Casement stories of armed raids in the forests (including an illegal foray into Colombian territory in the area of the Caquetá River, to the northeast), floggings, torture, and murder: a litany of horrors with which Casement was becoming all too familiar. Crichlow also provided Casement with more information about two station chiefs in particular, Alfredo Montt and Armando Normand.

Casement considered the stocks at Ultimo Retiro the most vicious he had seen. The leg holes there were considerably smaller than the ones in Occidente: "The ankle-holes were so small that, even for a well-built Indian, when closed the wood would often have eaten into the flesh. For an ordinary-sized European or Negro the top beam could not close upon the leg without being down upon the ankle or shin bone." Whole families could be held in the stocks for any amount of time, each confined in all the imaginable ways that the design of such an instrument of torture allowed.

While Casement and the commission members were examining the stocks, Casement had his first close encounter with an Indian. A "fearless skeleton," aged between thirty-five and forty, without warning started speaking in Huitoto to Casement. Fortunately, Sealy and Chase, who were both nearby and knew some of the language, helped with the translation. "Waiteka [the man's name] turned his thighs and buttocks, and showed us the broad weals on both, right down the back of the thighs, and he said he got this for not bringing *caucho* [rubber], and that they were put in this *cepo* here and starved to death—that they died in it; that many, that all of them there had been flogged. Many had died in this *cepo*."

Once they knew of Casement's plans to interview the Barbadians in La Chorrera, the commission decided on an itinerary for their journey that would get them back there on time to catch the *Liberal* to Iquitos. On October 11, after a stay of four days, the visiting party left Ultimo Retiro for the interior of Arana's territory, to visit the rubber stations of Entre Rios, Matanzas, and Atenas. This would take them more than a fortnight, and they would be trekking through the forest until they returned to the Igaraparaná for the short river trip back to La Chorrera.

Entre Rios, as the name suggests, was located between the Igaraparaná and the Caquetá rivers, the northern boundary of Arana's empire. It took the party most of the day, October 12, to get there through the forest from Puerto Peruano, where the launch dropped them off. The path was extremely well kept. Casement was quick to see the wretchedness that lay behind it:

> The land rises 100 feet or more and then sinks again to another stream—often with steps and big trees and stakes laid—all the work of the Indians. Every stream is well bridged. Some have five big trees laid parallel and notched so the feet won't slip—and often a liana rope banister. This road is a big work—seeing too that the wretched workers on it are drawn from far-off homes, many hours away, and get no scrap of pay and only just the food to sustain a starved existence.

There were no Barbadians at Entre Rios. The commission had come here to interview the station's chief, Andres O'Donnell. Casement was struck by the man's Irish name. When he asked him about his roots, O'Donnell, who spoke Spanish and Huitoto, told Casement that his grandfather had emigrated to Spain from Ireland. Casement's opinion of the man, even though he had read and heard about his criminal activities (from both Bishop and James Chase), was not as negative as his views of the other station chiefs he had met. It seems that his opinion of O'Donnell was tempered by the Gaelic connection, no matter how distant.

Four days later, the commission, with the exception of Walter Fox, the botanist, who remained to make a more detailed investigation of the *Hevea* species growing in the locality, moved off to Matanzas, a rubber station due east of Entre Rios. They reached Matanzas, which had the reputation of being one of the worst stations—it literally means slaughters or massacres, and it was the station referred to most frequently in the Hardenburg depositions—in about twenty hours. Armando Normand, the chief of the station, whom they were expecting to meet, was at La China, a rubber station ten hours away (perhaps hoping to avoid the visitors). If so, he failed—a messenger was sent to fetch him.

Casement expressed a kind of morbid fascination with Normand. In his absence, Casement was given Normand's sitting room in which to stay. If he didn't know it already, Casement soon learned that his host was English. The sitting room was a giveaway: "It is pasted round with pictures from the *Graphic*, largely dealing with the Russo-Japanese War of 1904. There are also certificates from the London School of Book-keepers of 1904, giving him a certificate as 'book-keeper' and a certificate from some senior school of earlier date." No sooner had Casement inspected the place than Normand himself arrived—"a little being, slim, thin and quite short, say, 5'7" and with a face truly the most repulsive I have ever seen, I think. It was perfectly devilish in its cruelty and evil. I felt as if I were being introduced to a serpent. All through dinner he spoke Spanish only, but whenever by chance a word came to me, I answered in English. As soon as dinner was over, he bowed and left us."

There was a lot of activity in Matanzas as the *fabrico*, one of two that year, was almost ready to move to La Chorrera. That evening, after Normand had excused himself, Casement turned in early. In the middle of the night he and the other commission members were suddenly woken up by the patter of small feet and low voices calling out, "Normand, Normand." A man with a rifle and a lantern was leading a group of women around the veranda. "I jumped from bed. Some voices shouted down the passage and they all bolted to the room Normand is sleeping in. It was the arrival of the Harem," Casement concluded, "making for the room where they presumed their sleeping lord was lying . . . They looked like tiny little things . . . poor little creatures pattering all day and night through the forest after this beast."

The next morning, October 18, Casement told Tizon that he intended to leave Matanzas to return to Entre Rios on his own, without waiting for the commission to wind up its business, and that he would leave just as soon as he had spoken to James Lane, a Barbadian working at Matanzas, and Westerman Levine, another Barbadian, who was due from La China. Lane was interviewed immediately. Stories of floggings—one only a month ago—and murders came pouring out of Lane's mouth, but Casement broke off the questioning for the time being, intending to resume it at La Chorrera. Later that afternoon, Levine turned up, and he, too, provided details of floggings, beheadings, burnings, and shootings. Many of the floggings, some of the most brutal, he had committed himself under orders from Normand. Casement gave strict instructions to Tizon that Levine should be immediately dismissed from the company's service and brought down to Entre Rios with the commission.

On October 19, 1910, about fifty Indians headed out of Matanzas laden with some seventy pounds of rubber per person, the first of ten trips they would have to make to get the whole of the *fabrico* to La Chorrera in time for its shipment to Iquitos. Casement, together with Bishop, Sealy, and James Lane, headed out a little later. After walking for most of the day and overnighting in an abandoned *maloca*, the party arrived in Entre Rios after noon on October 20. Fox and O'Donnell met them on their arrival.

Several hours later the rubber-carrying Indians arrived in Entre Rios. They had been marching since the morning, and as they began to arrive in the station, their driver, a man called Negretti, pushed them onward, not allowing them any rest. Casement was appalled. Just before this group had departed Matanzas, Casement had tried to carry a load of rubber, to see what it was like. "I could not walk three paces with it—literally and truly," he wrote. "My knees gave way and to save my life, I don't think I could have gone 50 yards. Yet here they were, coming in from 8 to 10 hours away, 25 to 30 miles, and with 45 miles through the forest before them to get to Puerto Peruano . . . The little boys, some of them of 5 or 6 . . . were coming along too, often with 30 lbs or more on their tiny backs." Now, as they struggled by, Casement and Fox tried to take photographs of the burdened Indians. The fading light made it nearly impossible. In exasperation Casement remarked that he had seen nothing as bad as this on the Congo—"It is indescribable and makes me positively ill."

Casement spent the next day in conversation with Fox—who had by now come to see the situation as Casement did and declared that unless something was done to end the atrocities immediately, he would kick up a stink on his return. A day later, the rest of the party that had remained at Matanzas began to straggle in. First came Normand, then the commission members together with Tizon. A little later Normand's harem turned up.

As in his first meeting with the man, Casement made a great deal of Normand's face as a guide to his inner being.

> It is a perfectly atrocious face—but there is no doubt the brute has courage—a horrid, fearful courage, and endurance, and a cunning mind too. He is the ablest of these scoundrels we have met yet, and I should say far the most dangerous. The others were murderous maniacs mostly, or rough, cruel ignorant men . . . This is an educated man of a sort, who has lived long in London, knows the meanings of his crimes and their true aspect in all civilised eyes.

Entre Rios was full of people, but Westerman Levine, whom Tizon was supposed to bring along to the station, was nowhere to be seen. Casement was perplexed by his absence, and as he mulled it over, he began to fear that a plot was being hatched to undermine his work in the Putumayo. There were plans, he concluded, to tamper with the evidence.

It occurred to Casement that the Barbadians, who had been gathered together in La Chorrera to await his return, would be a soft target for both Normand and Victor Macedo, the chief of La Chorrera. Casement was convinced that Macedo would try to bribe the Barbadians—not difficult, since most of them were deeply in debt to the company. In that event, it would be the word of eight men (the number who were expected to assemble in La Chorrera) against three—Bishop, Sealy, and Chase—whose depositions and evidence were watertight.

Casement had to act quickly. In order not to arouse suspicion, he decided to dispatch Bishop to La Chorrera to make sure that the Barbadians who were waiting there for Casement were "not tampered with." "As I am playing with the Devil," Casement commented, "I won't take any risks. I'll not go spades and let him double when I have such a good hand of Barbados clubs."

Casement was getting ever more anxious that his grand plan for evacuating the Barbadians might fail. He hoped that his preemptive strike would work, but only time would tell. In the meantime, he busied himself in Entre Rios learning more about the details of the *fabrico*, of the kinds of weights the Indians were expected to—and did—carry. He also spoke to Bell and Barnes of his fears about the La Chorrera plot and discussed with them the possibility, which he had already raised with Cazes in Iquitos, that he would leave La Chorrera with all the Barbadians and drop them on the Amazon in Brazilian territory, where they would await a steamer on its way to Manaus. Casement was certain that if the Barbadians appeared in Iquitos, they would be jailed immediately on trumped-up charges. He had put them in this dangerous situation, and he was determined to get them out of it safely.

Several days later, after the commission had gone to visit another nearby rubber station—its name, Atenas (Athens), must have evoked a wry smile—the party was ready to return to Puerto Peruano to pick up the launch downstream to La Chorrera, which they reached on October 28.

On October 29 Casement heard the best news possible: Tizon had agreed to let the Barbadian men go, even though they had admitted committing crimes themselves. The only condition was that Casement would have to pay their debts to the company.

The *Liberal* was due on or before November 5. There was no time to waste. Bishop had managed to get to the men before Macedo and Normand did, and they agreed to tell Casement everything. Over the next few days, on October 31 and November 1 and 2, Casement met and took depositions from nine men. Each of them, in his own way, confirmed all that Casement had heard. "The list of horrors," he commented with a degree of satisfaction, "has grown every hour to-day and yesterday and Monday. So completely are the Barbados men now vindicated that Tizon actually to-day asked me 'as a favour'—his own words—to let him have a list of the names of all the Agents of the Company incriminated by the men. High and low—he asks now they shall be judged by the blackmen! What a change from the first days of my coming to La Chorrera."

La Chorrera was abuzz. The *fabricos* from throughout the area administered by the La Chorrera headquarters continued to flood in, carried on Indian backs. Casement and Fox watched a *fabrico* arrive from a station a fair distance away. In the line of carriers were two young boys, one of whom was carrying about fifty pounds of rubber, almost his own body weight; the other boy was carrying more rubber than he actually weighed. "Fox and I watched this confirmation of so much—it told its own tale—with a sort of grim joy."

Over the next several days Casement pored over each of the Barbadians' accounts, checking wages paid against items purchased from the company store and gambling debts. Everything appeared greatly, arbitrarily overpriced. The Barbadians had been forced to part with their wages in a major swindle. But there was little time for argument, and no point, as he had already agreed to the company's condition for letting the Barbadians go.

On November 9, after Casement had been in La Chorrera for almost a fortnight, the *Liberal* finally arrived. Casement caught the air of celebration as the ship's white funnel poked above the bush as it approached. Some people cheered, and the ship let off a rocket. At six in the evening it anchored, and passengers started disembarking. Bishop, who went on board when the ship tied up, returned excitedly to Casement with the news that John Brown, Whiffen's guide and Casement's hope as an interpreter, was on board the ship and had finally answered Casement's call. What would Casement do with him now that the job was done? He would have to go back to Iquitos with them on the *Liberal*.

Casement received letters and news from home. One piece of news struck him in particular. Dr. Hawley Crippen, the notorious murderer who had managed to escape the authorities in Britain, had been caught. "But what a farce it seems," Casement remarked, "a whole world shaken by the pursuit of a man who killed his wife—and here are lots of gentlemen I meet daily at dinner who not only kill their wives, but burn other people's wives alive—or cut their arms and legs off and pull the babies from their breasts to throw in the river or leave to starve in the forest—or dash their brains out against trees." The public was fascinated and preoccupied with a gruesome murder in polite society while the systematic extermination of a people held little interest for them. The public's duplicity sickened Casement, while at the same time it showed him how alone he was in trying to right serious wrongs. "Why," Casement asked, "should civilisation stand aghast at the crime of a Crippen and turn wearily away when the poor Indians of the Putumayo, or the Bantu of the Congo, turn bloodstained, appalling hands and terrified eyes to those who alone can help?"

Rumors in La Chorrera were rife among the Barbadian men that there was a plot under way to have them "disappear" before they reached their destination. When Casement heard of the rumors, he knew that whether they were true or not, he had to make sure that the Barbadians avoided Peruvian territory. Fortunately, the Brazilian customs officer on the *Liberal* agreed to drop the Barbadians off in Brazilian territory on some pretext. Casement was mightily relieved.

On Wednesday, November 16, 1910, almost two months since he had arrived in La Chorrera, Casement was on his way out. "Thank God!" he exclaimed. "I left La Chorrera and the Peruvian Amazon Company's 'Estate' to-day. I am still their involuntary guest on their steamer *Liberal*, with the eighteen Barbados men, four Indian wives of these and the children of John Brown, Allan Davis, James Mapp and J. Dyall."

On November 20, having steamed down the Igaraparaná and the Putumayo, the *Liberal* entered the Amazon River. The next day, the captain and Casement agreed on the spot where they would drop off the Barbadians, a small place called Esperança, on the Amazon in Brazil. Casement had not told the Barbadians, apart from Bishop, of this plan; when it was made known, almost all of them agreed to it.

Only Bishop, John Brown, his wife and child, and Philip Lawrence, who had been a cook at La Chorrera, opted for Iquitos instead.

With a decent supply of food from the ship's stores, fourteen men, four women, and four children disembarked. They would now wait for a passing Booth steamer from Iquitos to take them to Manaus. Casement had written letters to the captains of the ships he expected to pass this way, explaining the situation and telling them that they could claim the passage money from the British vice-consul in Manaus. With all arrangements made, Casement and the others continued on to Iquitos.

11

GODFORSAKEN HELL-HAUNTED WILDS

After setting the Barbadians on their way to safety, Casement could relax and enjoy the journey back to Iquitos. The shimmering riverscape, which had escaped his attention on the way to the Putumayo, now prompted comment and reflection. Instead of being immersed in documents, he had leisure to appreciate the ebb and flow of one of the world's great waterways. "A beautiful natural history store" is how he summed up what he saw. Instead of the dark, menacing forests of the Putumayo, there were wonderful vistas of fruitful trees and shrubs, "a vegetable profusion." The Amazon personified bountiful nature, fertile as the Nile, laden with silt from lands stretching up to the Andes, rich black soil that formed islands that dissolved in the next flood, only to re-form again. Were it not for rubber, Casement concluded, the indigenous people would live in "absolute clover." There was no felling or clearing of timber required: "The great river does that. It just piles up millions of tons of gleaming drift, washed clean and harrowed and shining as the water subsides from the crest, and leaves them stretched out for miles to sun and rain for enough time annually to raise two crops each year." It was the Garden of Eden.

Yet as Casement surveyed the scene and imagined the benevolent possibilities it offered its inhabitants, he recalled the horrible actuality of the Indians' lives that his questioning of the Barbadians had revealed. Everything that sustained them and gave them pleasure in this remote forest—the plants, the animals, and the rivers—had been ripped from their grasp. It had been stolen from them "not by a Government, as in the case of the Congo pillage, but by an association of vagabonds, the scum of Peru and Colombia, who have been assembled here by Arana Bros. and then formed into an English Company with a body of stultified English gentlemen—fools or worse—at their head." As if that wasn't criminal enough, these "cut-throat half-castes" turned the women and children into playthings, while their husbands and fathers "are marched in, guarded by armed ruffians, to be flogged on their naked bodies . . . bearing the indelible marks of the lash over their buttocks and thighs, and administered for not bringing in a wholly lawless and infamous toll of rubber."

Casement's sympathy for the Indians and his profound understanding of their oppressive exploitation led to a plan to take back to England an Indian boy who, through the good offices of the Anti-Slavery and Aborigines' Protection Society or the missions, might persuade some wealthy and well-intentioned people to buy shares in Arana's company—not for rubber, but to save the Indians. His idea was that well-disposed English shareholders, hearing of what was happening from one of the victims, would be able to curb Arana's greed and force him to end his henchmen's reign of terror.

To this end, Casement looked around for a suitable candidate, and at La Chorrera, while waiting for the boat to take him back to Iquitos, he had spotted "a dear little chap" and invited him to England. As the child was willing, and his parents and his older brother had been killed by the rubber ruffians, his tribal chief accepted a present of a shirt and trousers in return for his agreement that the boy go with Casement. This virtual sale of the child, and the whole plan of using a native Indian to elicit help and sympathy for his fellows, may seem repugnant to us now, but at the time it was a recognized mode of behavior, and for Omarino, as the boy was called, it must have been a welcome release from almost incredible exploitation. When Casement weighed him, Omarino was 25 kilos, and the load he had carried to the company's scales was 29.5 kilos.

On the same day, a young Andoke man begged Casement to take him away with him. His name was Arédomi, and he was desperate to get away from the Putumayo. Both young Indians accompanied Casement to Iquitos.

When they arrived on November 25, 1910, Casement went to stay with Cazes while the remaining Barbadians and the Indian youths were placed in rented accommodations. Casement's relationship with Cazes was never warm. He felt that Cazes had failed to help the Barbadians when they complained to him years earlier about their treatment by agents of Arana's company. He also suspected that Cazes had known much more about what was going on in the Putumayo than he was prepared to admit, particularly to the Foreign Office. Moreover, Casement was afraid that the relationship between Cazes and Arana would compromise the commission's investigation. Casement knew of the letter Arana had written to Cazes in which he stated that the Peruvian Amazon Company Commission had only a commercial purpose and that the investigation of crimes was a matter for the Peruvian government alone. Casement's understanding was that the letter was meant to keep Cazes quiet.

Back in Iquitos, face-to-face with Cazes, Casement was certain that the consul had been withholding information. "Every time he opens his mouth he shows how very much more he knew about it all than he admitted to the FO when asked for information. He was cheek by jowl with Arana in London at that time. He knew heaps and heaps of things and yet in his letter to FO he pretended he knew practically nothing."

Despite his distrust, when Casement went to see the prefect of Loreto, Dr. Alayza Paz Soldan, he had to take Cazes along to translate. There, Casement suspected Cazes of mistranslating and speaking for himself instead of on behalf of Casement.

In spite of this, once Casement had related all that he had seen and learned in the Putumayo—including the names of the worst offenders—the prefect assured him that justice would be done. He also confirmed that the Peruvian government had already begun to make plans for its own commission of investigation into conditions in the

Putumayo. The attorney general of Peru, José Salvador Cavero, had successfully applied to the Supreme Court in Lima to instruct the court in Iquitos to investigate the alleged crimes. Cavero had been moved to do so after reading a disturbing letter printed on August 7 in the Lima newspaper *El Comercio* by Enrique Deschamps, a distinguished member of a newly founded and influential intellectual association in Barcelona, the Sociedad Libre de Estudios Americanistas, who repeated the allegations made in *Truth* and implored the Peruvian government, whose reputation was at stake, to investigate the matter.

Despite Paz Soldan's reassurances, Casement was unconvinced that any real investigation would take place, let alone that justice would prevail. Arana's grip on the town and the region was just too strong. As Casement was about to leave his office, Paz Soldan told him that the Peruvian government had consented to his visit—and that of the Peruvian Amazon Company Commission—only because they regarded the allegations as unfounded and therefore attached no importance to the investigations.

When Casement went to say goodbye to Paz Soldan at the beginning of December, he was informed that the Peruvian government's own commission would be on its way to the Putumayo by the end of the month. Casement was appalled to learn that the *Liberal* was heading back to the Putumayo the next day, and on board would be Pablo Zumaeta, Arana's brother-in-law, and Benjamin Dublé, a senior manager in the Iquitos office of the Peruvian Amazon Company. Ostensibly they were traveling to La Chorrera to dismiss the worst section chiefs. Casement, convinced that the company would do everything in its power to hoodwink its own government, concluded that Zumaeta and Dublé were on their way to interfere with the witnesses. He was contemptuous of the prefect's weakness in allowing the two men to preempt the investigation.

Casement was now even more determined that the truth should prevail and that the actions of the Peruvian government in trying to cover up the atrocities, as well as the atrocities themselves, would be revealed. He realized that all that was left to him was to "try and move the civilised world to action."

When Casement returned to Iquitos from the Putumayo and saw the Booth steamship the *Atahualpa* tied up at the pier, he was overjoyed. His feelings of delight and relief that he was back safe and sound were tinged, however, with the ambivalence of seeing, in the ship's English flag, a symbol of fairness and decency and, at the same time, an impediment to the independence of his own land. "Hurrah, I'll welcome the sight of the English flag . . . since there is no Irish flag—yet. I am glad to think there is a flag—red and all—that stands for fair dealing and some chivalry of mind and deed to weaker men."

During his time in the Putumayo, Casement had become increasingly sympathetic to the Indians and outraged by their plight. Although dispatched by the Foreign Office to investigate conditions in the lands belonging to the Peruvian Amazon Company, he had authority only with respect to the Barbadians who were British subjects. As he admitted privately in 1913, he had gone way beyond his remit: had he failed or got into trouble with the Peruvian authorities, he could have been disowned by the British government for exceeding their instructions. Casement's sense of outrage at greed and injustice, and his humanitarian sympathy for the victims, led him to take great risks, both with his career in the Foreign Office and with his life. He knew how easily people disappeared in the Amazon.

Casement's experience of conditions in the Putumayo emphatically led him to side with the Indians against their Hispanic oppressors. While catching up on the news that he had missed during his time in the Putumayo, he noticed in the November 12 edition of the newspaper *El Oriente* that the Huambisa Indians, who lived some four hundred miles to the west of Iquitos, had killed sixty-seven people, presumably Peruvians. He read the article with glee. His only regret was that it wasn't sixty-seven hundred people. As he remarked, "These gentlemen went to conquistar the Huambisas, but apparently they found that tribe still a pretty tough nut to crack, and able to do some conquistaring on its own account." This was in line with his earlier reactions in the Putumayo, when Andres O'Donnell told him of the murder of the Colombians by the Indians and Casement replied that his sympathy was with the Indians. Later, in his diary, he added, "I have more than sympathy—I would dearly love to arm them, to train them, and drill them to defend themselves against these ruffians."

Later, of course, when he came to see the Irish as the Indians of the British Isles and tried to put these sentiments into action, he paid for them with his life and reputation. But already in 1910 it's clear that he was willing to risk his own life to expose oppression and exploitation and to help these victims defend themselves.

On the day of his departure from Iquitos, Casement bade farewell to his friend the French trader Marius Vatan, who reminded him how dangerous the area was. "It was only because [you] had come in an official character that [you were] allowed out alive . . . Your death would have been put down to Indians." At about 11:00 a.m. on December 2, 1910, just a few days over three months since his first view of Iquitos, the *Atahualpa* cast off from the Booth Company's pier. "This is the last view I shall ever have of the Peruvian Amazon—of the Iquitos Indians and their pleasant cheerful faces—of the low line of houses fronting the wide, bold sweep of the [Amazon] as it comes down from its throne in the Andes—the mightiest river upon earth bathing the meanest shores." But Casement was wrong about never seeing the Peruvian Amazon again. Less than a year later he would be back, Vatan's chilling message echoing in his mind.

A SYSTEM OF ARMED EXTORTION

asement arrived back in London on January 4, 1911. He was now free of the responsibilities and charges he had undertaken in the Putumayo. He had extended protection to twenty-one Barbadians. Of these, three decided to remain working for the company, two remained as guides and interpreters for the commission, ten headed off to work on the construction of the Madeira-Mamoré Railway, and six, including Frederick Bishop, decided to return home. The Indian youths, Arédomi and Omarino, were sent to Barbados, in Bishop's care, to learn British ways before proceeding to London.

Casement lost no time in getting in touch with his superiors at the Foreign Office and his supporters at the Anti-Slavery and Aborigines' Protection Society. He had already primed the Foreign Office to expect revelations. He told Sir Edward Grey that his investigations fully supported the charges made against the Peruvian Amazon Company, that the commission members all agreed with his findings, and that the prefect in Iquitos was convinced also.

The following day, Casement met with Louis Mallet, the assistant undersecretary of state at the Foreign Office. The gist of their conversation was forwarded to Sir Edward Grey. Mallet stated that Casement had confirmed everything that Whiffen had told the Foreign Office in November of the previous year, and that "the cruelties practised on the Indian tribes exceed in horror the Congo atrocities." Casement promised an immediate report and warned that the Peruvian Amazon Company would probably try "to clear out but that their duty is to remain and put things right."

Two days later Casement sent a preliminary report. It was short and to the point, conveying succinctly the abysmal horror of the Putumayo. He stated that his conclusions were based on voluminous evidence and that he would be submitting a more detailed report in time; for now, he wanted his superiors to know the seriousness of the situation. His evidence came not only from the testimony of the Barbadians but also from his own eyes—"the marks of the lash were not confined to men or adults. Women, and even little children were more than once found, their limbs scarred with weals left by the thong of the twisted tapir-hide, which is the chief implement used for coercing and terrorising the native population of the region."

Appended to this preliminary statement was an annotated list of what Casement called the worst criminals in the Putumayo. They included six section chiefs he had met during the investigation, and he singled out two of them as being particularly vicious—Augusto Jiménez, the boss of Ultimo Retiro, and Armando Normand, the boss of Matanzas, "a man of whom nothing good could be said."

The report was eagerly received at the Foreign Office. Its preliminary nature was recognized, as was the fact that it dealt in the main with the Barbadians and their experiences. But as one clerk noted, "the report only gives one an idea of the condition of the natives, but one gathers enough to realise that it cannot be much less bad than that which prevailed in the Congo." The main arguments were summarized and distributed around the office.

Even in its preliminary form the report was a damning piece of evidence. Sir Edward Grey understood perfectly the publicity potential of the documents. He was happy to have its contents passed on, confidentially, through Lucien Jerome, the British chargé d'affaires in Lima, to the Peruvian government, and, through James Bryce, the British ambassador in Washington, to the United States government. He did not want to share Casement's draft report with the Peruvian

Amazon Company. Rather, he wanted to use the threat of publication to force it to reform its operations.

On January 31 Casement delivered his first complete report. Longer and more detailed than the preliminary one, it ran to nineteen foolscap sheets in its printed form and focused on the experiences of the Barbadians who had been interviewed. Casement described how they had been recruited in Barbados, the nature of their contract with Arana, and how they were hoodwinked. Having been promised work as laborers, they found themselves rounding up Indians at gunpoint and "acting as armed bullies and terrorists over the surrounding native population," and because of extortionate prices and their own gambling, they had fallen into debt and thus become peons in the service of the company, with little prospect of buying their way out. Casement provided detailed accounts of cruelty and murder as told to him by the Barbadians.

The report did not, of course, omit the condition of the Indians, although collecting testimony from them was outside his brief. Casement was careful to make sure his readers understood precisely what was going on in Arana's territory. His key point was that rubber collecting in the Putumayo was not a commercial operation, as that term was normally understood. It was an exploitative operation aimed at the Indians. "The true attraction from the first," Casement wrote, "was not so much the presence of the scattered *Hevea Braziliensis* trees throughout this remote forest, as the existence of fairly numerous tribes of docile, or at any rate of easily subdued Indians." The "'civilised' intruders" came to subjugate ("*conquistar*" is the Spanish word) the Indians, not to annihilate them. The exploiters kept repeating that they were extending civilization to the Indians in the shape of profitable occupations. This was a travesty. Searching for words to convey the true essence of the system, Casement chose "brigandage" and "a system of armed extortion."

News of Casement's report had leaked out, and its existence soon became a matter of public record. On February 8, 1911, the Liberal MP Joseph King questioned the Foreign Office. Was there a report from Consul General Casement? Were Barbadians employed in the Putumayo? Did they carry out acts of barbarity? The answer was simply that a report had been received and that it was being considered.

Two weeks later King returned to the issue. He pressed the government: When did the government receive Casement's report? When would its contents be revealed to Parliament? Had there been any communication about it with Peru? Questions like this, in particular about when the government intended to publish the report, were raised repeatedly for the rest of the year and into the next.

The Foreign Office's answer was anodyne and would continue to be so for some time to come. The parliamentary undersecretary of state, Thomas McKinnon Wood, simply answered that the government had received Casement's report and that communications with Peru had revealed that the government there had ordered a judicial commission to proceed to the Putumayo. Privately, however, the Foreign Office, which had the right to publish the report, decided not to reveal any more. As in the case of its dealings with the Peruvian Amazon Company, the Foreign Office decided that in its relationship with the Peruvian government, the threat of publication was a more effective weapon than publication itself at this moment. "If we were to publish," as Louis Mallet wrote in a departmental memo, "it would deprive us of our chief lever with the Peruvian Government."

Without the support of the United States, which didn't seem to be forthcoming, there was little else the Foreign Office could do. As Grey pointed out, Arana's territory was not British and the British had no jurisdiction there, just a few British subjects. All they had was Casement's damning and deeply embarrassing report, and the implicit threat to name and shame.

Behind the scenes, Casement continued to influence the Foreign Office through his confidential correspondence with Louis Mallet. In one of his early letters to Mallet (dated January 8), Casement was blunt about what he had seen in Arana's territory. There was evidence everywhere that Arana had the area under his thumb, that his crimes were well known, but no one dared say anything, and this included the prefect, Paz Soldan, "honest but weak—all around him at Iquitos are rogues and villains."

Casement suggested that it was the duty of the British government to make the Peruvians aware of what they had to lose by supporting Arana's empire. Peru needed to attract and retain foreign investment. It could not afford a scandal, and as Casement argued, "Once these

Putumayo atrocities were publicly vouched for and the shocking detail of the infamous treatment of the Indians made public all sources of foreign investment in Peru would dry up."

Casement was furious about the treatment of the Indians, and he assumed that all right-minded folk would feel as he did. "If only one of the ruffians were hanged," he wrote, "or imprisoned even, for a very long time—but hanging [is] best—it would go far to end their dastardly acts." Even the four members of the Peruvian Amazon Company Commission—Barnes, Bell, Gielgud, and Fox—had come around to Casement's way of thinking: "It wasn't hanging they wanted to inflict— that was far too mild—they wanted torture by their own methods to be inflicted on Mr Arana's principal agents and year-long friends."

Casement ended the letter with an anguished cry. "I will make any personal sacrifice in the world to help you," he wrote to Mallet, "and if it should come to wanting evidence I will get you the living personal witnesses of those on the spot at my own cost if needed."

While producing his first report, Casement was painfully aware that the sufferings of the Indians that had so aroused his compassion were not what the investigation was about. He was distressed that he had to leave out so much about the Indians and to include so much about the Barbadians and their ill-treatment, which was comparatively trivial, though "mean enough" in itself, as he put it. He began to write a second report "giving chapter and verse as far as I can" on the condition of the Indians in the Putumayo, but it was slow and grueling work. Toward the end of February he wrote, "I am 'full up' with atrocities and horrors at times—and it is only the thought of those poor, hunted, gentle be- ings up there in the forest that keeps me going." He finally dispatched it to the Foreign Office on March 17, 1911, St. Patrick's Day.

"I have the honour," Casement began his report, "to transmit here- with a report dealing with the methods of rubber collection and the treatment of the Indians in the region dominated by the Peruvian Am- azon Company on the Putumayo affluents of the Amazon."

In some twenty-five thousand words, Casement detailed the horror of the Putumayo. He began dispassionately, laying out the region's geographical and historical context, but a simple statement of the fall in population after the arrival of the white folk revealed the true and dreadful story. From an estimated thirty thousand Huitoto Indians (the largest group native to the area), there seemed to be, he wrote, only about ten thousand left. Even allowing for the depredations of disease and warfare, which were fairly constant, it seemed that the arrival of the *caucheros*, and in particular the rubber-collecting system favored by the Peruvian Amazon Company, had depleted the population by nearly two-thirds. It was, as Casement had remarked on previous occasions, even worse than the Congo. Paternoster had not been far off when he stated in his first *Truth* article that the population of the area had been reduced by tens of thousands.

Once he gave the reader a chance to absorb this dramatic drop in population, Casement began the catalog of what he termed "continuous criminality." He detailed the regime of violence, discussing the use of the gangs of *muchachos de confianza* to terrorize the Indian rubber collectors; the employment of Barbadians and others to round them up; the ritual nature of the *fabrico*; and the ubiquitous penal system— horrible floggings, sometimes to death, the use of the stocks, and deliberate regimes of starvation. Casement spoke about the Peruvian Amazon Company as operating with complete impunity outside civil authority, and of the perpetrators, the chiefs of sections, as being a law unto themselves, addicted to a cycle of criminality. "The freebooter on the Putumayo had [no care] for the hereafter to restrain him," Casement wrote:

> His first object was to get rubber, and the Indians would always last his time. He hunted, killed, and tortured to-day in order to terrify fresh victims for to-morrow. Just as the appetite comes in eating so each crime led on to fresh crimes, and many of the worst men on the Putumayo fell to comparing their battues and boasting of the numbers they had killed . . . Such men had lost all sight or sense of rubber gathering—they were simply beasts of prey who lived upon the Indians and delighted in shedding their blood.

Casement recounted the story of one Bora Indian, a young cacique or chief, referred to in the Barbadian depositions as Katenere, "the bravest and most resolute opponent the murderers had encountered."

The story went that Katenere, like so many other Indians, consented to bring in rubber for Armando Normand, the chief of the Matanzas section, but because he was being badly treated, he fled into the forest. After some time, Katenere and his wife were captured and returned to the station, where he was put into the stocks. One day Bartolomé Zumaeta, another of Arana's brothers-in-law and a senior agent of the company in Iquitos, arrived and raped Katenere's wife in front of him. Somehow Katenere escaped with his wife. He managed to get hold of some Winchesters and with a small band of supporters began to wage an offensive against the company's agents. This was sometime in 1908. For the next two years Katenere's mission was successful, including a major triumph when he personally found and shot Zumaeta dead. However, on one of the company's expeditions to hunt him down, Katenere's wife was captured and taken to the station, and when he tried to rescue her, he was shot down. So ended the only resistance to the company's ruthless system.

Toward the end of March, Casement sent the Foreign Office the verbatim transcripts of the thirty interviews with the Barbadians that he had recorded. The readers could immerse themselves in the horrible details, recounted by real voices, which, because of circumstances, had to stand in and speak for the missing voices of the Indians. This completed Casement's work. Mallet's first reaction was to the point: he warned Sir Edward Grey, "The details are so sickening that you may not care to read them."

Meanwhile, Arana's family had taken up residence in London, in a spacious house near Hyde Park. No sooner had Casement disembarked in England from Iquitos than he received the first of a series of letters from Arana asking to meet him and to discuss his ideas for the reform of the company. Casement thought the communication very cheeky; he simply wrote back to say that he had been on official business in the Putumayo and was not at liberty to discuss it. Still, Casement was curious. "It may do good to meet the rascal," he wrote to Mallet, but at this stage it went no further.

Several months passed. Arana had left London. Casement heard no more from him, but he then resurfaced. He had been selected as

141

the Peruvian representative at the International Rubber and Allied Trades Exhibition, scheduled to open in Islington's Agricultural Hall in late June. When in early March the Foreign Office had first heard of this appointment, Louis Mallet, who learned of it in a telegram from Lucien Jerome, the British chargé d'affaires in Lima, was absolutely livid. He had never heard of the International Rubber Exhibition, and as for Arana's presence at it as a representative of Peru, he was not short of words: "It is an outrage," he commented in a memo on the subject, "that Arana should be sent here as Peruvian representative to any exhibition." And he went on. "Can we object to Arana's appointment or move the promoters to do so? The Prince of Wales is a Patron of the exhibition and we have called the attention of foreign governments to it. Arana is a criminal of the most appalling type and ought to be hanged." A discussion followed among a number of Foreign Office clerks as to the best course of action. The matter was taken so seriously that they asked Sir William Davidson, the Foreign Office legal adviser, whether there was any possibility of charging Arana with murder once he stepped onto British soil. His answer was entirely in the negative. Arana could not be apprehended, but, Mallet suggested, if he did come to represent his country at the exhibition, "the King should be asked to withdraw his patronage."

Algernon Law, a senior clerk, came up with the most useful suggestion. The manager of the exhibition should be sent for and told that they should telegraph Peru to say that Arana was not a "persona grata" to them or to the delegates from other countries and that he could not be received. So the machinery of government began to move. Mallet met Mr. Staines Manders, the managing director of the International Rubber Exhibition, near the end of March. Three weeks later Manders let Mallet know that Arana had resigned his post as his government's representative at the exhibition.

Arana, always the one wanting the final word, told his London board a completely different story, an indication of the extent to which he deceived his own directors. The minutes of the Peruvian Amazon Company recorded that Arana had declined to accept his government's wish that he be the country's representative on the grounds that he had pressing business in the Putumayo.

142

DEUS EX MACHINA

After Casement left the Putumayo, the commission continued its work visiting, in addition to stations under the control of La Chorrera, those in and around the Caraparaná, which were under the control of El Encanto. Finally leaving the Putumayo on February 22, 1911, the commission, after a stay in Iquitos and Manaus, sailed for England on April 12—except for Gielgud, who remained in Manaus to attend to business matters there.

Since Casement had returned to London, he had been receiving, from time to time, news from and about the commission and its progress. Cazes kept him informed, but the commission members themselves also wrote with news and their sense of what was going on and what could be done. Louis Barnes, the commission's head, wrote to Casement from El Encanto toward the end of December 1910, shortly after Casement had left Iquitos for England. If Casement had any doubts that the members shared his views, this letter dispelled his uncertainties. Using language that Casement would have found familiar, Barnes informed him that at Santa Catalina, a rubber station to the east of La Chorrera, he "had the great pleasure of shaking by the hand

a Bora who was present at the despatching to a warmer land of Bartolomé Zumaeta, and I was told he took part in it." Barnes was referring
to that heroic incident, as Casement himself had put it, when Katenere killed Zumaeta in revenge. Barnes further endeared himself to
Casement in the next sentence: "After seeing the terrible way the poor
wretches have been treated one can only wonder how they left a
Blanco [a Spanish-Peruvian] alive or allow one to live." Barnes brought
Casement up to date about where they had gone and whom they
had met, and he suggested new names to put on the so-called blacklist
of criminals. He ended the letter on a note of solidarity: "Rest assured," he told Casement, "we shall be no party to any attempt at
white-washing or hushing things up in any underhand way, what you
told the Prefect . . . is correct and if necessary I will drive it home to
him and I know the others are with me."

So they were. Walter Fox, the rubber specialist attached to the
commission on the recommendation of the Royal Botanic Gardens at
Kew, was a soft-spoken, gentle man, and the oldest member of the
commission. Fox did not mince his words when he reported back to
Colonel David Prain, the director at Kew. Most of Fox's communication, naturally, concerned the flora of the region and particularly the
botany of the rubber trees, but he was so outraged by what else he had
seen that he could not withhold a stinging and shocking assessment:
"I wish not to anticipate our reply to that further than that I should like
to exterminate 5/6 of the employees here who are placed over the unfortunate aborigines. The whole system of management is wrong from
top to bottom."

Even Henry Gielgud, the secretary of the Peruvian Amazon Company and the individual in the commission whom Casement had had
the most trouble persuading that they were witnessing a crime and not
a commercial system, had come around. He, too, had written to Casement, commenting on the fact that Abelardo Agüero—the chief of
Abisinia section and the man accused of unspeakable acts of torture,
maiming, and murder as an agent of the company—had fled toward
Colombian territory to the north, his retinue of *muchachos* in tow,
when he got wind that charges might be on their way. Before he departed, he and his men had set fire to the Boras' *chácaras* (garden plots
where they grew their food) as his final act of evil. Gielgud recounted

this, adding that it was a pity that the Indians "couldn't tie [Agüero] up in one of the *chácaras* with his friends—it would have been an acceptable holocaust." Casement sent Mallet these choice quotes in order that the Foreign Office should know, in advance of the commission's arrival back in England, that its views of the Putumayo were no different from his own. Casement's persistence had scored a singular victory.

The idea that only a British public company, subject to British regulations—which would introduce a system of exchange to replace the one based on terrorism, exploitation, and quotas—could save the Indians had started to form in Casement's mind while he was still in the Putumayo. Whatever he may have felt about British rule in Ireland, no well-regulated British company, he believed, would resort to exploitative practices in its operations. It, Casement was convinced, would pay a fair wage for a fair day's work. He did not believe in turning the clock back. He had made this perfectly clear when discussing colonialism and Africa with Morel. "A gentler humanity" is what he believed in, and a British company founded on sound commercial and legal principles was now the only way to save the Indians.

The Foreign Office was keenly aware of Casement's deeply held view that the best future for the Indians lay with a reconstituted British company. Sir Edward Grey made this the goal of the Foreign Office also. The scene was now set for a battle for the control of the Putumayo. There were two possible outcomes. One was a reconstituted Peruvian Amazon Company, with headquarters in London, which appeared to be the best solution for the Indians. The second was a private company run by Arana and his men as a continuation of the same old system of terror and violence. Casement hoped that the Peruvian government could be urged, diplomatically, to prosecute Arana, making the second possibility less likely.

Casement's report was a major part of the Foreign Office's arsenal in its battle with Arana. In early March, Grey had asked Casement for his opinion on whether he agreed that his first report "might be communicated confidentially to the company at once with an intimation to the effect that the Secretary of State assumes that steps will be taken to put a stop forthwith to the practices disclosed." Casement's opinion was that it would be better to await the commission and its report before transmitting a copy of his own. On April 29 the commission members disembarked in England. Within a short time they would be delivering their report to the company. Grey agreed that timing was critical and waited for the right moment to strike. Grey's other plan was to have Casement attend those company board meetings when reform measures were under discussion. Confidentially, as he told Casement, he wanted to know the company's intentions and "to some extent impose [my] wishes on them through you in an unofficial manner."

On May 4 Casement went to the Foreign Office and agreed to attend board meetings under the terms Grey had outlined. Knowing that the commission's report would be delivered any day, Grey's plan was put into action: on May 13 he wrote to the Peruvian Amazon Company. In an attempt to get a positive response, he began by reassuring the board that it was not being accused of anything—he was convinced, he told them, that they were ignorant of the "appalling state of affairs"—but that, in return for this absolution, they should put in place a set of reform measures that would prevent the abuses from ever happening again. He then played his trump card.

> To help the Company in this object he would be willing to place at the disposal of your Directors unofficially and privately the services of Mr. Casement who from the knowledge gained from his recent tour and his previous experience in such matters would, it is confidently expected, be in a position to offer the Company valuable assistance. Mr. Casement has expressed his willingness to do all he can in helping to draw up a scheme of reform and to attend, if desired, any meetings which your Directors may hold with this object in view.

Though he agreed to attend board meetings, Casement was shocked to learn that Grey had exonerated the directors. Some were ignorant, he admitted to Mallet, but Arana was not, and "none of them *should have been ignorant*" (my emphasis). In a particularly astute reading of the situation, Casement reminded Mallet that from the outset the directors had chosen to accept Arana's word without question and had proceeded to hide behind "this error of judgement" in order to claim ignorance. "Support them in the future to do right as far as possible, and to repair the terrible wrongs of the past but don't think you are called on to explicitly champion their past ignorance."

Casement's criticism of Grey's hasty exoneration, what he termed the "unnecessary professions of faith," found favor with Mallet. In a memo to Grey, Mallet echoed Casement's view. Grey, clearly embarrassed, answered that he had only the "British" directors in mind. Grey had to backtrack, and so on May 31 he wrote to the company, under the pretense of asking for the commission's report, to clarify his position on the ignorance of the directors with respect to the abuses in the Putumayo. What came out was a bit of a fudge: "In expressing his opinion that your Directors were in complete ignorance of the appalling state of affairs revealed in Mr. Casement's reports Sir E. Grey is to be understood to refer only to the British members of the Board."

The commission's report, presented at a board meeting on May 17, was wide-ranging, but as expected from the brief given to its members, it touched mostly on commercial and financial matters.

It was mild compared with Casement's, a Foreign Office clerk noted. Nevertheless, though details were sparse, the analysis shallow by comparison, and the main concerns commercial rather than humanitarian, the commission came remarkably close to Casement's view in its conclusions. The management of the operation, the commission concluded, was hopeless, producing "abominable results from the commercial as well as from the humanitarian point of view." The management hardly ever visited the area and let the chiefs of the rubber stations do more or less what they pleased, as long as they got the rubber; and as their remuneration was based solely on how much rubber they got, they would resort to any method to get as much rubber as possible in the shortest time. The Indians were treated as a chief's property. Not collecting the required amount of rubber became a heinous offense and was treated accordingly. "The ultimate welfare of the Indians did not interest him, and such important matters as the planting of the 'chácaras' (garden plots for growing food) and conservation of rubber were allowed to go by the board." The report went on to repeat an observation that could be traced back to Saldaña Rocca in Iquitos in 1907, and to Casement more recently, that the Putumayo was a haven for convicts and that "unfortunately, too many of the Company's employees were recruited [from that class]." The chiefs of the rubber stations were, in the commission's opinion, totally unfit for the job. They were uneducated, lacked character, and had not the slightest idea about rubber. "One chief, who had been in the Putumayo for seven years, frankly admitted that he only knew a rubber tree when he saw it bleeding, and only a few even knew the native names for the trees," the report noted.

Getting straight to the point of the nature of the labor system that the company followed, the report concluded that "labour supervision as carried out by such men under the conditions above described and in the absence of any Governmental control rapidly became indistinguishable from slave-driving."

As Grey had hoped, Casement was invited to a board meeting to discuss the commission's report, set for June 1. He insisted that the Foreign Office provide him with a shorthand writer to take accurate, detailed notes of what was said. "I am not going to leave anything to chance," he told Mallet, "and to the 'recollection' of anyone after the event. A great deal is possible, to my mind, with men in such a desperate hole as these men are in, and my remarks might be misinterpreted, or misunderstood afterwards—so it will be as well to have a trusty record kept of anything I say apart from the desirability of a record of what they say."

The directors were all present, with the major exception of Arana, together with the members of the commission. The meeting lasted two hours, and according to Casement, nothing was accomplished. Casement was dismayed that the board's directors were "all at sea" and did not seem to "know what to do or have any ability to carry out a scheme of reforms. They are in the hands of Julio C. Arana and his informal gang of robber cousins and brothers-in-law out there."

At the meeting, Casement read out a letter he had just received from Arana. In it Arana expressed complete astonishment that, as he put it, "there existed a state of affairs which one could hardly expect of

Roger Casement on the deck of one of the ships he used
on the Amazon to get to Iquitos in September 1910

The Devil: Julio César Arana, 1907

The *Liberal* on the Putumayo, 1910

The headquarters of the Peruvian Amazon Company at
La Chorrera, 1912 (Stuart Fuller)

ABOVE: Captain Thomas Whiffen's exploration party, setting
out in search of the missing Eugène Robuchon, 1908. BELOW: A
Barbadian with two *muchachos de confianza*, the Company's hired guns

The Peruvian Amazon Company's commission, La Chorrera,
1910: (left to right) Juan Tizon, Seymour Bell, Henry Gielgud,
Walter Fox, Louis Barnes, and Roger Casement

Three Indian youths carrying substantial loads of
rubber, 1910 (Roger Casement)

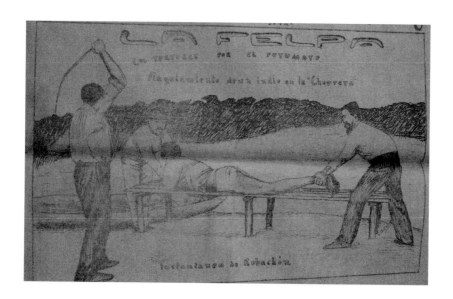

Image and reality: Cartoon printed in *La Felpa* of an Indian being flogged in La Chorrera (*above*); source photograph by Eugène Robuchon, 1903 (*below*)

The Mark of Arana: This photograph, taken by Henry Gielgud in 1910,
shows the scars on an Indian boy who was flogged at Ultimo Retiro
for not bringing in enough rubber. Casement sent a copy of it to the
British Embassy in Washington to help it put pressure on the State
Department to become actively involved in the Putumayo issue.

Slavery and the "civilising mission" on the Putumayo.
ABOVE LEFT: A terrified Huitoto woman. ABOVE RIGHT: Carlos Rey
de Castro stated that fifteen years earlier this woman had been nude and
tattooed; now she made her own clothes on the latest model of the Singer
sewing machine (Silvino Santos, 1912). BOTTOM: Chained Indian rubber-
gatherers in stocks (W. E. Hardenburg, 1912)

Adolfus Gibbs, one of the Barbadians interviewed
by Casement in Iquitos in September 1910 (Photograph
probably taken by Silvino Santos in Manaus, 1913)

One of the many political cartoons in the British press
following the publication of Roger Casement's report
in 1912 (*Westminster Gazette*, July 18, 1912)

mankind." He continued to thank Casement for all that he had done "to all concerned and especially to the natives of that region." Arana devoted most of the letter to congratulating himself for already having taken the necessary steps toward reform and excusing himself, because of financial problems with the company, for being unable to pay as many "visits of inspection" to the Putumayo as he wished.

Casement's reaction to the letter was clearly evident in his annotations to it, including phrases such as "liar" and "wholly untrue." Although he may have acted diplomatically at the meeting, Casement made it quite clear to the directors that Arana was culpable and that "no sincere reform was possible with him on the Board." Casement went on to suggest that reform might begin by sending a member of the commission or one of the British directors to El Encanto and another to La Chorrera to work with Tizon on changing the system. The board accepted this proposal.

A second meeting was called for June 28. But by then King George V had ascended the throne after the death of his father, Edward VII, on May 6, 1910. The honors list accompanying George V's coronation on June 22, 1911, included the conferral of a knighthood on Roger Casement. Sir Edward Grey, on whose recommendation the honor was conferred, was the first to congratulate him, Sir Roger Casement, "in recognition of your valuable services in connection with your recent Mission to the Putumayo District."

Casement was deeply troubled by the honor, even more than he had been six years earlier when he was made a Companion of Saint Michael and Saint George for his Congo investigation. Then he had felt that accepting an honor from the British would be frowned on in Ireland; now, he was sure that accepting a knighthood would be seen by the Irish as traitorous. He certainly felt a traitor himself. The tension between his sense of the injustice of British rule in Ireland and his allegiance to the British state, in whose service he had come face-to-face with gross injustices in the Congo and the Putumayo, was increasing. His problem with the new title was clearly evident in a letter he wrote to Gerald Spicer, head of the American section at the Foreign Office, a few days after his knighthood had been announced. "Thank you for your congratulations and good wishes," it began innocently enough, and then the tone changed abruptly: "altho' if you ever attempt to 'Sir Roger' me again I'll enter into an alliance with the Aranas and Pablo Zumaeta to cut you off someday in the woods of St James' Park, and convert you into a rubber worker to our joint profit." As with the earlier award, Casement's knighthood was only grudgingly accepted.

Arana was absent from the second board meeting. The board explained that it "had not invited him, thinking his presence would not be welcome to Sir R. Casement." Casement responded by pointing out that "as Senor Arana was a Director, and the most important one too, it might be well for the Board to ensure his presence at their further meetings, since their decisions must be largely dependent on their ability to carry him with them, or else on their power to compel his acceptance."

Then the directors dropped a bombshell: the company had no money left and was struggling to carry on the business. Rubber output from the Putumayo had fallen in 1910 by 20 percent on the previous year's figure, and world prices had taken a severe tumble, thanks largely to the appearance on the market of cheaper plantation rubber from the Far East. Added to that, the company's level of debt had risen to dangerous levels. There was panic among some of the rubber station chiefs in the Putumayo following Casement's visit, and they were demanding their commissions. In addition, Pablo Zumaeta—having mortgaged the Putumayo estates to his sister, Eleanora, Arana's wife, for £60,000—now claimed, with his power of attorney, the repayment of the principal plus interest on her behalf. The company's British bankers had refused to extend any more credit.

Once Arana saw that the company's own commission was not going to whitewash conditions in the Putumayo, and when he found out, as he must have done from Tizon, that Casement's findings were totally damning, he must have realized that he had exposed his operations to unnecessary scrutiny, that floating his company on the London Stock Exchange had been a big mistake. Though it had seemed at the time to make him a player on the world commercial stage, thanks to Hardenburg, Whiffen, Casement, and the company's commission, the true nature of his operation had been exposed and the Peruvian Amazon Company was now a liability. He had to retrace his steps and withdraw his rubber empire from the limelight. Behind the scenes

Arana sought a solution to his problems by financially draining the Peruvian Amazon Company, leaving it with as few assets as possible, effectively killing it as a going concern. Pablo Zumaeta's insistence on the payment of the mortgage was a major step in that direction. The company was to be "robbed left, right and centre by Arana and his gang," as Casement put it. What was left would not suffice, Casement feared, to serve as the foundation of the hoped-for British company.

It was evident that there was little hope of anything positive being done, because every reformative action, such as sending out people from England to the Putumayo, depended on funds that the company no longer had. As Henry Read, one of the directors and a highly experienced Latin American hand, put it when pressed by Casement to commit to some action and soon, "You cannot get blood out of a stone; we have no money to carry on anything unless something turns up." The meeting broke up, but not before a further meeting was set for July 5, at which Arana would be present.

Casement was despondent. After talking it over with Louis Barnes, he decided to suggest to Read and the other board members that their best option now lay in raising money themselves to pay for someone to travel out to the Putumayo and put the reforms in place. But Casement saw little hope that this desperate measure would succeed. As he remarked to Spicer:

> Their efforts seem hopeless. The business incapacity at this end has been on a par with the criminal neglect at the other (Manaos [sic] and Iquitos). The only men equal to their task were the murderers. They killed effectually and got rubber too, which the Zumaeta-Arana family seem to have appropriated in one way or another between them. Everything since the Company was formed has been left to J.C. Arana in London and Pablo Zumaeta in Iquitos.

A week later, the board met again, this time with Arana present. It must have been quite a scene: Casement glaring at Arana, suspecting him of trying to break up the company but not being able to prove it or even voice his suspicions, Arana continuing to act as though the problems had nothing to do with him. The meeting failed to solve the company's problems, and it soon became clear that its finances were even worse than they seemed. Arana cynically offered to help by halving his directorial salary, bringing it down to £1,250 per annum.

Casement left the meeting with the distinct impression that the Peruvian Amazon Company as currently constituted was unlikely to survive, something that was corroborated by a letter from the chairman of the board, John Russell Gubbins, asking for a private interview at Casement's home. At the meeting Gubbins told Casement that the news was very bad: the company had outstanding debts exceeding £100,000. Furthermore, the board believed, and had evidence to support, that Arana and family were determined to oust the British directors and liquidate the Peruvian Amazon Company as it was now constituted. Such a liquidation would mean that the company would cease to be a public concern, and as a consequence, the cloak of protection that Casement hoped a British public company would provide to the Putumayo Indians would disappear.

Time was now of the essence. Something had to be done to retain a civilized presence in the Putumayo for the sake of the Indians and to stop Arana from getting his way. Money was the only answer. As Casement told Spicer at the Foreign Office in the wake of his interview with Gubbins, Arana wanted the Putumayo to himself, and "when the company breaks up (which Gubbins thinks will be the 17th instant, if some *Deus ex Machina* does not offer £100,000 to start with) they may exploit the last rubber trees and last Indians to their private profit." Casement put it bluntly: "They and their Iquitos pals would want such a lot of bribing to get them out of the Putumayo that only a Carnegie, or some unusually philanthropic person, could afford to purchase their retirement."

At its next meeting, on July 14, the board, remarkably enough, turned to Casement to find money from among his "humanitarian friends" to buy out Arana and save the company. Casement had these contacts—such people as William Cadbury, the Quaker chocolate manufacturer and philanthropist; Charles Booth, the chairman and owner of the Booth Steamship Company and a great social reformer; and, through other contacts, the great industrialist of the age, Andrew Carnegie. Casement immediately threw himself into a frantic round of fund-raising.

Despite his heroic efforts, by the end of July most of Casement's attempts had failed. The reason he heard most often for not investing funds was that the time was not right for wild rubber. Rubber harvested mainly on British and Dutch plantations in the Far East, which had begun to arrive in European ports in significant volumes in 1909, looked as though it would soon outstrip wild sources. The output of plantation rubber had doubled in one year and was set to do the same again, while that of wild rubber had stagnated.

Amid the drama of trying to save the company and, therefore, save the Indians in the Putumayo, Arédomi and Omarino, the two Huitoto youths Casement had brought out of the Putumayo with him, had arrived in Southampton. Their stay in Barbados, which was only to prepare them for the English leg of their experience, had lasted longer than expected. On June 26 they were on English soil at last.

As he had planned, Casement used the two youths as publicity for the Putumayo as often as he could. It would not be unfair to say that he used them as exhibits. They were taken to the Foreign Office and shown off at various gatherings, some at the homes of close friends, at an Anti-Slavery and Aborigines' Protection Society meeting, and at the Universal Races Congress, which met in London between July 26 and 29.

Not long after that, the wider public was introduced to Arédomi and Omarino. On August 1 *The Daily News* printed an article with the title INFERNO IN A PARADISE, the bulk of which took the form of an informal interview with the two Huitoto youths. It was a unique moment. Readers were drawn straight into the lives of the Huitoto people with an immediacy they could never get from the reports already in circulation—the earlier articles in *Truth* and the parliamentary questions and answers printed in newspapers such as *The Times*. "It is already known in this country," the article began, "that the rubber merchants of Peru have exploited the Indians of the forests in the north-east of the country, and are forcing them to work by diabolical cruelty. Yesterday I heard from the lips of two young Indians who have escaped from this 'inferno in a paradise' a plain tale of the sufferings of their people, the Witota [sic] tribe." "I met them," the interviewer went on, "in the studio of an artist who is painting their portraits, and found them in native dress, a loin-cloth of white bark. Their brown bodies are finely built, and their faces bright and intelligent. They may be savages: they are certainly gentlemen. Their home is a forest on the banks of the Igara Parana, a tributary of the Putumayo, in that wild tract of country in the north-east of Peru."

The interviewer went on to ask the youths about the frightful abuses the Indians had been suffering in the Putumayo. Omarino told of how he had witnessed his own mother's beheading on the order of José Fonseca, the chief of La Sabana rubber station. He also recounted that women were being taken from their families and forced into harems for the rubber station chiefs and that his people were suffering terribly carrying the extraordinary loads of rubber through the forest and dying of starvation.

"There was no doubting the lads' sincerity," the article continued. "They told their hideous tale in a simple, straightforward way. They have escaped; others are being tortured and done to death. The rubber districts of Peru are far away from the civilized parts of the country. Iquitos, the headquarters of the rubber trade, is filled with adventurers lusting for rubber—godless men who hold nothing sacred. There is no church and no religious influence in the town."

Casement had wanted to use Arédomi and Omarino to publicize the horrors of the Putumayo, and the article in *The Daily News* certainly did that. But Casement had more long-term ideas for them, which included having them educated in Ireland at St. Edna's, a bilingual school (Gaelic and English), begun and run by Patrick Pearse, the Irish nationalist and political activist—a plan that did not materialize. Casement probably realized that taking the youths to Ireland was not in their best interests and would be difficult, since he would not be with them. It was, as he told his friend William Cadbury, an idealistic rather than a practical proposition: "I fear with me gone they might not understand things and give great trouble—and there is the far off, later future to think of." He would have to return them to Peru.

The final blow to the attempt to find a buyer for the company came on August 3, when Casement's last hope was disappointed: Andrew Carnegie failed to register an interest. With Gubbins also failing to raise funds, there was no doubt that the company was going into liquidation. It was only a matter of time—weeks rather than months.

Then, good news reached London. The Foreign Office had learned late in July that the Peruvian government's own judicial investigation of conditions in the Putumayo was under way in Iquitos. Several chiefs of rubber stations had been arrested in Iquitos for alleged atrocities, and warrants had been issued for more than two hundred people. With the Peruvian Amazon Company on the verge of liquidation, Casement hoped that the Indians might be saved through the judicial system, with some kind of protection afforded them against oppression and exploitation.

Perhaps it was a vain hope, but Casement was determined to find out more and be on the spot. On August 5, 1911, he wrote to the chairman of the board of the company with the news that he would no longer "be at liberty to attend further meetings . . . I am leaving this country at an early date."

14

THE VEIL OVER THE PUTUMAYO MYSTERY

It was near the end of July, as Casement realized that his fund-raising efforts had come to nothing, when he suggested to Gerald Spicer that he return to Iquitos. The Peruvian Amazon Company, he wrote, was on the verge of collapse, and recent telegrams had convinced him that events in Iquitos, including the Peruvian government judicial investigation, were moving quickly. These developments made it imperative, Casement argued, that "we should have someone at Iquitos with as little delay as possible to watch and as far as may be guide events locally." "I am quite willing to go out at once," he continued, "if it is thought I could be of service in this direction. I think I might be."

The tenor of Casement's letter became more insistent as it progressed. "I am quite ready to go," he wrote, "and should be glad to try and put a square ending to what has begun and carried so successfully to this length—and were I in Iquitos I could influence things a good deal in the right direction."

It was also clear that Casement saw his return to Iquitos as a covert operation. He suggested that the Foreign Office let it be known that he was returning to ensure that the authorities were not questioning the Barbadians who had decided to remain in Iquitos. Casement's real intentions—"to influence the authorities to take sincere and effective measures on the Putumayo"—were to be kept quiet.

Spicer had agreed with Casement's suggestion and pressed it on the department. "Sir R. Casement's idea is a good one," he urged; "there would be considerable advantage in his being at Iquitos to watch the course of events . . . Sir R. Casement's knowledge of all the circumstances is so extensive that he will be able to find out easily how the trials are conducted & what is now the actual state of affairs on the Putumayo."

On August 3, 1911, Casement visited the Foreign Office to make final arrangements with Spicer. He would leave London for Iquitos on the sixteenth of the month. The word was put around the department that he was returning to Iquitos on public service in his position as consul general for Brazil. A telegram containing Casement's plans was sent to Lucien Jerome, the British chargé d'affaires in Lima, who had authorization to pass the information on to the Peruvian government and to David Cazes, still the honorary British consul in Iquitos.

Henry Gielgud, Seymour Bell, and Louis Barnes, members of the company's commission, were given to understand that Casement was returning to Rio de Janeiro. He didn't want anyone on the board knowing his true destination. He wanted his arrival in Iquitos to be as much of a surprise as possible.

Casement's close friends, however, knew where he going and what he was up to. To his ally and fellow humanitarian Edmund Morel, Casement was particularly frank. "I go *again* [sic] to the forest . . . it is only a mission, a continuance of my work of last year and I hope to make a clean sweep this time. We have got the Peruvian govt. on its mettle and I am going to try and keep it clean and bright." Casement admitted to Morel that the Putumayo had been consuming all his energies. His return to Iquitos, a town he hated, filled him with moral purpose: "I shall here be an instrument of good and maybe the means of ending a ghastly system of wrong-doing." However, he also told Morel, he had not forgotten his primary objective in life. "This is my last external effort on behalf of others. Henceforth & for aye I shall concentrate on Ireland alone—& neither Congo, nor Hindu nor Inca shall haul me aside."

In fact, as it turned out, the Putumayo would occupy Casement for longer than he intended.

In June the subject of the Iquitos consulate had come up in the Foreign Office. Casement had commented when he was previously in Iquitos that the situation of an unsalaried consul could lead to conflicts of interest. David Cazes was an example; he supported himself in Iquitos as a trader, and since rubber was the main and most lucrative product, it was inevitable that his operations would involve the rubber trade. The time had come, Casement argued, to place the Iquitos consulate on a salaried, rather than an honorary, footing.

Spicer agreed, as did Mallet, to whom it fell to write to the Treasury for the necessary finance. Mallet told the Treasury, briefly, about the background of the Putumayo issue, stressing in particular the point that the process of getting reforms in the area was at a sensitive stage and that the Foreign Office was working closely with both the company and the Peruvian government to make progress. Explaining why he was writing to them, Mallet pointed out—as Casement had urged him to do—that the Foreign Office thought that reforms in the Putumayo would be neither far-reaching nor permanent unless they were supervised by a salaried British consul. Because of the difficulties of operating in such a distant part of the world, the Foreign Office requested a salary and allowances in excess of the normal rate.

It was essential to find the right man and install him as quickly as possible. "You should choose a good man for the Consul at Iquitos a young man (not too young of course, but one who can stand the climate and the heat)—a man . . . with brains, intelligence and a good, honest nature, who can put two and two together," Casement insisted, and he knew the man. George Babington Michell, at that time posted in Paris as acting consul general, had begun his diplomatic career in 1902 with a first posting to Morocco, where he remained for the next few years until, in 1905, he was posted to the Congo. He stayed in the Congo for two years, and it was because of their shared interest in the Congo that he became acquainted with Casement. They had recently met in Paris after Casement's return from the Putumayo. Michell was forty-seven, the same age as Casement, not exactly a young man, but he had "tropical" experience (in the Congo), and this counted for a great deal in the circumstances.

Three days after petitioning the Treasury, the Foreign Office learned that their request to fund a salaried consul in Iquitos had been granted. On July 21 Casement heard that Michell had secured the appointment. Although Michell was prepared to leave for Iquitos as early as late September, on Casement's insistence, his scheduled departure was taken out of Foreign Office control; it would instead depend entirely on the situation in Iquitos, something Casement himself would assess firsthand. Once Casement gave the go-ahead for Michell to go to Iquitos, the Foreign Office would terminate Cazes's appointment as honorary consul.

All was now set up. On August 16, 1911, after a flurry of letter writing and shunting between England and Ireland, Casement arrived at Waterloo Station to board a train for Southampton. With him were Arédomi and Omarino.

To see them off that day was William Rothenstein, one of the country's leading painters, and his wife. Casement had commissioned Rothenstein to do a double portrait of the two Huitoto youths. The first sitting took place in Rothenstein's Hampstead studio in the middle of July, both youths dressed as they were in the Putumayo. For authenticity, Casement presented Arédomi with a richly plumed headcovering he had brought from the Putumayo. Rothenstein had them to his studio several times, but on August 15 Casement told him that there would be no more sittings. He was taking them home, but not to the Putumayo. "I shall not leave them in the forest again," Casement wrote to Rothenstein, "but with a good friend in Iquitos where they will be happy and cared for and have some decent future—and I have no doubt, in many days to come they will think and talk of you and of the 'picture.'"

Later that day in Southampton, Casement and the Huitoto youths boarded the SS *Magdalena*, bound for Bridgetown, Barbados. "I return when Providence permits me," Casement wrote to Rothenstein, "but they, poor forest spirits never again!"

So far as the Foreign Office was concerned, Casement was going to Iquitos to keep his eye on events there, to help make sure that what seemed from a distance to be a genuine move for reform in the Putumayo succeeded. But his decision to go to the Amazon via Barbados suggests another plan. He was going to try to persuade one of the Barbadians, presumably Frederick Bishop, to act as his interpreter. Casement was intending to go to the Putumayo—"to the 'twilight,'" as he put it in his parting letter to Rothenstein.

Casement knew Barbados well, having spent two months there in the summer of 1908, recuperating from illness shortly after taking up his post as consul in Pará. "The place is so small a mouse could not hide" is how he summed up the island. To his enormous surprise, upon his arrival in Bridgetown on August 28 he was greeted by Andres O'Donnell, the chief of the Entre Rios rubber section in the Putumayo, who, Casement had felt, possibly on account of his Irish connection, had not plumbed the depths to which the other chiefs had sunk. O'Donnell had been living on the island for the past six months. He was owed quite a bit of money by Arana but had no hope of ever getting it back. Casement commented that "he looked abjectly miserable."

Although initially Casement had been generous in his assessment of O'Donnell, he was not about to conceal O'Donnell's presence from the authorities. "I don't think he killed Indians for pleasure or sport—but only to terrorize for rubber—a thing he was appointed to do by his superiors," he wrote to Spicer from Bridgetown. Although "he had a very well kept and well planted station and his Indians seemed happier than any others I met"—O'Donnell had served Arana for seven years—"it was just the same infamous regime of extortion and terrorism there as elsewhere—but with out the hideous torturings and indecencies of many of the other posts." Even if he was the "least criminal of the chief agents," Casement wanted Spicer to let the Peruvian government know that O'Donnell was in Barbados so that they could take the necessary steps to have him extradited to Peru to face charges there.

Casement, Arédomi, and Omarino did not remain long in Barbados. Aside from O'Donnell, Casement did not encounter any others who had lived in Putumayo, and he left the island without the interpreter he had hoped to enlist.

On September 4 they boarded their ship bound for Pará. Although he had failed to find an interpreter, Casement had met Herbert Spencer Dickey, an American medical doctor who was recuperating from an attack of yellow fever. It turned out that Dickey had been the medical officer in the Putumayo, working for Arana for almost a year, from July 1908 until June 1909, and based in El Encanto. Dickey knew South America well. After qualifying as a doctor, he had set out for Colombia to work for the Tolima Mining Company, a London-registered gold and silver prospecting and mining concern, where he remained for seven years. From Colombia, Dickey transferred to Peru and the Putumayo. After his spell with Arana, Dickey had moved to Brazil to work for a rubber concern on the Javari River. He was now returning there. Quite by accident, Casement found in Dickey an extremely useful resource: he could speak Portuguese, Spanish, and the Huitoto language, and he also knew a great deal about the rubber trade and about the Putumayo and the people who worked and slaved there. How much more he knew would emerge on the voyage.

Pará was reached on September 9. After a fortnight's stay waiting for the next available ship to take them upriver, Casement's party, including Dickey, left the port on September 23 on the *Hilda*. Dickey recalled the trip many years later. Casement, he remarked, was one of the most unusual and interesting people he had ever met. His singular choice of clothing said a lot about him.

> Embarking on the river steamer from Pará that day in 1911, when the temperature was floating around ninety-six in the shade, he wore a thick and very dark brown suit of Irish homespun. How he stood it I do not know, but then the rest of his costume was at least as strange. His straw hat looked quite as if it had been taken from an ash can years before. He wore a heavy flannel shirt, but did recognize the tropics to the extent of wearing white canvas shoes the soles of which were rubber. The final touch was a tremendous and very knobbly walking stick—a shillalah that must have been two inches in diameter at the very least.

Casement did just as he pleased, even if it offended others. At one point, Dickey remarked, Casement kicked off his shoes and removed his socks. The ship's captain was aghast at Casement's behavior—it did not "to his mind, go very well with the Irishman's post as British Consul General in Rio. I quite agreed with my friend the captain, but when I spoke to Casement as the captain had suggested, I was told to tell the captain to go to hell, that my companion's feet were hot and that he had no intention of putting on shoes and socks until he felt cooler. And he didn't. He went barefoot until we reached Manaos."

Dickey revealed that he knew quite a bit about what had happened in the Putumayo after Casement's departure at the end of the previous year. He had picked up tidbits of information while working in the Brazilian rubber district. He had heard that two men on Casement's most-wanted list, José Fonseca and Alfredo Montt, had been tipped off and had escaped into Brazil, forcing a number of Bora Indians to go with them. Casement had accused Fonseca of innumerable crimes against the Indians; Montt's alleged atrocities were, in Casement's estimation, even worse. Fonseca and Montt had gone to work rubber in an area on the Javari River at a placed called Santa Teresa, some forty miles from its confluence with the Amazon. Dickey, by a strange coincidence, was working close by.

Casement made plans to get as close to Santa Teresa as possible on his way upriver to Iquitos. He wanted to get the Brazilian authorities in Manaus to expel the two "wretches" and escort them to the Peruvian border at a point where Casement would arrange to have police officers arrest them and send them back to Iquitos to face the law.

In Manaus, while the ship was prepared for its final leg to Iquitos, Casement had a meeting with the governor of the state of Manaus, Colonel Antônio Bittencourt, who, according to Casement, had agreed to do what he could to catch Fonseca and Montt and, to that end, had released one of his own men, a Brazilian police officer, to join the ship.

Nine days later the *Hilda* reached the border town of Benjamin Constant, a little way up the Javari River from its mouth at the Amazon and not more than a few hundred yards across the river from the Peruvian border post. The Brazilian officer, José de Campos, had promised Casement that he would be going at once to Santa Teresa with a sufficient force of men to arrest Fonseca and Montt. The *Hilda* remained in Benjamin Constant for less than twenty-four hours, during which time Casement heard nothing more from de Campos. Casement did, however, see him in company with another police officer and the other partner, a Senhor Serra, of the firm that employed both Fonseca and Montt.

Fonseca and Montt slipped through the net and escaped arrest. De Campos, despite his fine, reassuring words, was clearly corrupt, and Dickey even went so far as to think that the two criminals had been tipped off by the Peruvian consul in Manaus, Carlos Rey de Castro, a name Casement knew well from Robuchon's posthumously published book.

The *Hilda* was ready to depart for its final destination. Several days later, on October 16, two months after leaving Southampton, Casement was back in Iquitos. He, Dickey, Arédomi, and Omarino left the ship.

For a short time Casement's faith that he could influence the course of events for the good in Iquitos was rewarded. Within the first week of his arrival, *El Oriente*, which during Saldaña Rocca's days was very pro-Arana, had printed an article eulogizing Casement's work in the Putumayo; and the prefect, Alayza Paz Soldan, had said that "the honour of lifting the veil over the Putumayo mystery" was entirely Casement's.

Then Casement had a meeting with the man behind the arrest warrants and arrests he had heard about in London. His name was Rómulo Paredes. He had recently returned from the Putumayo, having been appointed in March by the attorney general of the Supreme Court in Lima to head up a commission of inquiry into conditions there. Paredes had no legal training and was not the court's first choice. That had been Carlos Valcárcel, who had been made a judge in Iquitos in July 1910. Valcárcel fell ill just before his planned investigation in the Putumayo and had retreated to New York to seek medical help. Paredes was thirty-four years old and had come to Iquitos in 1907 from Lambayeque, on Peru's northern coast, where he had begun a career as a journalist. He had continued his work in Iquitos and had recently purchased *El Oriente*.

Events had, indeed, moved quickly while Casement was in London.

The commission of inquiry, which Paredes headed, was large and well prepared. Aside from Paredes, there was a physician, two interpreters, and a military escort of nine men. The commission had visited all of the rubber sections in the Putumayo. Paredes took depositions from chiefs of rubber stations, lesser employees, and many Indians, which he had gathered into a substantial three-thousand-page handwritten dossier that he used to write his report to the prefect. Paredes imparted the results of his investigation in the Putumayo to Valcárcel, who was now back in his judicial post following his medical treatment. Immediately Valcárcel issued arrest warrants for 237 people.

Casement enjoyed meeting Paredes, not least because of the compliments he was paid. "Says if it had not been for my prior journey," Casement commented in a letter to Spicer, "he could not have succeeded—it was my going that broke up the gang and [made] everyone else alert and 'ready to tell the truth' . . . He said openly that he had blushed with shame to be a Peruvian—and had he not known that I had been there and would report it all to my govt. he would not have gone on with it—the crimes laid bare were too atrocious."

Compliments and Paredes's good work notwithstanding, it soon became clear that the real situation in Iquitos bore little relationship to Paredes's optimistic picture. For one thing, only 9 of the 237 warrants issued by the Iquitos court had led to arrests, and almost all the men charged were minor agents of the company. Paredes's list of warrants had included the names of some of the worst perpetrators of atrocities—men such as Victor Macedo, Carlos Miranda, and the Barbadian Armando King—but all these men were still working and living in the Putumayo. Also, early in August, Valcárcel had issued an arrest warrant for Pablo Zumaeta, the managing director of the Peruvian Amazon Company in Iquitos and brother-in-law of Arana, but no arrest had taken place, although he was living quite openly in Iquitos. The superior court in Iquitos then quashed the warrant and, instead, issued Valcárcel an order of dismissal, arguing that he had earlier abandoned his post by going off to New York. Other arrest warrants made during the time Casement was in Iquitos also came to nothing, as the authorities always seemed to arrive just a little too late: many chiefs escaped into the forest, taking with them considerable numbers of Indians, either to work new rubber stands or to sell to other *cauche-*

ros. Too many people with authority in Iquitos were under Arana's influence. Justice was not being done.

Casement's confidence soon dissolved into frustration and despair. From several quarters he learned that many of the rubber station chiefs who had had arrest warrants issued against them were still working in the Putumayo and walking around freely, as though nothing had happened. His own failed attempt to get Fonseca and Montt arrested, he now realized, was not just bad luck, but part of a whole conspiracy against the implementation of justice.

While in London, Casement had clearly thought he could make a difference by going to Iquitos. Was he simply naïve? It is hard to believe that he failed to grasp the political situation in Iquitos and the degree to which Arana had the town wrapped up.

Whatever the explanation for Casement's misguided beliefs, he now realized how illusory they were, and his reports back to the Foreign Office reflected his disappointment. On reading one of his dispatches, a Foreign Office clerk noted that they

> reveal a hopeless state of affairs. There seems no doubt that the authorities are in connivance with the criminals, & that things are still about as bad in the Putumayo as they can be—in fact it is not improbable that the last state of the district will be worse than the first. The control now seems to be entirely in Arana's hands . . . & as long as the rubber is collected at the present rate there will always be money for purposes of bribery.

There was little more Casement could do in Iquitos. Arana had many friends in the Amazon who had helped to keep the true state of conditions in the Putumayo concealed. Carlos Rey de Castro, the Peruvian consul in Manaus, who watched over Arana's business in the city, was particularly instrumental in this, Casement learned. "This man's reputation for venality in connection with the Putumayo is so well known in Iquitos that I have heard him referred to by Peruvians there as a disgrace and discredit to their service." Paredes confirmed that Rey de Castro was "one of those primarily responsible for the ignorance in which the government at Lima had been wilfully kept of the true state of things on the Putumayo."

Another, particularly vile person Casement learned about was Benito Lores, a man who had been appointed by the Peruvian government as a special commissioner for the Putumayo. Lores, Casement
discovered, had been the captain of the launch *Iquitos* when it was
involved in the massacre of the Colombian *caucheros* at La Unión in
January 1908, and it was this same Lores who was involved in impris-
oning and then kicking Walter Hardenburg when he was forced on
board the launch after witnessing the atrocity.

Paredes also warned Casement off trying to go back to the Putumayo, on the grounds that there was little he could accomplish. Worse
still, without the protection of the commission, which Casement had
enjoyed on his previous trip, his life would be in great danger.

On November 30 Paredes called on Casement and handed him a
copy of his own confidential report, which he had completed and submitted to the prefect on September 30. Paredes had no authority to
hand the report over to Casement, and no one, it seems, knew that he
had done so. Casement read it with great care and attention.

Several days later Paredes went to see Casement again and surprised him with the news that he would be leaving Iquitos shortly for
Lima and for Lambayeque, his family home. He expected to return to
Iquitos in April. He was becoming increasingly uncomfortable in town.
One of the local papers, *El Heraldo*, began a series of attacks on Paredes, on the prefect, and on the Lima government. The British government, Sir Edward Grey, and Casement himself did not escape censure.
The British government was charged with acting improperly and with
having issued secret instructions to Casement to remove from the jurisdiction of Peru the "sole criminals . . . the Barbados negroes, who
alone had committed reprehensible acts." In the same article, Pablo
Zumaeta and his cohorts were lauded as "heroes and patriots who only
advanced the interests of their country."

Casement remarked that the situation now in Iquitos was the same
as it had been four years before, when allegations of the crimes committed in the Putumayo first appeared in *La Felpa* and *La Sancion*. Then,
the local newspapers attacked Saldaña Rocca before turning on Walter
Hardenburg. Now, Casement argued, "the people assailed are the Peruvian Government itself, the special judge sent by that Government to
the Putumayo, and the foreign Government charged with fomenting

the conspiracy against the local patriots who have done so much and suffered so many things in advancing the cause of Peruvian civilisation in the wilderness."

It was time for Casement to leave Iquitos for good.

On December 7 Casement boarded the Booth liner *Ucayali* for its voyage downriver to Manaus. This really would be the last time he would do the trip.

The despair he had felt in Iquitos stayed with him on his voyage down the Amazon. To add to his misery, he learned that the Peruvian Amazon Company had gone into liquidation. The decision was taken on September 12, after consultations with Sir Frank Crisp, the company's solicitor and one of the most influential company lawyers in Britain. On September 27, at an extraordinary general meeting, the board unanimously agreed to appoint Julio César Arana as the company's liquidator. There could be no more cynical a ploy than this. Arana could do exactly as he pleased. The shareholders in London were now entirely at his mercy, as were the Indians in the Putumayo.

Arriving in Manaus on December 11, Casement wrote to Spicer, summing up the situation as he saw it. The criminals had all escaped, some of them into Brazilian territory, and now that the heat was off, they were regrouping. Victor Macedo, the chief of La Chorrera, had gone to Iquitos. "The Superior Court will probably go down in a body to greet him & have him to dinner," Casement commented caustically. He wouldn't be surprised, Casement noted, if the rubber station chiefs with arrest warrants out for them all returned to Iquitos and brought criminal libel charges against Paredes, so pervasive and powerful was Arana's grip.

Casement now understood more clearly than ever the extent to which Arana and his henchmen had lied and how ruthless they were. He told Spicer that Dickey had been in the Putumayo when Whiffen passed through in the summer of 1908 trying to solve the mystery of Robuchon's disappearance. Dickey was disgusted to learn of Arana's accusations of blackmail against Whiffen. "Whiffen acted all the time on the Putumayo like a gentleman," Dickey said, "& the whole thing was a put up game to blacken his character when they found he knew too much." Pablo Zumaeta, Casement believed, was the worst of the pack. Apparently he had even kidnapped three Peruvian soldiers, his own countrymen, and sold them into slavery working rubber in Brazil. "Pablo is to me the essence of all that is contemptible. If you saw the little fat, cowardly, pale-faced beast you would want to kick him right away."

As if all this was not depressing enough, when Casement reached Manaus, none other than Julio César Arana himself arrived, fresh from his triumph in London at having been appointed official liquidator to the Peruvian Amazon Company. Arana made straight for Casement's hotel, but Casement refused to receive him. Most likely Casement was motivated by a sense of disgust, as well as being careful to maintain the distance required of him as an official of the British government.

Two days later, on December 17, Casement boarded the *Hubert*, another Booth liner, for the final leg of the downriver voyage to Pará and the mouth of the Amazon. The next day, still some distance from Pará, Casement completed a précis of Paredes's report updating the situation in the Putumayo. He wanted to get it to Grey and the Foreign Office as quickly as possible.

On arriving in Pará, Casement changed his plans. He decided not to return to London as intended. Instead, on December 24 he boarded the *Denis* for Barbados and arrived at Bridgetown on December 29. One of the first things he discovered was that Andres O'Donnell was not only still on the island, a free man, but that two days earlier he had married Miss Stella Bruce Turney, the daughter of the superintendent of Queen's Park. The news grated on Casement as yet another reminder of how little justice had been done. O'Donnell had become a well respected member of Barbadian high society. No one had arrested him; no one had asked for his extradition, as Casement had hoped would happen. The local press referred to the marriage as one of the chief "fashionable events" of the week. Attending the celebration, Casement noted, were a number of the British residents and a "strong contingent of the local Peruvian 'colony' who form now an appreciable element of Barbados social life. These Peruvians are mostly from Iquitos and more than one of them Putumayo murderers."

It was not Casement's intention to stay in the colony any longer than he had to. On the day he arrived, he learned that there was a ship scheduled to leave on December 31, and he booked himself on it. At 3:00 p.m., the SS *Terence* cast off from Bridgetown. It was not heading for Europe. Its destination was New York. Someone had to make the Americans put pressure on the Peruvian government to save the Indians. Who better than the Irish Knight himself?

PART
FOUR

15

PUBLISH AND BE DAMNED

When, in late November 1909, James Bryce, the British ambassador in Washington, asked the U.S. government for help in putting pressure on the Peruvian government to investigate conditions in the Putumayo, the State Department had replied that it was involved in delicate negotiations with both Peru and Ecuador about their common border and could do nothing that might jeopardize those talks. Bryce accepted the American position, but since then he had kept the State Department fully informed of developments in the investigation, including sharing Casement's reports with it.

Now that Casement had turned up in the United States, Bryce wanted to introduce him to State Department officials, to impress upon them the need "to co-operate energetically" in this humanitarian effort, as he termed it.

On January 10, 1912, Bryce wrote to Huntington Wilson, the assistant secretary of state, to arrange a meeting with Sir Roger Casement. The two men met and talked; Casement also had a few minutes with President Taft at a dinner. Recalling the president's meeting with Casement a few years later, George Young, the first secretary at the British embassy, left a vivid description of that encounter when, in a quiet corner of the British embassy, the two men first met. "A queer picture they made—the tall Celt haggard and livid from the Putumayo swamps, fixing with glittering black eyes the burly rubicund Anglo-Saxon. It was like a black snake fascinating a wombat." Casement explained to the president and later to other State Department officials that he was convinced that "no really serious efforts are being made to prosecute those responsible for atrocities in the Putumayo." American help was needed urgently.

Casement had come away from his second trip to Iquitos despondent. His efforts and, therefore, those of the Foreign Office, had hit a wall. There was nothing more that it could do. Only the U.S. government, he was convinced, could move things along. "So I went off to Washington," Casement later recalled, "—entirely off my own bat—without a hint that such a move was on—without letting the F.O. know and got . . . the thing taken up from there by a sort of personal assault on Taft and the State Department. Grey was delighted when he knew & spoke in the warmest terms to me."

Directly following Casement's meeting with State Department officials, U.S. secretary of state Philander Knox sent an urgent message to the American minister in Lima, Henry Clay Howard, informing him that he should make the details of Casement's concerns known to the Peruvian government—to impress upon them that they should take drastic and effective action in the region and to emphasize that the British government was intent on publishing the reports of Casement's investigations and that this exposé "might induce public opinion of the world to believe that Peru has shown herself unable effectively to exercise sovereign rights over the disputed region."

Casement also suggested to the State Department that it should reopen its consulate in Iquitos, which had been effectively closed down in 1908. The State Department agreed.

It now looked as though the U.S. government was getting involved in the Putumayo cause at last.

Casement's trip to the United States was short but extremely fruitful. He was back in England on January 20, 1912. Partly because of his success in Washington, where he had "worked up the State Dept. to a high pitch of feeling in the matter," and partly because of his now unassailable knowledge of the politics of the Putumayo, Casement had put himself in the role of gatekeeper at the Foreign Office in London: nothing was decided at the highest levels without first finding out his opinion. Almost as soon as he disembarked in Southampton, he was at the Foreign Office consulting with his superiors, particularly Gerald Spicer.

Energized by his American detour, Casement emphasized that time should not be lost, that the Foreign Office should "strike while the iron is hot," and that his reports should be published as soon as possible. Leaving anything to Peruvian justice alone, he felt, would be a mistake. His bitter experience in Iquitos several months earlier had convinced him that initiatives from the Peruvian authorities, whether they were in Iquitos or in Lima, meant nothing. When, for example, the president of the Iquitos court made a judicial order at the end of December 1911 to accelerate the criminal procedure against the men being held in an Iquitos jail awaiting trial, Casement had become so mistrustful of justice in Iquitos that he remarked to the Foreign Office, "They are put forward merely to deceive, and give the impression that the matter is being dealt with in due process of law. If we were to wait the development of the proceedings, it might well be that the nine men in custody would die in jail before the final stage of investigation were reached—but I fear the remaining Indians on the Putumayo would also be dead—or killed." Casement had also learned that Arana was saying in Peru "that as soon as what he called 'this fuss' was over, the natives would be set to work again." To Casement this meant the extermination of the Putumayo Indians.

The Peruvians needed to face up to their responsibilities in the Putumayo, and the best weapon the Foreign Office had to put pressure on them to act was publicity. Casement began his campaign of pressuring the Foreign Office. In early February 1912 he prepared a memorandum outlining his vision for the steps that should be taken following publication of his report. Publication, he insisted, would show the world "how Peru has used her primitive, defenceless, innocent populations in this greedy rush for rubber." "The surest check against continuance of these cruelties," he continued, "is to drag into daylight and hold up to universal reprobation the authors and abettors and criminals of the Putumayo slavery." Concentrating on punishment was not, he argued, the best way forward, for that would allow the Peruvian government to drag its heels, as it had done already, and open the British government to a charge of duplicity. He was thinking here of Andres O'Donnell, now living the life of Riley in Barbados, where the authorities were turning a blind eye to his presence on the island. "We should look rather foolish," Casement remarked, "with one of the criminals marrying 'with pages in white satin' and English girls as bridesmaids in 'pink voile' dresses (they should have been crimson!), at a British church in a British colony, with a 'highly fashionable' colonial gathering, and nothing said by us."

At the same time, Casement presented the Foreign Office with a report of his findings from his most recent trip to Iquitos. The report showed that nothing had been done to stem the atrocities perpetrated on the Indian population. Paredes had taken thousands of pages of evidence on the Putumayo, and according to his calculations, the Indian population had fallen to a new low. "Human bones," Casement wrote, "the remains of lost tribes of Indians, are so scattered through the forests that, as one informant stated, these spots 'resemble battle-fields.' One Peruvian officer, who had been through the Putumayo since the date of my visit in 1910, said that the neighbourhood of one particular section he had visited recalled to him the battlefield of Miraflores—the bloodiest battle of the Chilean war [the War of the Pacific]."

Casement also took the opportunity to remind the Foreign Office that Britain should take the moral high ground and concentrate its efforts on improving conditions for the Indians. Anything that deflected from this purpose, such as insisting on punishment or raking over the past, could backfire. It might also give the Peruvians a moment to reflect on the salient fact that Britain's stake in the Putumayo rubber trade and its impact on the commerce of Iquitos was substantial: "the whole of the rubber output of the region, it should be borne in mind, is placed upon the English market, and is conveyed from Iquitos in

British bottoms [ships]." If the Peruvians countered with an observation such as this, it would be difficult to get the argument back to the issue of the welfare of the Indians. It might seem a little hollow for Britain to contend that it was a champion of Indian rights.

Casement also wanted the Foreign Office to impress on the Peruvian government that it, too, should concern itself with reforms, and those that Paredes had recommended to the Iquitos court should form the basis of an overall plan. Of course, Casement had already seen Paredes's report in Iquitos, and now he handed over his précis of it to the Foreign Office so his colleagues could see for themselves the reforms being suggested, the most important of which was that the Peruvian government should begin to administer the area responsibly by having salaried magistrates installed in four rubber sections, with full powers of investigation and arrest.

However, the Paredes report had not yet appeared in Lima, despite being sent—or so Casement was told—four and a half months earlier. This was further proof that the Peruvian government, if left to itself, would do nothing. The delay, if that was what it was, in getting Paredes's report from Iquitos to Lima prompted Casement to remark cynically,

> had I not gone back to Iquitos it is pretty clear we should never have known anything of this document at all. Probably it would never have left Iquitos. Its existence would have been denied—that is to say we should have been told only of the "Expediente" or dossier forming the judicial part of Paredes' work while the other, or political report, he compiled on his return to Iquitos would have been omitted from official reference.

Casement worked feverishly to try to convince everyone who had influence that the reports needed to reach the public. Apart from colleagues at the Foreign Office, Casement turned to his friends and to the officers of the Anti-Slavery and Aborigines' Protection Society: "The gang of ruffians need frightening I assure you & the only weapon is the fear of publicity."

Casement wasn't alone in pressing for publication. Members of Parliament, such as Joseph King, who knew that Casement had completed a report as early as February 1911, kept asking the government for a date of publication, but all they got from the foreign secretary was that he was giving the matter his careful consideration. In July of the previous year, when Josiah Wedgwood, Liberal MP for Newcastle-under-Lyme, asked the same question, he had received the same reply; and on March 5, 1912, eight months later, when Noel Buxton, Liberal MP for North Norfolk, raised the issue yet again, Sir Edward Grey simply said that he was not in a position to give a definite answer.

Grey was holding back on publication. His hands were tied: the Monroe Doctrine meant that he could do nothing without consulting the State Department. Grey was pleased that Casement had been so warmly received in Washington and that the Americans seemed to be on board, but he felt unable to publish the reports on his own. He was holding back until he heard what Henry Clay Howard in Lima reported back to Washington. The waiting now began.

Casement, however, was not as sanguine as Grey. He had his own contacts both in Washington and Lima who were providing him with off-the-record information, which suggested that the American position was more complicated and contradictory than was understood in London. One of Casement's informants, George Young at the British embassy in Washington, suggested that there was "backsliding at the State Department" and that it might not be as willing to involve itself in the Putumayo as Casement had been led to believe. Casement responded to this worrying news by sending Young a batch of Putumayo photographs to pass over to Huntington Wilson, the acting secretary of state. These pictures, together with accompanying notes, Casement hoped, would stem the "backsliding." But he had little confidence in Henry Clay Howard. Lucien Jerome, the British consul general in Callao and Casement's close confidant with a pulse on the diplomatic scene in Lima, had little good to say about Howard. Whether this was because of his lack of diplomatic experience—Lima was his first and only post—or for some other reason, or because he didn't seem to take warmly to the British, Howard made a poor impression on Jerome: "The USA Minister in Lima," he wrote, "is a kindly old ass who believes all they tell him—and we have the clearest proof that they have lied to us again & again—& of course to him."

Casement was growing increasingly agitated about the situation. He fired off a salvo to James Bryce in Washington. "I hope most sincerely," he wrote, "that the State Department will not try to prevent us from publishing the Putumayo papers. If they do it will be a sin—and a sin of selfishness that God will not forgive. Our wrong doing will be one of weakness if we give way to their deprecation—but theirs will be something more than weakness." Only compulsion and international pressure could move the Peruvian government to act, Casement argued: it had already shown that its promises lacked any substance. "The U.S.A.," Casement continued, "will be doing a grave disservice to humanity and civilization if they, for purely selfish ends, oppose the letting in of light upon this den of thieves and murderers."

Casement's fears were well founded. Early in March, Charles des Graz, the British first minister in Lima, passed on information to the Foreign Office that Howard was going to tell his superiors in Washington that in his opinion, publishing Casement's reports would "do more harm than good by its effect on the Peruvian Government and check any present endeavour or future practical scheme of reform when devised." Howard believed that pushing the Peruvian government by embarrassing them publicly was counterproductive.

Casement feared the worst—that the Foreign Office would not publish without the State Department's support. So he stepped up the pressure. He started feeding his Foreign Office colleagues as much information as he could honestly garner from his contacts in Peru and in Washington so as to undermine the hold that the United States had over decision making in London. Casement was no great fan of the Monroe Doctrine, and he took every occasion he could to criticize it, while putting the civilizing position of both Britain and, for that matter, Germany on a higher moral level. If the United States wanted exclusive influence in Latin America, it also had to take the responsibility that went with that position, and this included chiding its neighbors in cases of humanitarian abuses, such as the Putumayo.

Casement repeated that Howard was being fed a pack of lies. The Peruvian government, Casement emphasized, depended on Arana in the Putumayo, since his presence there guaranteed their claim to this territory. At the same time, Peru depended on foreign investment, and only a threat to that flow of capital would make the Peruvian government cut its ties with Arana and improve the lot of the Indians. Both the British and the American governments had a moral duty to their publics to warn them off investing in "such coffin ships as the Peruvian Amazon Company." Publication of his reports was essential, for "to purify the Putumayo through Peruvian official agency alone would be like referring the keeping of Lent to a jury of butchers!"

At the end of March, Casement's pressuring received a substantial boost when the London *Morning Post* broke the silence. On March 25 it printed an interview with Seymour Bell, the merchant who was one of the members of the Peruvian Amazon Company Commission to the Putumayo. Whether the members of the commission were under some code of honor to keep quiet is not clear, but Bell's interview came out of the blue. The article recounted the cruel conditions under which the Putumayo Indians collected rubber for the company, many details of which closely adhered to Casement's own reports. That Casement had accompanied the commission, and had already written reports for the government that had still not seen the light of day, was emphasized by Bell in the interview.

The article ended with a challenge to the government. Now that "the light of publicity has been shed upon the situation by Mr Bell's statement," the government was obliged to publish Casement's report.

Several days after the *Morning Post* story, *Truth* weighed in to the fray by pressing Bell on his observations. Could he be clearer on whether the cruelties he documented were a thing of the past, or was he implying that they were still continuing?

At this point Bell turned to Casement for assistance, and they exchanged ideas about how he should answer the question in *Truth*. On April 17, under the banner of PERU AND HER "CONGO," *Truth* had its answer and told its readers that hardly anything had changed in the Putumayo and that the Peruvian government had not established the rule of law in the region. "Englishmen," it stated, "were justly indignant a few years ago at the diabolical atrocities perpetrated in the 'Red Rubber' days of the Congo. This is a far stronger case." The British government, it argued, had a duty to bring an action against the Peruvian Amazon Company, which, though in liquidation, was still in existence as a British company. "As a preliminary step toward that end," the article continued, "the publication of Sir Roger Casement's report to the Foreign Office should be pressed for."

Public pressure on the Foreign Office was growing. The newspapers were doing their bit, as were the parliamentary questions about the government's plans to publish the report, which had been repeatedly fired at the Foreign Office since February of the previous year. On March 28, just a few days after Bell had spilled his story in the *Morning Post*, James Bryce finally informed the Foreign Office that the news from Washington was not as bad as they had feared. Howard, it was true, was against publication, but Huntington Wilson, the acting secretary of state, had used his influence and replied that the United States had decided to defer to the judgment of the British government regarding publication of the reports.

The ball was back in the British court, and it was becoming clear that it would now be impossible to resist the clamor for publication. Plans were rolled out to publish Casement's reports, together with dispatches and telegrams, in what was termed a "Blue Book," an official publication whose name derived from its rich blue paper cover. But then, in early April, the State Department looked as though it was about to change its position again. It had heard from Lima that the Peruvian government was about to appoint a committee to study the administration of the Putumayo and make reforms to guarantee the rights of the Indians. Everything was up in the air again.

The Foreign Office seemed pleased with the news from Lima and concluded that if it was correct, publishing Casement's damning report would be harmful, as Howard had warned. It decided to hold off on the decision to publish for the time being. Casement, however, was not so easily taken in. Over the next month and more, he continued his campaign of undermining the trust that the two governments were placing in Peru. He pointed out, for example, that one of the members who was going to be appointed to the Peruvian government's committee, Senator Julio Ego-Aguirre, representing the department of Loreto in Congress, was legal adviser to the Arana brothers. Senator Ego-Aguirre, who, incidentally, had been one of Hardenburg's students in

Iquitos, had also come out publicly in a Lima newspaper accusing Hardenburg of blackmail. To Casement, at least, appointing Senator Ego-Aguirre to study conditions in the Putumayo was tantamount to planning a whitewash. As if that wasn't enough to cast doubt on the Peruvian government's true intent, Casement also learned that Arana had been buying political favors in the capital—"spreading a lot of money in Lima," as he put it. As for Henry Clay Howard, Lucien Jerome had told Casement that he was not taken seriously in diplomatic circles in Lima, preferring to drum up business for American companies rather than worry about humanitarian issues. "He carries no weight here . . . He never goes to his office but spends his time in the different business houses in Lima trying to work up business for the American exporters for the Panama Canal. He is certainly energetic about that line." Jerome also mentioned that Howard was not sympathetic to the British.

Perhaps the most worrying news for Casement was that the Putumayo was now producing more rubber than it had in the previous year, and Casement feared that Arana's system of terror and violence was, if anything, getting worse. While the American and British governments dithered, time for the Indians was running out.

At the end of May it became official that the State Department was following Howard's advice. It was giving the Peruvian government time to initiate its own reforms. Bryce, in Washington, took a dim view and expressed his concern that the United States wanted to remain "at our expense as the benevolent guardian of Peru."

Throughout June, news filtered back to London to the effect that the Peruvian government was simply playing for time. Casement had had it right all along. It had, for example, made everything more complicated. In addition to its own committee, the government had created an auxiliary commission, to be headed by Paredes, who was to return to the Putumayo for more information and then report back to the committee in Lima to consider its next move. When Casement learned of this, he was incredulous—Paredes had already supplied the government with all the facts it needed. The composition of the auxiliary commission, moreover, was simply a farce, as Casement pointed out. One of its members, Dr. Don Julio Maradiegue, had actually worked as an advocate for the Aranas. This new tier of organization would mean that instead of producing concrete proposals of reform by the end of July, as the Peruvian government had promised the State Department, a delay until the following January was now inevitable.

Everything seemed to be conspiring against the publication of Casement's reports. Eduardo Lembcke, the chargé d'affaires at the Peruvian legation in London, began bombarding the Foreign Office with dispatches, reporting that Lima had already undertaken to reform the rubber regime in the Putumayo and that conditions for the Indians had already improved. Publishing, Lembcke repeated, should be withheld. Lembcke then proceeded to place all the blame for the atrocities squarely on the shoulders of the Barbadians, and he accused Casement of perverting the course of justice by spiriting the criminals away from Peru.

The Foreign Office was in a quandary. On the one hand, from a diplomatic point of view, it had to submit to Washington's reading of the political situation. On the other hand, it was convinced by the evidence that the Peruvian government was playing for time or, worse, that they had no intention whatever of intervening in the Putumayo. Early in June, Pope Pius X had issued a papal encyclical (a letter sent to all bishops) *Lacrimabili statu*, which deplored the conditions of the Indians and called for a missionary presence for the first time in the Putumayo. Public opinion in Britain, too, was pressing hard for publication. But what to do? Diplomacy or action? The crunch came at the end of June, when the Foreign Office learned that the auxiliary commission would not be meeting its deadline of reporting by the following March and, more worryingly, that Paredes had changed his tune and, while spending time in Lima, had fallen under Arana's spell, publicly blaming the British for what had happened in the Putumayo.

That was too much to bear. As far as Louis Mallet was concerned, Paredes's defection was the final straw. Mallet urged immediate publication of Casement's report.

On July 2 the Liberal MP Joseph King asked in the House of Commons whether Arana had been arrested and when he would be brought to justice. Sir Edward Grey replied that this was beyond his jurisdiction, and he had no further comment. Moments later another Liberal

MP, Noel Buxton, rose and asked, "When will the Report of Sir Roger Casement on the Putumayo rubber atrocities be published?" For the first time since early 1911 Grey gave a straight answer to that question: "I propose to lay the Papers before the House very shortly—at any rate before the end of the month."

On Saturday, July 13, 1912, the Blue Book was finally published. The British government had gone out on a limb and followed Casement, and its own instincts, rather than the Americans.

"I've blown up the Devil's Paradise in Peru," Casement exclaimed with glee when he heard the news. "I told you I should—and I've done it. It is a good step forward in human things—the abetters of cruelty are not so secure as they were—& their tenants are getting very scared. Putumayo will be cleansed—altho' nothing can bring back the murdered tribes—poor souls."

16

AN INTERNATIONAL SCANDAL

Monday, July 15, 1912, was a very hot day in London. The temperature reached 90 degrees Fahrenheit. There, in *The Times*, was the shocking headline that said it all: THE PUTUMAYO ATROCITIES: A SOUTH AMERICAN CONGO — SIR ROGER CASEMENT'S REPORT PUBLISHED. Readers were instantly transported to the steamy jungles of the Amazon, to a vast territory "within a square formed by the Equator, 5 deg. South lat., and 70 deg. West Long, the sovereignty of which is in dispute between the three Republics of Peru, Colombia, and Ecuador."

No sooner had they been taken through the geopolitics than readers were thrust into harrowing details of flogging, torture, and murder reproduced from the report. At one point in the article the editor broke off, remarking, "Far more terrible examples of cruelty are quoted on the direct evidence of witnesses of the crimes. We cannot reproduce them. It must suffice to say that all of the Indians of such a district, without discrimination of age or sex, became the helpless victims of the lust, cupidity, and savage cruelty of its conqueror." The article reminded readers that the story of the dreadful events of the Putumayo was first brought to the public's attention by an American engineer and published in *Truth* in the latter part of 1909, and that his allegations were fully borne out by the investigations of Casement, whose evidence came from a group of Barbadian men who had been forced by company superiors to carry out heinous acts against the Indians. At no time during Casement's questioning of the men, the article noted, were their claims disputed by the agents of the Peruvian Amazon Company who were present at the time.

The article concluded thus: "No one who reads Sir Roger Casement's Report can fail to wish it means and power to extend its civilizing influence. The existing system cries aloud to Heaven."

On the following page, readers could continue to digest these revelations with the help of the editorial. There, under the banner of SLAVERY IN SOUTH AMERICA, the writer took a broader view of the whole story. "Systematic slavery" was the key term used, "enforced by the lash and the bullet and enforced by every excess of cruelty and lust." The result was that the Indian population had declined from 50,000 in 1906 to 8,000 in 1911. There was no evidence that their conditions had improved: indeed, judging from the level of rubber exports that were leaving the region, the real fear—and this was attributed to Sir Edward Grey—was that they were worse.

The editorial did not dwell on the details of the atrocities. Rather, it emphasized the lack of reform and warned that the consequences, for Peru, of failing to act could be substantial. The article pointed out that though the authorities had issued warrants galore, virtually none of them had led to arrests. Many of the worst criminals were living openly in Peru, and excuses were still being made about the impossibility of policing such an out-of-the-way region at the same time as claiming sovereignty over it. The editorial praised Sir Edward Grey and especially Sir Roger Casement, who "has deserved well of his countrymen and of mankind by the ability and zeal with which he has investigated under very difficult conditions an appalling iniquity." It ended with a reminder that governments have responsibilities. "It is for the Peruvian Government," the editorial remarked, "to remember that sovereignty has its duties as well as its rights. It is for the Governments and peoples of this country and of the United States to stimulate them to the discharge of those duties, to lend them moral support in the task, and to bring home to them that failure to perform it must fatally compromise their credit and their future."

Soon most newspapers in Britain were carrying the story. The *Daily Chronicle* provided a little more information than most in an article written by the Reverend John Harris of the Anti-Slavery and Aborigines' Protection Society. Harris reminded readers that it was Walter Hardenburg, who had arrived in London at the society's offices in the summer of 1909 with a manuscript of a book titled *The Devil's Paradise*, who first exposed the horrors of the Putumayo. Soon thereafter, in the weeks to follow, most of Britain's periodicals—such as *Truth*, *The Saturday Review*, *The Spectator*, *The Economist*, and *The Nation*, and specialist magazines such as *The India Rubber Journal* and the *Anti-Slavery Reporter and Aborigines' Friend*—carried a considered piece on the Putumayo.

Thanks to the world's extensive telegraphic connections and their use by a core group of news agencies—Reuters, Associated Press, and Agence France-Presse—news of the publication spread rapidly. Most papers reported along the lines of *The Times*, though sometimes with many more sensational details. One was the New York *Sun*, which published attention-grabbing headlines such as BUTCHER NATIVES TO GET RUBBER; NEGROES OF BRITISH COMPANY COMMIT TERRIBLE CRIMES; ENSLAVED, BURNED AT STAKE AND MAIMED—JUST A FEW OF THE HORRORS; and ONE TRIBE DECIMATED. *The New York Times*, too, publicized the story, with the headline RUBBER ATROCITIES SPARED NO VICTIM.

The Blue Book, or Command Paper 6266, *Correspondence Respecting the Treatment of British Colonial Subjects and Native Indians Employed in the Collection of Rubber in the Putumayo District*, to give it its full and official title, was a hefty document. It ran for 165 pages and was nearly 100,000 words in length. The volume contained both of Casement's reports, written after his visit to the Putumayo; statements from thirty Barbadian men, which covered about half the total length of the publication; and a list of those people Casement considered to be the worst offenders in the employ of the Peruvian Amazon Company. The book concluded with Casement's report concerning his recent visit to Iquitos. Interspersed with these pieces were dispatches from British consular officials in Peru and from James Bryce and his colleagues in Washington, providing information on the diplomatic position of the United States leading up to publication. Alfred Mitchell Innes, of the British embassy in Washington, suggested that the Blue Book should include a photograph of a young Indian boy that vividly showed innumerable lesions on the back of his body—the "Mark of Arana." When he showed this photograph to James Bryce, Innes recalled that Bryce "nearly wept and, to tell the truth, so did I." However, Sir Arthur Nicolson, the permanent undersecretary of state, felt that it was inappropriate for a Blue Book to have photographs in it. The Blue Book was put on sale, as were similar government publications, at a reasonable price of one shilling and five pence, equivalent to about £5 today.

The Blue Book presented a wealth of details on all aspects of the Putumayo rubber trade—how rubber was extracted; how collections were organized around the *puesta* and the cyclical *fabrico*; how systems of oppression worked and were enforced; the history of a region hardly anyone had ever heard of; and so on. Besides exposing the atrocities, the volume gave a unique insight into the underbelly of one of the world's newest and most important industries and one of the world's most remarkable materials.

Part of the lasting impact of the Blue Book is that the horror is told through intimate stories. Sometimes Casement let the men tell their own stories, sometimes he presented their stories in the form of narratives, but in most instances the statements were a mixture of narrative and near-verbatim conversations. It was presented very personally and directly. Everyone had an identity—name, age, place of birth, and length of employment in the Putumayo. Frederick Bishop, Casement's guide and interpreter, was there, as was James Chase, the twenty-three-year-old who gave evidence "under a sense of fear; his agitation was plainly marked, and he was greatly disconcerted," and whom Casement found in La Chorrera. Chase's substantial statement, the longest of the thirty such statements, was enough in and of itself to provide Casement with all the evidence he needed of criminality. Chase also told Casement the heartening story of the fatal revenge of the Indian chief Katenere against his oppressors.

Never before had colonial subjects had their voices heard in a public document like this.

These thirty Barbadian men made history within the Blue Book, and their names became known the world over. The Blue Book also gave rise to spin-off stories such as the one carried by *The New York Times*. In early August 1912 Robert Isaacs, an elevator operator in a New York apartment building, contacted the paper and claimed that he, too, had worked in the Putumayo for Arana.

Isaacs's story appeared a day later, on August 4, under the headline SAW WHOLESALE MURDER IN THE AMAZON. It strongly resembled the Barbadian statements told to Casement. "Over and over again, [he] has cut into its almost impenetrable jungle lands, with his Winchester on his shoulder and his machete in his hand, on the search for Indians; who at the command of cruel Captains, has burst into peaceful Indian villages, helped round up the inhabitants, helped drive them back along the trail to slavery." Isaacs told of how he was enticed to sign up with the Aranas in Bridgetown; how when he got to the Putumayo "he suddenly found himself not a rubber hunter but an Indian hunter, not a laborer but a warrior, armed to the teeth, flanked by murderous companions, doomed to live in a hell of bloodshed and torture"; how finally, after witnessing and taking part in such horrors, he managed to get away from the Putumayo and ended up working for three years in the engineer's mess on the site of the Madeira-Mamoré Railway building project before coming to New York to work running an elevator in an apartment building. "I'm speaking the truth," he exclaimed at the end of the piece. "I can go back to the Putumayo forests and show anybody heaps of rotting skeletons at the places where we surrounded and massacred the Indians."

Casement had left England for the Putumayo in August 1910 and had delivered his final report at the end of March 1911. After a gap of fifteen and a half months, the story was finally in the open, an international scandal. But now what?

By the time of the Blue Book's publication, Iquitos had become home to two new consuls. The British consulate had been there since the latter half of the previous century, but it became for the first time a salaried post. George Michell, the man recommended by Casement, was the consul now fully representing British interests. The Americans also had a new consul, thirty-two-year-old Stuart Jamieson Fuller.

Fuller had received his first instructions from Huntington Wilson early in April 1912, while he was en route to Iquitos. By this time the State Department had laid its hands on Charles Eberhardt's reports, when he was the first American consul in Iquitos in 1907 and 1908. Where the reports had been all these years, or whether they were for some reason suppressed, is not known.

Wilson remarked that when Eberhardt visited the Putumayo in 1907, he reported that the Indians were being so exploited that he feared they might soon be extinct. Fuller was told to keep in close contact and co-operate fully with Michell, the first such Anglo-American collaboration in the region, and to get to know the rubber district of the Putumayo— "to visit, at intervals which may appear . . . advisable, the rubber stations along the Putumayo region in order that the department may have before it your views based upon personal observation." The rather vague language veiled a specific question: Had the cruelties so graphically described by Casement ceased? The Peruvian government still insisted, as it had when the allegations first appeared in the September 1909 issue of *Truth*, that the cruelties described were "historic," having happened before 1907. Conditions for the Indians, the Peruvian authorities contended, had vastly improved since then.

Fuller arrived in Iquitos near the end of May 1912. He immediately got in touch with Michell, who was about to go off on a tour of inspection of other major rivers that joined the Amazon. Like others before him, Fuller learned very quickly that this river town was far from being paradise. His first dispatch caught something of his desperation. Iquitos was a difficult place to settle in, he told his superiors. Prices were impossibly exorbitant.

Aside from the difficulty of settling in, Fuller soon learned that, in his own words, "the Putumayo question proves on examination to be considerably more complicated than would at first sight appear."

There was little sign locally of much overt concern, or indeed appetite for reform. Casement had found the same; most people thought the storm of international attention would soon pass. The attitude was exemplified by the case of Pablo Zumaeta, the head of the Peruvian Amazon Company's Iquitos operations, and Arana's brother-in-law. He was still under indictment, but that didn't stop him from being a well-respected man in town. Fuller observed that he enjoyed "most of the local honors, vice alcalde (vice mayor of the municipality), vice president and acting head of the chamber of commerce, president of the benevolent society, etc., to all of which he was elected subsequent to his exposure."

Fuller soon discovered, as had Casement, that the Aranas were not only among the wealthiest and most influential people in Iquitos and Loreto, but their influence stretched all the way to Lima. Their grasp on local politics was absolute. Fuller continued: "They would bring pressure to bear on many people who might otherwise strongly support a movement to protect the Indians and improve their condition." Fuller had learned what Casement and Hardenburg knew well—that Arana and his family were not just a local power. They had strong connections with the Lima political elite. Indians didn't figure into their equation except as expendable commodities.

There were many obstacles to overcome, but Fuller and Michell wanted to get to the Putumayo as soon as possible. In late May, Fuller reported to Washington that he and Michell were planning to visit the Putumayo either in late July or early August on a government vessel—"a launch other than those belonging to the parties responsible for the atrocities."

Chartering a vessel was simply out of the question, he wrote, the rates being astronomical. This left two possibilities. They could go by the Peruvian Amazon Company's launch, which headed up the Putumayo at the time of the *fabrico*, visiting both La Chorrera and El Encanto; but that posed the problem, as Fuller put it, that "anyone who went up in this way would be allowed to see exactly what the company wished him to see and no more." The government launch, which made the trip every four or five months taking supplies for the garrison, would allow them more freedom, but since it only went to La Chorrera, this option would limit the scope of their investigation.

By the end of July it had become clear to both Fuller and Michell that the departure of the government launch would be indefinitely delayed. No one seemed willing to explain the delay. Fuller suspected that the Peruvian government was behind it, as it did not want Fuller and Michell poking their noses into the region, not wishing anyone to challenge their proclamation that conditions had already improved. Disappointed, Fuller and Michell had no choice but to take passage on the *Liberal*, the company launch with which Casement was so familiar, which they were told would leave Iquitos on August 6.

As the day of the scheduled departure approached, both Fuller and Michell did all they could to avoid dependence on the company once they got to the rubber stations. "To see anything at all of the local conditions," Fuller explained, "it is going to be necessary to do some travelling in the interior, owing to the fact that the dispatch of the company's launch is to be only to single ports and to each of these on separate voyages from Iquitos." To get around on their own, they would need to take everything with them—a tent, food, cooking equipment, a cook, an interpreter, and Indian bearers. To pay the bearers, Fuller and Michell would have to stock up on merchandise—"cheap clothes, sugar, salt, knives, and handkerchiefs"—because "there is no money in the whole district and the Indians do not know what money is and would have no use for it."

The interpreter they hired was John Brown, who had appeared too late to be of any use to Casement when he went to the Putumayo, but had stayed on in Iquitos. His connection with the Putumayo went back a long way, and he had traveled with both Robuchon and Whiffen. He could speak the Huitoto language and other local languages as well. The consuls could have found no one better. The cook was a Barbadian named Simeon Ford.

As they were packing their bags, the day of departure was put back twenty-four hours in order to accommodate a contingent of twenty-five gendarmes. They were being dispatched to the Putumayo ostensibly "to keep order and protect the Indians" and were under the command of Benito Lores, the special commissioner appointed by the Peruvian government for the Putumayo district. Lores was known only vaguely to Fuller and Michell—what they did know was that he had business and political interests in Iquitos unrelated to his official duties. Not exactly an impartial government official.

On the evening before departure Fuller and Michell learned from the acting prefect of the department of Loreto that Carlos Rey de

Castro, the Peruvian consul in Manaus, was going to meet the *Liberal* at the mouth of the Putumayo and join them on their voyage. The Peruvian government had commissioned Rey de Castro to undertake an investigation on its behalf in the Putumayo "for the purpose of ascertaining the fulfilment of the measures taken, with the object of observing the manner in which the instructions issued to the authorities of that zone were being carried out." Both consuls knew something about Rey de Castro's relationship with Arana; they had read a report that Casement had written for Sir Edward Grey in November of the previous year, in which he produced evidence that the Peruvian Amazon Company had advanced the vast sum of £5,000 (£380,00 in today's money) to Rey de Castro. Rey de Castro, as Casement put it, had been "purchased."

If they had had any doubt that the authorities and Arana were conspiring against their investigation, now, certainly, they knew a stitch-up was under way. But they still had no idea how far Arana would go to keep prying eyes out of the Putumayo.

17

THE OLD GANG

In London, Casement followed closely the events unfolding on the Amazon. He was in constant touch with the Foreign Office—he wrote to Sir Edward Grey and others at least once a week, commenting on the constant dispatches that were arriving from the British legation in Lima. He also heard frequently from Lucien Jerome, the British consul general in Callao, who fed Casement with local stories, rumors, and newspaper clippings. Casement knew all too well what lay in store for the two consuls and the nature of the people with whom they had to contend.

It was going to be a charade. Rey de Castro's appearance was proof of this. When Casement learned that Rey de Castro was on his way to the Putumayo, he could not withhold his incredulity: it was a scandal, pure and simple. Casement had heard more than enough on his previous trip to Iquitos of the extent to which Rey de Castro had misinformed Lima concerning the true state of affairs in the Putumayo.

Benito Lores and his troop of special police was further evidence of the cover-up. Casement suspected that they were being sent to the Putumayo to "scare the Indians so that the two Consuls will see none!" "These poor beings will be alarmed at the soldiers & this domineering bully will take good care to have news sent round to all the Sections so that . . . the Indians with any grievance will be kept out of the way." Casement was also convinced that the rubber station chiefs would even go so far as selecting "parties of specially selected 'muchachos de confianza' in pants & shirts etc. [to] play the role of the native population."

When Rowland Sperling, an assistant clerk at the Foreign Office, read about Rey de Castro and Lores, he concluded that "the Arana gang are already doing all they can to prevent the Consuls discovering the true state of affairs now existing, but we can do nothing until we get the Consul's report. They may be able to get behind the scenes in spite of Arana."

Stuart Fuller admitted that on the evening before the *Liberal* left Iquitos, when he learned that Rey de Castro would be accompanying them, he seriously considered canceling the trip, but he "decided to continue in view of the arrangements already made at considerable expense and the doubt as to facilities for going up at a future date."

What he thought when the *Liberal*, on August 11, four days out of Iquitos, pulled up at Colonia Riojana, an Arana outpost in Brazil (named after Arana's birthplace, Rioja) where the Putumayo meets the Amazon, we can only imagine. Waiting for the *Liberal* was the *Napo*, a Booth steamship heading for Iquitos from Manaus. Getting off the *Napo* and transferring to the *Liberal* ahead of Carlos Rey de Castro was Julio César Arana.

Some ten days later the news of Arana's appearance at Colonia Riojana had reached Casement. If Rey de Castro's involvement was a scandal, then how would one describe Arana's?

Everyone at the Foreign Office agreed that this consular tour of inspection was a farce. Casement summed up what they must have thought in a lengthy memorandum he wrote to the Foreign Office from Belfast toward the end of September. Arana's objective was to get two favorable reports, one from each consul. Casement painted the scene for his colleagues: "The Consul General at Manaos [*sic*], an old hand at the game—gets instructions to intercept the two Consuls and accompany them on their journey—and the better to ensure the success of this scheme Arana himself returns in supreme control while a special police force is hurried to the spot which will be at his disposal to impede the Consuls' enquiries and intimidate the wild Indians from approaching them."

Casement expected a whitewash. The two consuls would be forced to see everything through Rey de Castro's eyes (unlike his own true viewpoint, through the "eyes of another race"); they would conclude that the Putumayo was tranquil and that the Indians were not being forced to work. All sorts of promises would be made "and the entire region will be closed again for years to the world and we shall never know how the Indians are faring under 'the change to humanitarian methods.'" In reality, Casement continued, "everything will be done to aid [Arana] in profitably exploiting the patient native race. The leopard does not change his spots; and the Aranas and Zumaetas have no more feeling for Indian humanity today than when they began their career of murder and pillage on the Putumayo."

Transferring to the *Liberal* that day as well as Arana and Rey de Castro was a whole contingent of people, including Dr. Herbert Spencer Dickey, now back in Arana's employ as medical officer for La Chorrera, and seven others: Rey de Castro's personal servant; an agronomist; an accountant; an Italian telegraph engineer; Marcial Zumaeta (Arana's brother-in-law); a Huitoto woman called Julia whom Zumaeta had brought from Barbados to return her to the station of Entre Rios (she was reported to be Andres O'Donnell's Indian "wife"); and a photographer, Silvino Santos.

The party, consisting of Fuller, Michell, and the ten others, arrived in La Chorrera on August 17. As Casement and others in the Foreign Office had anticipated, Rey de Castro and Arana did everything they could to manage the two consuls, to prepare the ground for their various visits, and to prevail on them to see everything through their eyes: "Señor Rey de Castro," Michell remarked when they were watching the Indians at work, "kept pointing to their fat and prosperous condition, and expatiating on the happiness and obvious contentedness of the people." Fuller's version of Rey de Castro's interference differed little from Michell's. "He insisted on stopping at unimportant places," Fuller wrote, "where he apparently did nothing but take meaningless photographs of Indians. He continually attempted to take direction of the whole thing into his hands and ordered the company's men about to suit his convenience, apparently with the intention of conveying the impression that this was an inspection tour under his sole direction."

The two consuls were hardly ever free of their hosts. Conversations were monitored; itineraries changed without warning or reasons given; and delays were the norm. Rey de Castro was their constant companion. "Under a pretence of allowing us a complete freedom of action," Michell reported, Rey de Castro did everything he could to impede their progress, partly by foisting the agronomist and the photographer on them, pestering them with questions, and insisting on taking photographs. "His anxiety not to lose sight of us was amusingly evident. Though totally unfitted physically for severe exercise, he followed us over fatiguing roads, through heat and storms, wherever we went, while Señor Arana, a heavy man, no longer young, and suffering acutely from sciatica, also accompanied us, uncomplaining but indefatigable."

Hemmed in, the consuls saw far less than they wanted to see. Arana and Rey de Castro excelled at keeping Fuller and Michell from seeing too much. They hardly caught a glimpse of any Indians—except during a three-day period when they managed to slip away with the connivance of one of the Barbadians who had remained in the region—and visited fewer stations than they had hoped. In the end, they were only in the area for just over a month, far less time than Casement on his tour.

When they returned to Iquitos on October 6, both consuls retired to write their reports, and both came to the same conclusions: from their limited vantage point, conditions seemed to have improved, in that "no evidence of cruelties now being perpetrated came to our notice." Most of the personnel who were alleged to have committed the worst crimes had vanished, replaced by new faces, yet the old system of quotas and percentages was still in force. The consuls' key finding, however, was that there was no evidence that the government was taking any interest in the region: "The fate of the Indians," they concluded with some trepidation, "lies almost wholly in the hands of a commercial concern."

Casement's fear of a complete whitewash was not fully realized. To their credit, Fuller and Michell did not fall into Rey de Castro's trap, and they used their ingenuity to see as much as they could without his interference. On the other hand, the reports seemed to conclude that the worst of the excesses was over and that the Peruvian government took little interest in the Putumayo. The Indians' fate was not in their own hands, but still in those of the company.

Arana had won this round of the battle. The old gang, Arana and the Zumaetas, was still in charge, the region even more tightly in their grip than before. Despite the fact that Paredes's arrest warrants had been issued almost a year earlier, and despite the boast that the jails in Iquitos would not be big enough for all the criminals they were going to arrest, no one was being held in custody. The old station chiefs had scattered to other parts of Peru, other parts of South America, or even farther, and no one was trying to get them back to face charges. Fonseca and Montt were living openly in Brazil. The Brazilian authorities were reluctant to get involved, as there was no extradition treaty between Brazil and Peru.

Andres O'Donnell managed to get himself safely to Panama even though he had been arrested. A legal quibble over the extradition papers had led the chief justice of Barbados to order O'Donnell's release from custody, and he promptly made his way to Bridgetown's wharf to get out on the next available ship. Armando Normand had escaped to Bolivia, was living in Cochabamba, in the center of the country, and was appealing to the Peruvian courts to quash his warrant. Victor Macedo, according to Consul General Lucien Jerome, was living openly in Lima; when the police went to the address they were given, there was no sign of the man, though he had been there until very recently. Jerome suspected that Macedo had been given a tip-off.

Arana was ensuring that none of the station chiefs would appear in court. Their silence was important, but Arana went beyond evasive measures. He turned to the press, not for the first time, to attack his enemies directly. A perfect example of this strategy was an interview given by Abel Alarco, Arana's brother-in-law and the man behind the recruitment of the Barbadians in 1904, to the Lima paper *El Comercio* on July 22, 1912. In the interview, Alarco, sensing that Peruvian pride was under threat, played the nationalist card. Colombians, he insisted, had been behind all the attempts, including the publication of the Blue Book, to discredit his country because they would stop at nothing to get the Putumayo and its wealth. Alarco accused Hardenburg (and

Perkins) of being puppets of the Colombian president Rafael Reyes, who, for the sum of £4,000, had purchased their services to spy on the operations of the Peruvian Amazon Company and to start a propaganda campaign against Peruvians by selling stories of atrocities in London. According to Alarco, when Hardenburg got to Iquitos, he made a proposition to Arana's solicitor, Julio Ego-Aguirre, that for £8,000 he could be persuaded to write very favorably about Arana's operations in the Putumayo. When Ego-Aguirre refused, Hardenburg set off for London with his defamatory dossier and "sold" his story to *Truth*. Alarco maintained that Peru was doing in the Amazon only what European powers had been doing for centuries worldwide: subduing local populations, often by force, and deriving great commercial benefit therefrom. "For we need not hesitate to declare," he remarked, "we who have opened the Putumayo to commerce and the world, that we have used force when force was indispensable. One does not conquer by caressing."

The world, and especially Britain, owed a great debt to Peru, Alarco argued. Peruvians laid down their lives in order to defend themselves against the "savage, an unintelligent and unproductive being," to deliver rubber, "a product which is quoted in Liverpool as if it were gold." The "Englishman who spends his mornings speeding along the broad dusty highroad in his 40 horsepower 'Argyll' car," Alarco asks, "[does he] know not or does not wish to know how great the daring of the Peruvian who produces the rubber for the tyres of his car?" "The issuing of arrest warrants against innocent, brave men," Alarco thundered, was "bleeding the Putumayo dry, as these heroes of commerce are forced to disappear into the 'depths of the forest'" to escape rough justice. "One more act of complacency from our Government," Alarco concluded, "and the Putumayo will be finally lost to Peru."

Giving interviews to the press, especially those that stirred patriotic emotions, was an excellent way for Arana's people to get their message across in Lima. But not everyone in Lima saw it Arana's way. *La Prensa* was one paper that tended more toward an anti-Arana position. On July 8, just days before the Blue Book's publication in London, *La Prensa* made a major attack on Arana and his methods of guaranteeing silence. In an article that was part obituary and part editorial, *La Prensa* announced that Benjamin Saldaña Rocca had died recently "in a state of cruel abandonment." It was Saldaña Rocca, the paper reminded its readers, who first brought attention in Peru to Arana's dark world in the Putumayo. The article went on:

> His efforts were completely wasted because, in those quarters where he did not find the gold of the Firm of Arana in his path sealing the lips of the Government officials, the circumstance that the frontier controversy with Colombia as to the ownership and possession of the Putumayo had at that time been rekindled, forced honourable men to observe a patriotic silence. And that humble defender of Right and Humanity had to fly from Loreto and died miserably in a wretched hole in order that he should not in his turn be the victim of the criminal exploiters of that river.

And the article continued in this vein, emphasizing the veil of secrecy and obfuscation over Arana's operations, citing, as another victim of the Putumayo silence, Eugène Robuchon "in that obscurity which covered up the investigations, the denunciations and the deaths—in that same Putumayo—of the French explorer Rebuchon [sic] whose photographs reproducing the 'macabre' orgies of the servants of the Firm of Arana even now pass from hand to hand." The Putumayo was not, in La Prensa's opinion, a challenge to Peruvian patriotism, as Alarco suggested in his article in El Comercio, but a "great National shame."

Soon La Voz del Oriente, a newspaper published by a club called the Centro Loretano, an organization founded to promote the interests of the department of Loreto in the political life of Lima, appeared. Its very first issue signaled that it, too, was joining in the battle of words over the Putumayo. It carried an attack on the "blackmailer" Hardenburg, and the editor vowed to his readers that he would continue to publish the truth of the events in the Putumayo and that the paper would make the Putumayo a central feature of its concerns. Subsequent issues carried vicious attacks on both Casement and Whiffen, accusing both of attempted blackmail and extortion.

In Iquitos, the Arana gang continued to fight back against its critics.
On November 4 Consul George Michell reported that the municipality threw a lavish banquet in the "Hall of Mirrors" in the Hotel Continental in honor of their favorite son, Julio César Arana. Local merchants
and public officials applauded the master of ceremonies, the merchant
Luis Morey, when, in eulogistic tones, he reminded his audience that
Arana had brought civilization and work to the Putumayo. Arana replied that words failed to express his gratitude for the sympathy and
understanding of the guests—"all men of honour and sound judgement." The banquet in his honor, he said, had inspired him with
greater courage in his struggles.

Arana then turned briefly to Luis Morey and repeated his words
that as far as his countrymen were concerned, his name and the Putumayo were synonymous. Arana explained to the audience that he had
sacrificed much to bring civilization to the Putumayo.

> It is a region, watered by the river of that name, which has remained
> unexplored until a few years ago and which with part of its forests
> inhabited by *cannibal natives* [my emphasis] has for a long time re-
> sisted every attempt at civilization. It was necessary to establish enter-
> prises strong and powerful in capital and resources in order to achieve
> the domination over the tribes which were an obstacle to the march
> of progress.

Peru, though, had its enemies, he continued, and they were intent on
besmirching his good name. "Elsewhere, to the foreigner, the Putumayo is a vast region which has become celebrated through attacks
and criticisms of which it has been and still is the object." Then, taking the moral high ground and, on a rousing patriotic note, he ended
his thank-you speech.

> I do not defend nor shall defend those who, calling themselves civi-
> lized, have perpetrated cruelties through degeneration or greed but I
> shall do all in my power that light should be shed and that the name
> of those men should be rehabilitated who acted in defence of the
> National territory, contributing to assuring our sovereignty. I do not

know if perseverance in work and faith in the destiny of my Country, stimulated by our valuable and benevolent friendship, will lead me on to commercial success but in exchange I am certain that in all adverse vicissitudes of fate, I must preserve stainless the name left me by my fathers and which, with fortune or without, I wish to leave equally pure and clean to my children.

Whether Arana really believed that patriotism justified his exploitation of the native population or was cynically manipulating his audience's jingoism is not clear; probably both—he certainly knew how to appeal to his fellow *blancos*. Who would stand up for the "cannibal natives" when the defense of national territory was at stake? Arana's florid rhetoric echoes that of colonial exploiters like King Leopold in the Congo; the Peruvians' independence from Spain had not changed the Hispanic attitude toward the indigenous people.

PART

FIVE

18

THE CANON AND THE BOARD

On August 4, 1912, a cool and overcast Sunday morning, Canon Herbert Henson took the pulpit in Westminster Abbey and, in a fiery sermon, named and shamed the British directors of the Peruvian Amazon Company. Until then, the public knew only that the company had British directors, not who they were. Thanks to Henson, they would soon be in the public spotlight and become household names.

Henson had a fierce reputation as a preacher and polemicist. Canon of Westminster Abbey, he used the pulpit, not just at Westminster but at other sacred venues, to address, principally, religious issues of the time. Concerns such as nonconformity, communion, Christian socialism, and religious education received a thorough examination in sermons that he carefully timed to last thirty-five minutes. He was no stranger to political controversy, using the letters page of *The Times* to give vent to his views on themes as widely diverse as the Irish Land Bill, the Education Bill, and women's suffrage, to which he was strongly opposed.

A few days after the Blue Book's publication, Henson expressed in a letter to *The Times* his outrage at the atrocities that had taken place on the Putumayo. It gave a clear sense of his stand on the issue. He began by attacking what he called the "gainers," whose "gains are dyed deep with innocent blood." "Not the least painful feature of the Blue-book," Henson wrote, "is the repeated reference to the truly humiliating fact that a great British company has been the cardinal criminal in this miserable business." "Who are the directors?" he asked. "Who are the shareholders? Perhaps some of your readers conversant, as I am not, with mercantile affairs and affinities will tell us."

He pleaded that the British public should rush out to buy copies of the Blue Book and, for the petty amount of one shilling and five pence, see for themselves the extent of "commercial greed in the twentieth century." He then turned his attention to the United States. "If the 'Monroe Doctrine' carries to American minds any moral connotation," he pointed out, "then the great Republic which fought the greatest civil war of modern times in suppressing slavery cannot stand idle while the dependent Republic of Peru fails in the alphabet of humane government."

On past performance, Henson would have taken his politics no further than *The Times*, but on this Sunday morning he daringly brought politics into Westminster Abbey. His preparation for this sermon was meticulous—nothing was left to chance. He had already preached a trial run a fortnight earlier at Shrewsbury School and only a week before at Westminster Abbey's adjoining parish church of St. Margaret's, where he was also rector.

The congregation was packed that morning—American tourists and visitors from the provinces joined regular London worshippers, according to the *Manchester Guardian's* correspondent. Perhaps they knew in advance what was coming their way. For them, Henson had prepared an uncharacteristically long, forty-five-minute "passionate sermon"—a full ten minutes longer than he usually allowed himself—to expatiate on the Putumayo atrocity.

In "A Sermon on a Blue Book," he reminded his congregation that it was Sir Roger Casement who had exposed this "most infamous oppression that has ever served the interest of cupidity or stained the record of despotism," in the famous Blue Book, "this black record of painful and violent crime [which] will form part of that literature in which perplexed and undone races confess their mysterious and inscrutable anguish." Basing his sermon on the Blue Book as his text,

Henson described the barbaric methods of collecting rubber in the Putumayo and demanded that the "employers of the malefactors"— they are among us, he proclaimed—"should be arrested and brought to trial. Justice demanded no less." He also demanded that some international agreement be put into operation by the Great Powers to save the Indians from their misery.

This was pretty strong stuff, but then Henson ventured into even more dangerous territory. After referring to the "Arana brothers" as adventurers, "able, uncommissioned and uncontrolled, to set up over a great territory an infamous despotism, and destroy in a decade the greater part of the native inhabitants," and to Arana himself as "the arch-organizer of the whole tragedy," he turned on the "great financial syndicates of Europe and America, wealthy companies and individuals, who gain the double advantage of moral anarchy in the rubber yielding forests, and legal security in the civilized communities which provide their markets and revere their wealth."

A little later Henson did what no one else had done. He named the directors—"Mr. Henry M. Read, Sir John Lister-Kaye, Bt., and Mr. John Russell Gubbins." Henson rounded on these men. What had they done for their remuneration? he asked his congregation. Surely, he answered, to assure the shareholders that the company "was an honourable business, earning an honest profit." And when the allegations first appeared in *Truth*, he continued, did these same men try to find out the truth? "Far from it," he answered.

As Henson put it in his memoirs, he "resolved . . . to pillory the British company which had brought such great disgrace on the British name, and lent itself (either in conscious collusion or in indefensible ignorance) to such infamies." Writing to *The Times* was one way to do it. Another way was to buy up a great many copies of the Blue Book and distribute them freely, which he also did, but using the pulpit was the most audacious strike of all.

Neither in the letter to *The Times* nor in the two previous sermons had Henson named names. According to his own memoir, it was not until after the sermon at St. Margaret's that he learned the names of the British directors, and he decided there and then to preach, as he recalled it, "with the gloves off."

Large parts of Henson's sermon, especially the names of the British directors, appeared in the British press over the next few days. Now that the names were out, Henson demanded that the directors be arrested and brought to trial and said, "The time has come for such change of commercial law as shall render it impossible for those who make money by the oppression of native races to wash their hands of all responsibility for the crimes of their agents in those regions, however remote, where their wealth is gained."

Henson later said that he deliberately made these defamatory remarks to force the directors to proceed against him—in other words, to get it all out in the open. The Peruvian Amazon Company's firm of solicitors, Ashurst, Morris, Crisp and Company, lost little time in replying to Henson. They were indignant—"The statements which you made . . . in regard to our Clients can only be characterized as absolute untruths and they constitute an outrage upon every aspect of fair play and justice"—but they did not threaten nor proceed with any legal action. Rather, they stated that the directors knew nothing of what was going on in the Putumayo, and that as soon as they learned from *Truth* what was alleged to be taking place there, they dispatched a commission of inquiry to find out the truth. They demanded to know from Henson what measures he was going to take to make amends for conduct which "our Clients are justified in describing as unworthy of a Clergyman of the Church of England—unworthy of a Gentleman—unworthy of a man."

Henson was not one to be cowed. In response, he refuted each and every one of their "facts" and ended the letter with the following remark:

> I differ so completely from your Clients in their view of what is befitting a Clergyman, a Gentleman, and a man, that you will not be surprised to learn that I think nothing is required from me in any of those characters which would abate anything of the severity of the censure which I conceived myself called upon to pass on the Directors of the Peruvian Amazon Company preached in the Abbey Church on the 4th of August last.

Henson decided to make the correspondence public. On August 19 he read the letters from the solicitors and his answers at a meeting of the Anti-Slavery and Aborigines' Protection Society. He told the

Reverend John Harris that he was free to keep the correspondence and get it published.

Readers of *The Times* were treated to a remarkable public display of acrimony when, on August 24, the newspaper published the exchange of letters between Henson and the directors' solicitors. Henson had staged a significant publicity coup. The public mood was already unsympathetic to the directors' plea of ignorance. The newspaper's editorial, which chastised the solicitors for the tone and temper of their letter, came down firmly on Henson's side and turned on the directors, asking them to explain how they were so "innocently misled as to the character of the enterprise in which they recommended the public to participate," how they were kept in the dark about how the profits of the company were made, and what they had done "to stop the atrocities and to make amends to the victims."

Henson took the bold step of naming the directors, but his was not the only pressure on them. Before Henson's sermon, on July 19, Michael Reddy, an Irish Parliamentary Party MP, had asked the foreign secretary bluntly whether the government intended to take action against the company's British directors. Francis Acland, the parliamentary undersecretary of state and Foreign Office representative, that day sidestepped the question, but when pressed by another member of Parliament, he admitted that the government hoped its actions were "amenable to English law." Another member of Parliament managed to squeeze a cautious affirmative answer to his suggestion that the government should publish the names of these directors and bring them to justice.

The next day, the parliamentary exchange was printed, as usual, in *The Times*. Reading his newspaper in his fine Georgian home in London's Manchester Square that day was Sir John Lister-Kaye. Sir John had been a director of the Peruvian Amazon Company since its foundation. The parliamentary questioning unsettled him. If the government were to publish the names of the directors, as it seemed likely to do, his good name would be forever associated with a horrible atrocity. Taking advice from the company's solicitors, Sir John and the other directors decided on a preemptive strike. They prepared a letter for

circulation in the press, which recounted the setting up of the Peruvian Amazon Company Commission to the Putumayo and Casement's
attachment to it. It then stated that after the return of the commission, Sir Edward Grey had written to the company with these words:
"The Secretary of State is convinced that your Directors were in complete ignorance of the appalling state of affairs now revealed and that
they will lose no time in elaborating a scheme of reform which will
effectually prevent the recurrence of these grave abuses." (At the time
when Grey wrote the letter, Casement had been appalled by the exoneration.) The directors' letter suggested that in light of Sir Edward's
statement, Acland should retract his own.

Lister-Kaye used his excellent connections to pull strings. Personally contacting Sir Arthur Nicolson, the permanent undersecretary of
state, he explained that he would prefer Sir Edward Grey to clear his
and the other directors' names in the House of Commons rather than
sending the letter to the press. Grey replied that the matter would be
cleared up in a further round of parliamentary questioning.

In Parliament on Tuesday, July 23, just a few days after Lister-
Kaye's meeting with Sir Arthur Nicolson, the Liberal MP Joseph King
opened the questioning, asking the foreign secretary whether the directors might face criminal charges. Sir Edward Grey answered ro-
bustly: "[When] the matter was first brought to their notice the British
directors made it clear that they had no knowledge of the state of affairs; they appointed a Commission, which was evidently sent in good
faith to inquire on the spot. I am not aware of any ground on which
His Majesty's Government could take action respecting them." This
statement was not precisely the same as was contained in his letter to
the company in 1911, for in Parliament, Grey did not say that he was
convinced of their ignorance, but rather that they claimed ignorance.
Not quite the same thing, but it seemed to assuage the directors, and
their threatened letter was never sent to the press.

As soon as Grey sat back on the bench, Douglas Hall chimed in
with a question about responsibility: "Is not the principal responsible
for his agents?" Grey didn't answer the question, and it was Joseph
King's turn again: "May we take it," he continued, "that the directors
fully recognise the validity and truthfulness of Sir Roger Casement's
Report?" "Oh yes," answered Grey. "So far as I am aware the directors

have never disputed the state of affairs which was disclosed. What they have contended was that they were entirely ignorant of the state of affairs before Sir Roger Casement's and their own Commission went there."

But Grey's answer still did not satisfy the House. The next day, King pushed further by asking whether the Blue Book had been sent to the director of criminal prosecutions to see if they considered whether there was a case to answer—if charges could be brought against the directors, "who have profited financially from the cruelties practised in collecting rubber in the Amazon basin?" Sir Rufus Isaacs, the attorney general, thought that the English court would not entertain such an indictment.

The questioning had reached an impasse, but on August 1, thanks to pressure from the MPs who had been most insistent on it in the Commons, the Putumayo atrocity came to be debated in Parliament for the first time, instead of being subject to questions, as had been the case until now.

Liberal MP Joseph King, who in February 1911 first raised the issue in Parliament of the publication of Casement's report, spoke eloquently and pointedly. This was essentially a British matter, he emphasized. The location of the company's operations was not germane to the situation. "British honour and policy are deeply concerned," King stressed. He then went on to explain that a not insignificant part of the labor force was British, that the company was British, that the rubber was shipped in British vessels, and that it was worked on by British manufacturers. Casement had made similar points. "Under these circumstances," King continued, "it is humiliating and intolerable that we cannot bring the criminals to justice. It is also most unsatisfactory, to my mind, that we cannot with a clear conscience say that the British company which has command of this trade is clear of blame, and that its directors and officials are clear of knowing what was going on, or, at any rate, that they did not blindly pass over those methods which have been going on." Nothing short of a proper and full investigation into the matter of corporate responsibility would satisfy the country.

Behind the scenes, preparations were already under way to satisfy King's demand. On August 6, 1912, the day before Parliament adjourned for the summer recess, the pressure finally came to a head. Lord Robert Cecil, the Independent Conservative MP, turned away from asking questions of the foreign secretary and instead inquired directly of Prime Minister Herbert Asquith whether

> in view of the accusations which have been made against the Peruvian Amazon Company, particularly in foreign countries, the Government will consent to the appointment of a Select Committee to inquire whether any responsibility rests upon the British directors of the company for the atrocities on the Putumayo; and whether any changes in the law are desirable to prevent the machinery of the English company law being used for such nefarious practices?

Select committees, the members of which could come from either the House of Commons or the House of Lords, were appointed to inquire into specific matters of public interest. While the select committee was not a court of law, its powers were substantial and judicial. It could compel witnesses of any rank to appear and to produce evidence.

Cecil had already proposed this idea privately to Sir Edward Grey, who said he would discuss it with the prime minister. Asquith was in favor of an inquiry and replied that his government would approve the appointment of a select committee to investigate the issues raised and that it would begin its work once Parliament reassembled in October.

Not long after the House of Commons returned in October 1912, the Select Committee on the Putumayo was constituted, with Charles Roberts, MP for Lincoln, as its chairman. Roberts had the reputation of being unerringly impartial. His politics were firmly liberal, supporting, among other causes, female suffrage. *Truth* strongly supported Roberts's appointment, emphasizing his compulsive search for facts. "As a licensing justice," the magazine reminded its many readers, "he was regarded as the Torquemada of the Trade. Like the inquisitors of old, whom he resembles in countenance, he always warmed to his victims, whom he regarded, not as deliberate evildoers, but as the unhappy creatures of an iniquitous industry . . . Mr. Roberts . . . whose giant frame and gaunt arms loom above and around . . . always had the facts."

On October 30 the House of Commons was informed of the terms of reference of the select committee. It was to inquire whether the directors of the Peruvian Amazon Company were responsible for the atrocities in the Putumayo and whether the law needed changing "to prevent the machinery of the Companies Acts being used in connection with similar practices in foreign countries."

It would soon be calling its witnesses.

19

LA SELVA RETURNS TO PARLIAMENT

The select committee planned to meet weekly until all of its witnesses had been heard. The hearings would take place in the Palace of Westminster, in a spacious, wood-paneled Gothic-looking room, with two full-length windows overlooking the Thames on one side and an enormous fireplace on the other. Committee Room 11 was large enough to cope with the expected numbers: fifteen members of the committee, including its chairman, the witness, and his counsel, together with a number of newspaper reporters and as many members of the public as could squeeze in. Reporters from *The Times* and the *Manchester Guardian* were always present in the audience. Both papers carried a full report on the day's proceedings every week. By the time the first round of hearings was complete before Parliament's Christmas break, it became clear that the weekly schedule was too infrequent to accommodate the number of witnesses. In the following year, the committee often met three times a week, calling its final witness on April 30.

Roberts made it clear at the outset that his committee was not there to repeat the facts of the atrocities: they accepted that these were as Sir Roger Casement described them in the Blue Book. The committee's job was not to judge or take action, but rather to present information and recommendations to the House of Commons on the specific question of the responsibility of the British directors of the Peruvian Amazon Company. It was Parliament's business to take the matter further, both in the specific as well as the more general issues that this case raised. The key question that concerned the committee was: Who knew what, and when?

The answer to that question required background information that neither the Blue Book nor any other public document had revealed. Roberts had a large pool of potential witnesses from which to draw— the Foreign Office, the Colonial Office, the Anti-Slavery and Aborigines' Protection Society, and the Peruvian Amazon Company itself were obvious choices. Roberts hoped that other witnesses, as yet unknown, might emerge from the proceedings.

One of the first things Roberts did, even before the committee had been formally constituted, was to contact Sir Roger Casement. Beginning on October 24 and continuing for the next eight months, throughout the period of the hearings, the two men kept in close touch, sharing ideas on whom to call as witnesses, what kind of questions to ask of them, and what documents to have submitted. When not writing to each other, the two men met, often in Casement's London flat or at Roberts's house in Kensington.

In this they were taking a risk, as they both realized, because it could be construed that Casement was leading the chairman. But it was a risk Roberts was willing to take in order to sharpen his investigation. Roberts clearly wanted Casement to provide him with the kind of insight into the whole Putumayo world that only Casement had. Simply having him appear as a witness in front of the Committee, which he did on two occasions, was not enough. Casement, on his part, saw the select committee as yet another part of an investigation in which he had been involved for more than two years and on which he could continue to make an impact.

The committee called Gerald Spicer of the Foreign Office as its first witness on November 6. As head of the American department and a senior clerk, Spicer could take the committee through the role that the Foreign Office had played since the revelations of atrocities in the Putumayo in *Truth* in September 1909. Spicer confirmed that the department's *locus standi*, its only jurisdictional interest in the case, was the allegation that certain Barbadians had suffered at the hands of employees of the Peruvian Amazon Company. Spicer went on to acquaint the committee members with how the Barbadians came to be employed by Arana; he described the company's commission of inquiry and Casement's attachment to it, the Blue Book's main conclusions, and the relationship between the Foreign Office and the Peruvian government. Spicer's testimony was factual, providing dates and places. The exchanges with committee members were entirely amicable, and Roberts seemed pleased with how this first day went.

One week later it was Casement's turn. During his hearing, he described what he had come to see so clearly about the Putumayo—the criminality of the forced labor system, and how culpability rested entirely with Arana, his brother, and his brothers-in-law, the Peruvian directors of the company. The system, Casement emphasized, was deliberately designed: "It did not grow up by chance or by error or by neglect." The Peruvian directors knew just what they were doing.

Casement did everything in his persuasive powers to make the members of the committee understand that at the heart of the entire system lay a basic issue of human rights. Casement explained that the commission payment scheme to the company agents and the system of terror were

> not necessarily [connected], but they follow upon the absolute denial of all protection to the Indian by the civilised authorities in these regions. There are no civilised authorities in that part of the country. The rubber man goes out into an unknown region with his rifle and associates, and he looks for Indians rather than for rubber. The rubber is always there; the forest is full of rubber trees, but they are valueless unless you can get labour; they are hunting for labour, and the labour is that of the wild Indians; they can conquer and subdue the Indian, who is a grown-up child.

The problem in the Putumayo, as in the Congo, was quite simply forced labor.

Lord Alexander Thynne, the Conservative MP who prompted Casement for this exposition, continued the questioning. "Would it have been possible to have got the labour by other means?" "If they chose to pay them they could, of course, get it," replied Casement.

On his second appearance in front of the committee, on December 11, Casement—in response to Roberts's request for him to clarify the value of trade goods the Indians received for their loads of rubber—produced "ocular proof," as he called it. He held up examples of the meager goods that constituted the Indians' wages, waving them in front of the members and the gathered public:

> I have here a hat, a pair of pantaloons, and a shirt. These three things . . . represent 60 kilos of rubber . . . Here is a belt, I think, of cardboard. That was given for 5 kilos of rubber . . . Here is a flask of powder and some fish-hooks and some beads. They never gave a whole packet of beads, but two or three strings. They are all things of very trifling prime cost indeed, and of very inferior quality. What I have produced here represents, I am convinced, more than three years' work to an Indian; and, besides, he would have to feed himself and his wife and children all the time, in addition to which he would have to carry the heavy loads of rubber on very long journeys . . . I do not think he would voluntarily and willingly have worked for this trash except under compulsion.

Roberts urged him on. Were Indian workers, he asked, "supposed to be in debt to the company?" In other words, were the Indians the peons of the company working off their debt? "No," answered Casement. "That would relate to the more civilised regions. The hold on the Indian in the Putumayo was that he could not escape."

These goods, Casement told Roberts, should be placed on exhibit in the museum of the Board of Trade. "Those evidences of swindling," Casement remarked, "are as eloquent in their way of the whole blackguard system as the brands of the lash on the limbs of the poor Indians." As for the latter, at his second hearing Casement produced photographs for all to see: one was of a woman starving in a hammock, taken sometime before July 1911, which appeared in a Lima newspaper; others, taken by Casement himself, showed clear proof of horrible

217

punishments. Some showed the scars of flogging and maiming while others showed Indians in an emaciated condition. Casement also produced photographs of Indians carrying rubber loads, demonstrating how their bodies were distorted. These were important because "a great many deaths took place owing to the long journeys and the heavy weights imposed upon the Indians."

Casement could provide a vivid picture of the Putumayo abuses, but he could not directly answer the committee's key question: Did the London directors know the state of affairs in the Putumayo? The only observation he could make was personal; he recalled that when he returned from the Putumayo and told them what was going on there, they seemed ashamed but did not "resent" the information.

Once he had finished giving his evidence, Casement handed over to Roberts documents that no one else had. He let him see his own annotated copy of Robuchon's book, pointing out that even though it had been edited by Rey de Castro, certain passages, which Casement précised for Roberts, should have warned anyone who read it that rubber collecting was coercive and that the Indians were always under pressure. No mention was made of payments to them. Though it described itself as bringing civilization to "the cannibal tribes" of the Putumayo, this, Casement repeated, was no civilizing company.

Handing Roberts a number of articles from Peruvian newspapers, Casement described the kind of men who spoke for the Peruvian Amazon Company and for the Arana family. In particular he highlighted the interview Abel Alarco had given to *El Comercio* in July to show Roberts Alarco's "intimate knowledge of the true state of things on the Putumayo." Roberts learned that Alarco accused Hardenburg of blackmail and also admitted that to get the rubber out of the wild, uncivilized forests, coercion was required: "One does not conquer by caressing" was how he put it. Using another article that appeared after Alarco's, Casement vividly showed Roberts how widespread was the culture of denial and counterattack in Peru. This article quoted Dr. Carlos La Torre, a representative of the department of Bajo Amazonas to the Peruvian Chamber of Deputies, accusing not only Hardenburg but also Casement of blackmail. "In all those who came forward in the discussions of this campaign there is only revealed the thirst for gold," La Torre remarked.

Casement's appearance was followed by that of Gilbert Grindle, principal clerk of the West Indian department of the Colonial Office, who repeated the facts of the Barbadian immigration to the Amazon and the complaints by some of the men of ill-treatment at the hands of the Arana company, complaints that had been received in both Bridgetown and Iquitos.

Once Roberts had got as much out of the government as he could—and it wasn't very much—the committee called on others in the story. The first to come forth was Horace Thorogood, at the time a reporter on the London newspaper *The Star*, but back in 1909 he had been writing for the *Morning Leader*. Thorogood's story, first recounted in his own newspaper, was sensational. On September 23, 1909, the day after *Truth* published its first Putumayo article, Thorogood went to the offices of the Peruvian Amazon Company asking for an official reply to the allegations made in the magazine. He said that five or six directors of the company were there and that they denied the allegations and accused Hardenburg of trying to blackmail the company. They were not prepared, at that time, to add more details to their denial, and they invited Thorogood to return the following day. The next day, none of the directors were there, just a man who appeared to be the company's secretary. He told Thorogood that he should write no more about the allegations and handed him an envelope that contained a banknote. "For how much?" asked Roberts. "I do not know," said Thorogood. "I did not take the banknote out; I returned it to him and I said, 'What is this for?' He said, 'Well, we are much obliged to you for the trouble you took on Wednesday,' and I said, 'But you surely know that it is very improper to offer a reporter money.' He said, 'Oh, it is not a bribe; it is in recognition of the trouble you took on Wednesday.'"

Other witnesses had their own reasons for appearing in front of the committee. Travers Buxton and John Harris of the Anti-Slavery and Aborigines' Protection Society had no material evidence and used the occasion simply to keep the record straight, to reiterate that their society had played a critical role in the unfolding of events from the very beginning: namely, that it was they who had not only believed Hardenburg's allegations against Arana but had insisted that he take his amazing story to the offices of *Truth*; that they were the first to write to the Peruvian Amazon Company to seek an urgent meeting with the board of directors to discuss the allegations; and it was they who first suggested that Roger Casement be sent to the Putumayo.

A fortnight after Buxton's and Harris's appearances, Louis Barnes—who had become the leader of the Peruvian Amazon Company Commission after Colonel Reginald Bertie fell ill in October 1910—appeared. Barnes was responsible for the commission's report, which had not been made public. It was Casement who had suggested to Roberts that the select committee summon Barnes to give evidence. It was the first time, but not the last time, that Casement would steer the investigation.

Whether Roberts would have called Barnes in any case is not known, but Casement certainly stage-managed the event from behind the scenes. He provided Roberts with a long series of detailed and pointed questions for the committee to put to Barnes, through which the culpability of the directors would be revealed. "You will see the points I seek to bring out," Casement told Roberts, "the dire neglect of what should have been a duty & the easy confidence in Arana—the line of least resistance."

The questions were typical Casement, full of insight and drive. Had Roberts used them verbatim, the source would have been obvious. Framing Casement's questions in his own words, Roberts put them to Barnes, who appeared in front of the select committee on November 27.

Barnes was an excellent witness. His was the first testimony that allowed the members of the committee an insight into how the Peruvian Amazon Company worked from a managerial point of view. Barnes made several important points. The members of the commission came to precisely the same conclusion as the Blue Book did about conditions in the Putumayo. It was a criminal system. Local chiefs of rubber stations did just as they pleased and were seldom visited by the managers in Iquitos. The managers, in turn, hardly ever communicated to the board in London, and instructions sent from London were simply ignored in Iquitos. Indeed, Barnes emphasized, the London board was wholly ignorant of the management in both Iquitos and in the Putumayo. The directors in London had no idea how money was being spent—including, especially, how labor was being paid. There was no evidence that they ever asked. The management was a shambles.

Barnes concluded his testimony by stating that all of the company's officials he had spoken to in Iquitos and Manaus denied that atrocities had been committed, and "if the English directors had asked for reports from the same source no doubt they would have received the same answer as he did." So far, then, it looked as though the directors were really in the dark, but the committee was still perplexed as to why they didn't ask any questions of the management on the ground.

Then, on December 4, it was the turn of Sidney Paternoster, the assistant editor of *Truth* and the very man who had met Hardenburg and accepted his story. Paternoster reminded the committee that he believed in Hardenburg from the first time he met him, and it was this feeling of trust that compelled him to bring the Putumayo atrocities to public view. He assured the committee that had there been the slightest evidence that Hardenburg was interested only in financial gain, he would not have written and published the piece. Paternoster told the committee that Hardenburg had come to see him in August 1909 and showed him issues of *La Felpa* and *La Sancion*, the depositions he and Saldaña Rocca had collected in Iquitos, and his own book manuscript. Roberts asked, "Did you know nothing of him before?" Paternoster answered that he did not.

Roberts then drew out of Paternoster that he had gone to see Cazes at his London flat, where he confirmed Hardenburg's allegations. Cazes told Paternoster that "his lips were sealed officially; that privately he had never been on the Putumayo or any of its affluents to search for himself, but he had heard all these stories; he knew that a previous American consul had been up those rivers, and that in the American Consul's office he had seen a report which contained very similar allegations to these."

Cazes would be the next important witness. So far, Casement and Roberts had agreed on most things in the committee's proceedings, but when it came to Cazes, who was scheduled to appear on December 17, they were at odds on the issue of how he should be questioned. Casement did not want Cazes to be put through the ringer. It was not his fault that he was in such a difficult position in Iquitos. The Foreign Office was as much to blame as he was, "for they were quite content to leave those parts in the hands of local traders, only consulates in name, until the avalanche fell."

In the bundle of documents Casement handed over to Roberts was a copy of the letter Arana had written to Cazes in July 1910, alerting him to the imminent arrival of the Peruvian Amazon Company Commission in Iquitos and explaining that its terms of reference were commercial alone. Casement clearly explained how this letter had come into his possession and what significance it had.

> Cazes behaved rightly to me as his official senior etc. & gave me a copy of the letter and any assistance he could to investigate. Arana's intention, of course, was quite clear to me. He counted on Cazes, as a local merchant, considering his wishes as perhaps of more importance than the passing influence of a British consular officer sent to investigate and clearly implied his hope that Cazes might remember that trade friendships were of more value than a Consular post valued at £21. per annum.

By sharing the letter with Casement, Cazes showed that his allegiances were to Casement over Arana. Casement did not want Roberts to use the letter in a question to Cazes—he did not really want Cazes to be dragged into a public inquiry at all. As he put it to Roberts, "[He] has already lost the Consulate & all its attendant prestige—and really through me and my representations on the need of an official, paid Consular officer at Iquitos. So, if you can see your way to suppress that question, all the better perhaps." As Casement had pointed out previously, by using local British businessmen as unpaid honorary consuls, the Foreign Office put them into an impossible position.

Casement was clearly anxious about the letter, writing again to Roberts the same day, setting out his argument more forcefully. "On fuller reflection I would beg of you not to make any public use of the letter from Julio Arana to Mr. Cazes. Let it be solely for your personal guidance & help." The caution Casement urged was not only about Cazes but also reflected his anxiety that he might be recognized as the source of Roberts's material and line of questioning. No one apart from Casement could have had a copy of this letter, and if anyone was curious about its provenance, the trail would lead directly to Casement. "My name," he concluded, "can in no circumstances transpire as your informant on anything."

Casement was displaying a kind of nervousness that, until now, had not been usually apparent. He was a driven man, wanting to root out crimes against humanity whether in the Congo or in the Putumayo. But the Putumayo, which had now absorbed two years of his life, was having an impact on both his physical and mental states. Casement's doctor confirmed that he was suffering from severe pain in his back and side, which may have been caused by arthritis. His friends, in whom he confided that he was getting "seedier and seedier daily," certainly attributed his change in demeanor to the Putumayo. He appeared debilitated, "bent double with pain," "suffering from severe mental strain, in a highly nervous condition and quite incapable of discussing anything but the horrors of the investigations with which he seemed obsessed." No doubt, trying to manage the affair from behind the scenes added to his increasingly nervous disposition.

In the end, Roberts did refer to the letter, but it played no substantive part in the questioning. The committee was much more interested in what Cazes could tell it about Arana and his relationship with the London board. One of the committee members, the Liberal MP Hubert Carr-Gomm, took up that very issue. "I presume Señor Arana was a very plausible gentleman, and there was apparently a great deal of candour about him?" "Yes," replied Cazes, "he certainly gave me that idea. I have known Mr. Arana for, I think, 11 years, since I have been out in Iquitos; and I have always known him to be courteous, and he has always struck me as being a very honourable man." Carr-Gomm continued the questioning. "Do you think he was the kind of man who, knowing what we know now, would quite easily have turned a Board of English directors round his finger?" Replied Cazes, "I think it is quite obvious that they believed most of the statements he made, as I should have done. I should have been probably hoodwinked."

The select committee ended its first session before Parliament's Christmas recess on December 18, 1912. By that time, a dozen witnesses had trooped in and out of Committee Room 11, some of them appearing more than once. What they said in front of the committee had generally been known to only a few insiders in the Foreign Office, the Anti-Slavery and Aborigines' Protection Society, and, of course, Casement. But now, as witnesses spilled all they knew, ever more damning details of the Putumayo story emerged. Still more revelations would come out in the next session after Parliament's return, when the board of directors would be questioned.

Meanwhile, Casement was advised to have a well-deserved break, "to sweep all this off my mind." He was going to go to the Canaries at the end of December, he told Roberts, to recuperate. Before leaving, he promised Roberts the rest of the documents in his possession pertaining to the Putumayo, including the diary he had kept while there. "The diary makes me sick again . . . it brings up so vividly that forest of hell."

Casement docked at Las Palmas on Gran Canaria, on January 3, 1913. The next day, he fired off a letter to Roberts. In it, Casement candidly reflected on his part in the Putumayo story. He told Roberts to bear in mind that it had "been practically a one-man affair—my own. I must tell you the truth—so that you may understand—and you will acquit me, I know, from anything like boasting. It was really my doing from the day Grey sent me off until the Report was published two years later."

Recounting how the events of the past years had unfolded, especially how he had gone beyond the Foreign Office's relatively narrow concern for the Barbadians to look into the bigger issue of the atrocities perpetrated on the Indians, he stated, "Now I tell you these things because I want you to fully realize that the carrying through of the Putumayo question was a personal thing & once the personal factor goes the matter will, of necessity, relapse into the ordinary routine methods of diplomatic effort." He held out no hope that diplomacy would lead to a better life for the victims of Arana's brutality. "The outcome then is certain. The Peruvian Govt. will really do nothing. They will promise & leave everything as before to the men on the spot & the F.O. will, perforce, be required to accept this ending & so the whole question closes. The other blackguards will lift up their heads, & in a brief space the old game will go on with renewed vigour."

Casement confided in Roberts that as far as he could see, the Putumayo was not an isolated incident. He feared that other companies, both British and American, were taking advantage of what he termed "the Peruvian ideas of the 'whiteman's' claim to Indian labour."

Meanwhile, in London, it was time for the directors to be questioned. The first to be called was John Russell Gubbins, chairman of the board of directors of the Peruvian Amazon Company until its liquidation in September 1911. Gubbins had had long experience as a businessman in Peru. He explained that when he joined the company in July 1908, he was convinced that it was a sound business. Gubbins told the committee that Abel Alarco, Arana's brother-in-law and the man responsible for recruiting the Barbadian workers, had explained to him how the rubber-collecting system worked and that the Indians were paid in goods, cash being useless in the forest, all of which he accepted without question.

Gubbins then repeated under close questioning a version of events that had by then become familiar: that the first he or any of his directors heard of the alleged atrocities was in the publication in *Truth*; that they accepted Arana's story over that of Hardenburg's, who they thought was a blackmailer; and that as soon as it was possible, they arranged for their own commission of inquiry to proceed to the Putumayo.

After a grueling three days of cross-examination, the most that the committee could get out of Gubbins was that the relationship between Arana and the British board was probably not as it should have been. Gubbins admitted that the board could do nothing without Arana; that they had responsibility without control; that they were mere figureheads; and that they relied entirely on the information Arana supplied to them. Gubbins stressed that the atrocities were committed without their knowledge and consent: their consciences were clear.

Once Gubbins had been excused from the hearing, Sir John Lister-Kaye was sworn in. Though he had no background in South American business, nor in rubber, and did not speak or write Spanish, he, too, was convinced that the company was sound. When he was pressed on why he inquired only about the company's creditworthiness and not about the condition in which it held labor, he simply answered that he thought "there were plenty of labourers, and that was the main point to consider in the collection of rubber." Like Gubbins before him, he claimed innocence on the grounds of ignorance.

For most of the time, Lister-Kaye remained calm, his answers concise and to the point. But one committee member, the Liberal MP Willoughby Dickinson, was determined to get to the bottom of one key issue: Precisely when did the board of directors decide to send their commission to the Putumayo? Was it, as the directors claimed, when the article in *Truth* appeared, or was it later, after they had been pressured by the Foreign Office? The calm was broken.

Lister-Kaye insisted that the decision was taken in October 1909, before the Foreign Office's involvement. When Dickinson pressed him for further confirmation of that date by asking him when the name of Colonel Bertie was first discussed, Lister-Kaye could not recall. The British directors, he said, met frequently to discuss various matters, and the details of many of these meetings, often held privately, went unrecorded. Finally Lister-Kaye's discomfort at Dickinson's doggedness overwhelmed him. "We three British directors frequently met together and talked over things. Cannot you understand the immense anxiety we had in our minds, and is it not likely that we three Englishmen should meet continually and talk over them? . . . Cannot you understand the horror I felt at this hideous situation? I expected to find some sympathy, but you are combating the idea."

Lister-Kaye then apologized for his show of emotion, but despite being questioned on three separate days, he added nothing that had not already been established, namely that the directors were ignorant and eventually set up a commission to find out the facts.

The next day, January 22, was the turn of Henry Read, the last of the British directors to be sworn in. Read had joined the company as a director in December 1907 and had had extensive experience in Latin American business and banking.

Roberts, as usual, began the questioning. One of the things he wanted Read to comment on was why the board had accepted at face value Arana's version of events in the Putumayo. Read answered, "Because there was so much against Hardenburg and so much in favour of Arana. I do not know whether you care to go into the reasons why we had more trust in Arana than you gentlemen appear to have?" "I think perhaps it would be well," countered Roberts.

So Read began to tell his tale. He couldn't quite recall which, but he maintained that the suggestion of sending a commission to the Putumayo came from either Alarco or Arana. If crimes had been committed, why would anyone they implicated suggest sending a commission to investigate, thought the directors. Furthermore, Alarco had told them

> that Hardenburg was a bad man, and . . . had tried to blackmail the Aranas . . . Then came other episodes which were in favour of Arana. Arana, instead of paying a thousand pounds (blackmail), refused, and that does not look like guilt; and we knew Arana; we had been with him some time; we were very much impressed with his quiet reserved manner, but when we asked questions he appeared to speak with the greatest frankness, and Alarco as well.

Roberts, of course, had to ask Read, as he had asked the other two directors, about why he hadn't inquired into the conditions of the Indians: "You are English directors of a company trading in a foreign country, and, after all, the credit of England was to some extent at stake; but it never seems to have crossed the mind of any director that he had any duty to see whether these unfortunate natives were ill-treated?"

"Why should I think anyone was ill-treated? The thing never occurred to me. When I asked Alarco he told me that the man went into the shop, took a knife or gun, and went into the woods for three or four months for rubber; and it struck me as a free-and-easy life."

Roberts, impatient with the answers he had been receiving for days, asked Read again about why the directors never inquired into the conditions of the Indians: "Did you, the English directors, know enough about the conditions of Peru to make you feel that it was very undesirable to inquire into the Peruvian conditions for fear you should find what you could not defend upon any British standard?" "No, sir," replied Read, "decidedly not. The only reason we did not look into the past was because we felt we could not, and that the Peruvian Government alone must do it. If we attempted such a thing we should mortally offend them, and that, instead of getting help from them, we should probably be met with indifference and difficulty."

The day was drawing to a close, and Roberts asked Read a final question about whether he had acted appropriately and whether the directors did everything that was required of them. "So much so," answered Read, "that if it were to begin all over again to-day I would do it in exactly the same way."

When Casement read the minutes of the evidence given by the three British directors, he was enraged. He wrote back to Roberts that their lack of action was due only to cowardice and their desire to save themselves. They cared nothing for the wrong they had done—"they did not draw their Directors fees from peonage—but from piracy pure & simple"—and showed no remorse or wish to put things right. Casement also congratulated Roberts on learning more about the Peruvian Amazon Company in three months than all the British directors put together in four years.

A few days later Casement wrote to Roberts again, saying that he was not coming home as planned but had decided to continue to warmer climes in Cape Town to visit his brother. He would be out of touch for at least three weeks on the long voyage south and would not be home until April at the earliest.

On January 29 Read was recalled for a second day of questioning, but instead of one of the committee members starting the proceedings, the Peruvian Amazon Company's counsel, Raymond Asquith, spoke first, and he had startling news: Arana had cabled, announcing his intention to come to London and face his accusers.

20

THE PERUVIAN, THE AMERICAN, AND THE SELECT COMMITTEE

The Foreign Office had been tracking Arana's movements on the Amazon ever since Judge Valcárcel issued a warrant for his arrest in mid-December 1912. Arana had left Iquitos a month earlier, shortly after his celebratory banquet, and headed to Manaus. The British vainly hoped that the Brazilian authorities would extradite him in accordance with his arrest warrant. The unlikeliness of this happening was evident when the British chargé d'affaires in Brazil mentioned to the former head of the Colombian delegation in Lima the sterling efforts made by the Brazilian government to expel the Putumayo criminals that had taken refuge there. The Colombian just laughed, saying no more than that Arana was the most powerful man in Peru and that "all these men had money and were therefore masters of the situation."

Arana remained in Manaus for two months without any interference from the Brazilian authorities. While there, he lodged an appeal in the High Court in Iquitos against his arrest and issued a declaration to his fellow Peruvians in the form of a telegram, which he sent to the Peruvian press. Dated December 30, 1912, it appeared in Lima's *La Prensa* the following day. In it, Arana provided a clear statement of where he stood on the events of the preceding years. He began by arguing that Judge Valcárcel's warrant for his arrest was proof positive that the Colombians had finally been successful in their plan "to convert Peruvians themselves" into agents for their country. For his part, Arana had been rewarded with an arrest warrant for resisting their attempts to do the same to him. He had proof that would establish once and for all that what had been said against him had been a series of lies and that attempts had been made to blackmail him. He would be making all of this public in a book he was preparing, and he would tell his story to the European press. The telegram ended with the following statement:

> I would proceed to Iquitos were not my presence indispensable in Europe to undo the machinations against me and to save the prestige of my Country. But I am confident that the high Tribunals of Peruvian Justice will annul the Order of Judge Valcárcel, who has abandoned Iquitos in a quasi-clandestine manner. I beg my Countrymen to suspend judgement until they know the defence I am about to make and which will produce a worldwide reaction in favour of Peru and leave my named unblemished.

The British vice-consul in Manaus was watching Arana carefully. On February 12, 1913, he reported to the British consul in Pará that on the previous day Arana and his brother-in-law Marcial Zumaeta, who was now acting as his secretary, had boarded the *Lanfranc*, a Booth liner bound for Lisbon and England.

Arana had nothing to fear. Such was his popularity and influence in Iquitos that when Valcárcel issued a warrant for his arrest, the town erupted in riot against Valcárcel, who promptly fled because of ill health. A month later, the High Court in Iquitos quashed the arrest warrant on the grounds that the charges were too vague.

Not only was the Foreign Office tracking Arana but the British press had got hold of the news that he was on his way to Europe. When the *Lanfranc* docked in Lisbon on February 26, a London *Daily Mail* correspondent was waiting for him and, managing to get on board ship, persuaded him to answer a few questions. Arana maintained that the Putumayo atrocities had been grossly exaggerated, probably by his rivals in the rubber business. No doubt, he added, natives in remote localities had been ill-treated, but not by him—he had never been to those parts.

Before leaving Lisbon, Arana issued a fuller statement in which he explained that he had agreed to appear in front of Roberts's committee

> to give all of the explanations in my power in respect of the present state of things, having paid a visit of inspection to the region between August and October last at the same time as the Consuls of Britain and the United States and the representative of the Peruvian Government visited the region . . . I think my conduct and innocence will be properly judged there on this occasion, my case having already been rigorously investigated in my own country, where I have been entirely freed from responsibility by the higher tribunals.

Several days later, on March 2, the *Lanfranc* docked at Fishguard. Waiting for Arana on the quayside was a crowd of newspaper reporters. The photograph taken of him at the time shows a portly, aging man—not the trim, youthful Arana pictured in Robuchon's book and in the Manaus *Jornal do Commercio* of June 1908. A description in *The Observer*, accompanying the photograph, was favorable:

> He is a stoutly built man of forty-five, about five feet nine inches in height. His short-pointed beard is growing somewhat grey, but, as one would expect from a man of Spanish race, he is naturally dark. In manner he is simple and kindly, and quite free from affectation. That he is a good businessman is abundantly clear, but he is at the same time most charitable. He assists not only his friends who need help, but some who are not his friends.

A *Daily Mirror* reporter managed to get a short interview with Arana through Marcial Zumaeta, who spoke English, in the small interval between his leaving the ship and boarding the express train for Paddington. "I have come to tell the truth," declared Arana. "It is time it should be told." "There was a look in his eye," the reporter interjected, "which foretold many an hour of stonewall response to the questioning of the most bitter critics for months. Ever since the publication of Sir

231

Roger Casement's report on cruelties . . . Senor Arana has been the most bitterly attacked millionaire in the world. But he only smiled to-day when he landed."

Zumaeta was carrying a large bag stuffed with important documents, and the weighty trunks were filled with newspapers and photographs that "when published would prove that the reports were grossly exaggerated." Zumaeta then told the reporter that what he saw in the Putumayo was completely at odds with what Casement saw:

> We were in the region where the atrocities are reported to have taken place at the time of the publication of the Blue-book, and after a journey of 1,200 miles up the Amazon we visited many of the places mentioned in the Blue-book. All we can say is that we found no trace of any atrocities at all. The natives seemed to be well treated and there were no complaints . . . in many of the villages of their territory of 10,000 square miles we asked innumerable questions of the natives and the officials. But we could hear of nothing wrong.

Arana, Zumaeta said, would tell all this to the committee. "He has come to England to defend his honour and to justify his career. He need not have come, but he felt it was his duty."

Arana had made the decision to come to London initially to defend himself, not before the select committee, but rather in the High Court of Justice. There, several shareholders of the Peruvian Amazon Company, with the help of the Anti-Slavery and Aborigines' Protection Society, which had initiated the action (presumably as a way of punishing Arana), were bringing a winding-up order to effect the removal of Arana from the position of voluntary liquidator, to which the board had appointed him unanimously late in 1911. He was to be replaced by an official receiver. When Charles Roberts, as chairman of the select committee, first got news of Arana's intentions to come to London, he sent him an invitation through the company's solicitors to attend the committee's hearings as a witness.

The hearing, originally set for October 29, 1912, was postponed, the judge agreeing that Arana should be given an opportunity to answer the charges made against him.

As it turned out, there were several delays in getting Arana's evidence presented. When the petition to wind up the company came up again in the High Court of Justice on March 4, 1913, Mr. Justice Swinfen Eady refused an appeal by the counsel for the creditors for yet another postponement, arguing that the appeal should be heard as soon as the select committee had had its interview with Arana. He told Arana's counsel that his affidavit of evidence should be prepared for a hearing set for March 18.

Though Arana's counsel argued that the High Court was not the place to discuss questions of allegations of ill-treatment and atrocities in the Putumayo, Justice Eady disagreed and referred explicitly to the report by the company's commission of inquiry. He also referred to the conduct of the chiefs of sections, the allegations as they were reported in *Truth*, the culpability of the managers, the atrocities, and, finally, the condemnation of Arana himself. Justice Eady relied heavily on Casement's Blue Book for much of his information. The day after the affidavits were presented, Justice Eady passed judgment. There would be a compulsory order to wind up the Peruvian Amazon Company. He had no doubt that Arana was the last person who should be entrusted with this responsibility. "In my opinion," Justice Eady pronounced, "Arana and his partners sold a business whose profits were derived from rubber collected in the atrocious manner I have indicated, and it is impossible to acquit all of the partners of knowledge. Certainly [Pablo] Zumaeta knew, and if Arana did not know then he ought to have known. Under those circumstances I make the Compulsory order."

In case the public had missed Justice Eady's comments and judgment on the case as they were reported in the British press, the Anti-Slavery and Aborigines' Protection Society, intent on making Arana's life as difficult as possible, published a handy little booklet containing all of Eady's pronouncements on the case.

The British public had been primed for Arana's appearance. His interviews in Lisbon and Fishguard and the proceedings at the High Court in London raised expectations of a gripping hearing in Westminster. The committee members, too, were excited about his arrival, but like the showman he was, he made them wait. On March 20 Arana and Stephen MacAndrew, the Peruvian Amazon Company's solicitor, successfully petitioned the committee for a postponement until early the following month because Arana's wife, Eleanora, it was claimed, was ill and undergoing medical treatment in Switzerland, and he needed to go to her without delay.

Almost three weeks later Arana presented himself with his counsel and interpreter in front of Roberts and the committee. The *Manchester Guardian* provided a vivid portrayal of the opening scene on April 8:

> The much-talked-about Julius Cesar Arana came before the Putumayo Committee to-day—a heavy, yellow-faced man, with black-grey hair and beard, who gave his evidence in rapidly spoken conversational asides to the interpreter beside him, emphasising it from time to time by a quick gesture of his fat, short-fingered hands. He had put in a printed statement of his evidence-in-chief, which was in the nature of a general denial of the case against him, and his counsel Mr. Douglas Hogg [later the 1st Viscount Hailsham], sat behind him to watch his interests. He had, however, no occasion to interfere. The proceedings moved slowly, for every question had to be interpreted to the witness, and in turn his answers to the Committee, and the interpreter went deliberately about his work. Both English and Spanish shorthand writers were occupied taking down what was said.

The *Manchester Guardian's* reporter was transfixed by the performances given by Arana, his counsel, and his interpreter that day. Of the three, it was the interpreter who interested him the most, and that was partly because of the constant interventions of one of the committee members, William Young, Liberal MP. Young was a merchant with extensive experience in Mexico and "discovered to-day an extraordinarily fluent colloquial command of Spanish which enabled him to correct or define translations made by the interpreter, and to put fresh questions to the witness straight in his own tongue—a gift which had, of course, to be sparingly exercised for the sake of his fellow-members."

Roberts asked almost all the questions on the first day. Arana did not deny that atrocities had taken place. But he was adamant that he knew nothing about them until the reports were published.

Roberts asked Arana whether he knew of Robuchon's book. Yes, he did. Roberts then asked Arana about a passage in the book that referred to the Indians' loss of liberty after the arrival of the white man. Oh, said Arana, liberty in this instance referred to the fact that "they could not make war from tribe to tribe as they used to before." Roberts then tried another approach:

> Among your papers here is the original French basis of this book, which was edited by Senor Rey de Castro. I have looked through that and I find this passage omitted in the Spanish, "the Indians care nothing for the preservation of their rubber trees, and rather desire their destruction. Eager to recover their lost liberty and their independence of former days, they think that the whites who have come into their dominions in quest of this valuable plant, will go away when it has disappeared. With this idea, they regard with favour the disappearance of the rubber trees, which have been the cause of their reduction to slavery. Without ambition or knowledge of the value of goods, they give their labour for a few worthless beads, for an old gun, an axe, or a cutlass."

Did Arana know that Rey de Castro had cut that passage out of the Spanish translation? "No," Arana replied.

The point of the question, which Casement had insisted Roberts ask Arana, was to show that Rey de Castro had tampered with Robuchon's original French manuscript—a copy of which was found in the London offices of the Peruvian Amazon Company—before it was translated into Spanish. By omitting passages such as the one above, which described the Indians wanting the white man to get out of their lands and to leave them alone, Rey de Castro was helping to portray Arana's company as bringing civilization and its material benefits to the region. But Arana did not rise to the occasion, and the matter was dropped.

Throughout the questioning that day, Arana continued to maintain that he knew nothing about the conditions in the Putumayo as they had been described in *Truth*. When asked why Paredes could "get at the stories of cruelty from the Indians," Arana replied that "he was in the centre of Putumayo, and had a certain amount of authority in the matter." When asked a similar question about Casement's discoveries, Arana retorted that "it was necessary to have the experience of Sir Roger Casement, to have been in the Congo and lived there, and also to know the English language to be able to do this."

Arana had a knack for sidestepping awkward questions. Roberts wanted to find out from Arana about the use of firearms in the Putumayo. He read from a letter written by Miguel Loayza, manager of El Encanto, in June 1909: "'It has not been possible to send the six single-barrel shot guns, as we have none here, but in order to deal with the Indians who run away we are now sending three double-barrelled guns.'" When asked what he thought these guns were for, Arana simply answered, "I do not understand what they were for; but what I can make out, they might have been for giving to the Indians—dividing among them—to give them guns in exchange for rubber." Guns, Arana insisted throughout the day, were used to protect the employees from wild animals and to shoot game for the table. Shooting Indians, Arana added, was something he had learned about only since attending the select committee's hearings.

Questioned about the rights of the Indians in their relationship with the company, Arana replied that the Indian "only recognises his master, the man who pays him." When asked whether such a system was not open to abuse, Arana typically evaded the issue, preferring to answer an imaginary question about employment contracts: "With the whites," he said, "it is a question of having a document signed or endorsed to do it; but the Indian cannot sign—he cannot sign his name—he cannot write."

At that point Douglas Hogg, Arana's counsel, turned to Roberts, stating that Arana had heard that his wife was worse and that though he could appear again on the following two days, he could not stay longer than that.

The *Manchester Guardian*'s reporter was distinctly unimpressed by Arana's performance. He commented sarcastically that Arana "left the witness-chair this afternoon on his own showing a much wronged man, accused of bribery, cruelty, or connivance in cruelty, and partici-

pation in a system of unspeakable savagery, while all the while his relations to the natives were those of Robinson Crusoe to his man
Friday—of a paternal agent of civilisation towards a friendly and con-
tented race."

The next day, Arana appeared as promised. He began by repeating
his well-rehearsed theme that the problems in the Putumayo were the
fault of the Colombians. They, Arana insisted, had originated the system of abuse. The people he employed, by contrast, were the best
available. When asked to explain two entries in the company accounts,
one called "*Conquistar*" and the other "*Gastos de Conquistacion*," translated as "To conquer or subject" and "Expenditure of a Capital Nature
Incurred in Reducing Indians to Subjection," Arana responded by saying that the first meant "distributing goods and fitting out expeditions
with a view to converting the Indians to the system of barter"; the
second term referred simply to the costs involved in this "pacific
conquest."

At one point Roberts asked Arana again about guns in the Putumayo, and why, in addition to a substantial sum spent on "*Gastos de
Conquistacion*," there was also a large sum spent on rifles. Arana repeated that the Winchesters ordered from London and New York were
used solely for protection, stressing that "there is no rubber collector
in any region who does not carry with him one of these rifles."

Roberts, finding it impossible to get a straight answer from Arana,
changed topics abruptly in the hope of tripping up his witness. Asked
about the incidence of flogging Indians, Arana replied that he knew
nothing of this until he read about it in Hardenburg's and Casement's
reports. Wasn't Arana aware that before these reports Saldaña Rocca
had accused Arana's employees of flogging? asked Roberts. Arana replied that Saldaña Rocca's papers were considered rags, and in any
case, other papers had contradicted these accusations.

At this point committee member John Gordon Swift MacNeill, the
firebrand Irish MP for South Donegal, sensing the frustration in the
room, exclaimed, "This witness never answers a question Yes or No,
and the first thing I submit is to tell him to answer Yes or No, and
make his explanation afterwards."

But MacNeill's outburst was as useless as the questioning that pre-
ceded it: no one could get Arana to give a straight answer.

The questioning turned to the subject of Walter Hardenburg. Willoughby Dickinson asked whether Arana would recognize Hardenburg if he ever saw him again. Arana, typically noncommittal, answered, "Perhaps I might. I only saw him once, one night when he came to visit me."

Now the critical question of Hardenburg's veracity was broached. Joseph King produced the circular Arana had written to the shareholders of the company back in late December 1909, in which he wrote, "I produce to the board evidence of forgery on the part of Hardenburg." This statement referred to a check for £830 drawn on an Iquitos bank, which Hardenburg, as the bearer of the check, presented and cashed in Manaus at the Bank of Brazil. The check was sold on and made its way to the Rothschild bank, but they protested that it had been tampered with and refused to accept it as a negotiable instrument. King then put it to Arana that the circular was an attempt to portray Hardenburg "as a mere adventurer if not a criminal." Arana sidestepped, and then King read out the passage from the circular where Arana accused both Hardenburg and Whiffen of blackmail. Arana remained silent.

Roberts would have none of this. "Answer the question, please directly: do you charge Hardenburg with having committed the forgery or not?" Arana now found his voice and answered, "That is entirely another thing." Roberts asked again. "Do I understand then that you do not charge Hardenburg with the act?" Arana sidestepped again. "I do not know who was the forger," he protested, "Hardenburg or someone else." Joseph King tried once more to get Arana to give a straight answer to a straight question. "Then I will only ask you one more question on this subject. You do not now charge Hardenburg with forgery—do you or not?" "No," said Arana finally. "I do not accuse him now."

At the end of the day's proceedings Swift MacNeill took over the questioning of Arana. The subject was again Walter Hardenburg.

"When was your last interview with Hardenburg—was it not in April 1908?"

"The last was when I was in Iquitos in April, 1908."

"Then did Hardenburg tell you what was going on in the Putumayo?"

"He spoke to me with great seriousness on the matter of my trying to get or making inquiries about his lost luggage."

"And nothing more?"

"This was the object of the visit."

"Did you say anything about blackmailing?"

"No."

"Do you call him a forger now?"

"I have to repeat what I said before, that the suspicion falls on two persons, on the buyer or on the endorser."

Swift MacNeill motioned to a man sitting in the audience to stand up.

"Turn around," said MacNeill to Arana, "and see Hardenburg before you. Do not you know him?"

"Yes, I am very pleased to see him here, because we can then enter into other details."

Walter Hardenburg had left England in February 1910 for Canada. After a period of two months in Toronto working for a local newspaper, he had headed out west for Alberta, where he worked in several jobs, including that of a surveyor for the Canadian Pacific Railway.

While Hardenburg was in Canada, both John Harris and Travers Buxton had been writing to him, keeping him abreast of developments in the Putumayo and sending him copies of published documents that otherwise he wouldn't have been able to obtain. Hardenburg knew, therefore, that Casement had gone out to the Putumayo with the Peruvian Amazon Company Commission, that he had reported to the Foreign Office with material backing up Hardenburg's allegations, and that the commission's report did the same. He knew that Casement had returned to Iquitos a second time, and he knew that Dr. Paredes, in his report, had also supported his allegations.

Roberts had thought of asking Hardenburg to appear as a witness, but when, in December 1912, Thomas Fisher Unwin published Hardenburg's book, *The Putumayo: The Devil's Paradise*, the manuscript of which he had brought with him from Iquitos, it seemed there was no need to bring him to London from so far away. After all, what could he add to what he'd said in the book? No one, apart from Arana and his henchmen, had any doubt about Hardenburg. His book was widely and favorably reviewed. John Harris, for one, praised Hardenburg and claimed that had the two Americans gone to their destination by the usual route, they would never have encountered Arana's empire, and the fate of the Indians would have been sealed. No one would have ever heard of the Putumayo.

Now the public could read for itself how he and Perkins had planned to cross the South American continent from the Pacific coast of Colombia and how, instead of paddling down the Putumayo to the Amazon, they unwittingly found themselves in the heart of Arana's empire; how they had witnessed the slaughter of David Serrano and other Colombians; how he and Perkins had become separated in the Putumayo and their eventual reunion in Iquitos; how, while in Iquitos, Hardenburg had come into the possession of Saldaña Rocca's documents and back issues of *La Felpa* and *La Sancion*; and how, through this material, as well as the depositions and testimonials he had collected himself, he had learned of the horrible acts committed not only against the Colombians, which he had seen with his own eyes, but against the Indians, whom he had only glimpsed.

On his own account, then, Roberts had no reason to bother Hardenburg. But the Anti-Slavery and Aborigines' Protection Society had grown increasingly concerned that witnesses connected with the Peruvian Amazon Company—the likes of John Russell Gubbins, Sir John Lister-Kaye, and Henry Read—kept telling the committee that they had consistently refuted Hardenburg's allegations, siding with Arana against him. In their testimony, these men continued to refer to Hardenburg as a blackmailer and forger, allegations the society felt that Hardenburg should answer in person. On January 18, 1913, Travers Buxton, the society's secretary, wrote to Roberts: "As the Directors have repeatedly stated that they still consider him to be a forger and blackmailer, it has occurred to us that it might be well to suggest to Mr. Hardenburg . . . that he should consider coming over to this country in view of these persistent charges to clear his character."

Roberts agreed, and Hardenburg was contacted in Alberta. He replied quickly that he was willing to come but could not afford to do so. Over the next couple of months Buxton went around raising money for Hardenburg, and finally, on March 18, 1913, with the finances secured, Hardenburg set off from Red Deer, where he was living, for London.

The *Mauretania* docked on April 8 in Liverpool. Hardenburg disembarked and was met by John Harris of the Anti-Slavery and Aborigines' Protection Society and Richard Mudie-Smith of the *Daily Chronicle*. Harris had told him that under no circumstances was he to say anything to the press, except to Mudie-Smith. Harris warned Hardenburg that "the crowd behind Arana is composed of a very clever and unscrupulous lot of men, and they will take every advantage of anything you may say." Arana had already been injured by the High Court of Justice's decision to remove him as the company's liquidator.

Although Hardenburg did just as Harris told him, news of Hardenburg's arrival quickly spread. The *Manchester Guardian* reported that Hardenburg, "whose clean-shaven face gives small clue to his age" (he would soon be twenty-seven years old), had arrived in England "to confront those who have accused him of blackmail and forgery."

Hardenburg's first stop was Bolton, where he was invited, through the Anti-Slavery and Aborigines' Protection Society, to make a short speech at a public meeting to celebrate the hundredth anniversary of the birth of David Livingstone. This was the first time Hardenburg had spoken in public about his part in the Putumayo story. "Nearly four years ago," he began, "I came to England with the terrible story of the Putumayo atrocities. That story, which I knew to be absolutely true, was generally regarded as incredible. To-day, upon returning here, I find that every allegation I made has been more than confirmed, and that the British public is taking every step within its power to put a stop to the horrible conditions which prevail on the Putumayo." Hardenburg turned on those who were responsible for the atrocities, stating that instead of accepting responsibility, they were confusing the issue by charging him with forgery and blackmail. He welcomed the opportunity to clear his name in front of the select committee. In comparison with the crimes of the Putumayo, this was only a trifle. "The great thing is to do everything we can to put an end to the horrible conditions which have in ten years reduced the numbers of the Indians in the Putumayo district from 40,000 to 10,000."

The next day, April 9, Hardenburg was in London. He entered committee Room 11 and took a seat behind Arana and listened to his questioning.

Hardenburg was scheduled to appear on Tuesday, April 15.

There was a sense of theater in the committee room on the day of the confrontation between Arana and Hardenburg. Arana was described by a reporter from the *Daily Citizen* as a "full-figured, swarthy product of his climes and his prosperity," while Hardenburg appeared as a western hero—"well-built, but on the small side, he is the essence of quick life and alertness, the sort of man to sum up a difficult situation at a glance, a man, too, of lightning decision and immediate action." Hardenburg, the reporter added, "looks exactly what he is, an engineer. There is about him, too, an air of courage—the courage that led him to face the Putumayo officials, to journey on to Iquitos, then to set out for London to tell his story to Truth and the Anti-Slavery and Aborigines Protection Society, and now officially to retell it to the committee."

Hardenburg was taken through the events that led up to his first arrival in London. Once the background information had been covered, he was asked directly about the charge of blackmail. "Have you ever been convicted, arrested, or charged in a Court either with forgery or blackmail?" asked Roberts. "Never to my knowledge," was Hardenburg's answer.

Roberts asked Hardenburg to clarify the episode of the banknote. Hardenburg explained that he had arrived in Manaus in June 1909 with a man he had met in Iquitos, in the rubber business, named Julio Muriedas. He had with him a check drawn on an Iquitos bank for £830. Muriedas wanted the check cashed in Manaus so that he could avoid the extortionate charges in Iquitos, but when they got to Manaus, Muriedas, suffering from fever, was unable to get to the bank. So Muriedas asked him to write "Pay to the order of Senor W. E. Hardenburg" on the reverse side of the check and get it cashed. Hardenburg did this and duly went to the bank, where he successfully cashed the check and handed the money over to Muriedas. When Muriedas got better, the two men continued their trip down the Amazon to Pará, where they separated. Hardenburg caught the next ship for Liverpool. It was only in February of the following year that he learned that the check had been forged.

Roberts produced the check and showed it to Hardenburg. Yes, that was his handwriting on the reverse. Hardenburg then told the committee that at the same time he learned that the check had been forged, he also found out that Muriedas was in prison in Pará, having been found guilty of forging another check.

Hardenburg had come well prepared and was able to provide ready answers to the committee. He had already written a lengthy explanation of the tale about the check to Robert Bennett, the editor of *Truth*, and a copy of this letter had been passed on to Roberts and the committee. Hardenburg also presented to the committee a sworn affidavit from Walter Perkins, who at the time in late March 1913 was based in Lovington, New Mexico. Perkins backed up everything Hardenburg had said about the events in Iquitos and wrote eloquently about Hardenburg's good character.

Once the committee members were satisfied with their questioning, Raymond Asquith, the Peruvian Amazon Company's counsel, was given the opportunity to cross-examine the witness. The two men talked about the trip down the Putumayo, about the habits of the Putumayo Indians, and about the Colombian rubber concessions. Asquith seemed satisfied that Hardenburg had cleared his name. Hardenburg had accomplished what he set out to do by coming to London. When the hearing ended and he was free to go, Hardenburg went over to Queen Anne's Gate to thank the owner and staff of *Truth* for all they had done and for their support.

A week later *Truth* published a spirited defense of Hardenburg and a denunciation of Arana and the company's directors, whom they accused of hiding behind the untenable charges of blackmail and forgery. "I think," the writer commented, "no one who read the evidence which he gave last week will doubt that he fully vindicated himself, and the impression which he made upon those who were present at the time was much stronger than what could be conveyed by the mere printed report of his evidence."

Flushed with success and with an untarnished reputation, Hardenburg made appearances at a number of public gatherings, talking about the Putumayo. These engagements culminated at the annual meeting of the Anti-Slavery and Aborigines' Protection Society on April 23 in the Westminster Palace Hotel. Hardenburg was the society's guest of honor that day and, in front of an esteemed audience, delivered an extremely well-received account of his Putumayo experiences, which ended with a call to support the society's work in "stripping off from the limbs of the slaves the corroding chains of a slavery of the most detestable kind known in modern times."

Julio César Arana had by now left London and would soon be returning to Manaus and Iquitos, never to visit England again. On May 1, 1913, Walter Hardenburg was on board the RMS *Majestic* of the White Star Line, on his way to New York. He, too, would never return to England.

When, on April 30, the Select Committee on the Putumayo had completed questioning the final witness, it had met on thirty-six occasions, thirty-one of which were in public, and had interviewed twenty-seven witnesses, a thorough cross section of the principal characters in the affair.

The committee members spent a month discussing their findings and preparing a final report. Presented to Parliament in early June, the report, which ran to more than six hundred pages, contained the questions and answers of all the witnesses and the committee's conclusions and recommendations.

Arana was singled out as being responsible for the atrocities. Despite his claims of ignorance, the committee was unconvinced and concluded that not only had he known what was going on, but he had withheld this information from the British directors. The committee agreed that the directors had learned of the atrocities only in September 1909, when the first reports were published in *Truth*.

The Peruvian Amazon Company, the committee continued, therefore could not be held liable under British law: neither the Companies Act, which provided the legal framework in which companies with limited liability worked, nor the Slave Trade Acts, which provided the legislation to make the traffic in slaves illegal, applied in this case. However, the committee censured the British directors for "culpable negligence as to the labour conditions that prevailed under the company . . . they should not lightly have exposed to risk the good name of

England." "We now know," the report emphasized, "what has been possible under the negligent ignorance of one section of the directors and under the callous indifference and guilty knowledge of another section of the board."

Each of the directors came under the committee's scrutiny, but Sir John Lister-Kaye probably came off the worst. He, the committee stated, knew nothing about the company he had agreed to join, nothing about the country where it operated nor of the trade in which it was involved nor the language often used at board meetings. In short, "he deserves censure for taking a directorship under conditions so humiliating, and for allowing his name to be used as an inducement to attract investors into a company of whose business and proceeding he knew nothing at all." For a man who shunned the public gaze, this was terrible. Lister-Kaye's life was beginning to unravel. The shame of this exposure, together with his own mounting debts, finally led to his being declared personally bankrupt.

By singling out Lister-Kaye, the committee was sending a clear and strong signal that the directors of an incorporated company had a responsibility to their shareholders (and therefore the public) to know as much about the concern as they could. For directors to do otherwise, as Lister-Kaye had done—to sit on a board, ignorant of its operations while being rewarded for doing very little—was tantamount to being negligent in their duties. Unfortunately, the signal was not translated into legislation.

The report reiterated that as Casement's and Paredes's reports both clearly and starkly showed, horrible atrocities had taken place, and that the British directors were both lazy and unconcerned, content to be hoodwinked by the Peruvian directors. It seemed incredible, the committee pointed out, that the British directors accepted the interpretation of the Spanish words "*conquistar*," "*conquistadores*," and "*reducir*" as referring to some peaceful and ordered labor system rather than grasping their true meaning as the subjection of the Indians by force. The committee concluded:

> There appears to have been a tendency to acquiesce in the view of the Peruvian directors that the use of force by the Company was legitimate. On the lowest ground a British trading company had no right to

spend the money of its shareholders on the conquest of the Indians; the Company had taken no power to do so under its Memorandum and Articles of Association, and any money so spent was spent *ultra vires* (that is, beyond its powers). Apart from any financial question the Committee cannot but express their regret and surprise that any British directors should have thought fit to entertain such ideas.

Deception, which the committee felt was at the heart of the relationship between the British and the Peruvian directors, could also be seen in Carlos Rey de Castro's creative editing of Robuchon's travel journal, particularly the excising of Robuchon's passages relating to the Indians' lament for their lost freedom. Life in the Putumayo thus came across as (unrealistically) idyllic and peaceful. Furthermore, by having the journal published in Lima and publicized on its front page as *"Edicion Oficial,"* Arana, who used the publication as a prospectus for his company, was giving it a (false) official status.

The committee clearly understood that the knowledge of what was going on in the Putumayo had come to light only because of the "public spirit of a chance traveller and of an English journal." The truth, the report continued, had been established thanks to the initiative of the Foreign Office and "the remarkable work of Sir Roger Casement." Yet, in what was a very disturbing observation, the report pointed out that the committee members were convinced (after sifting through the mass of written documentation—most of it supplied to Roberts by Casement) that the Putumayo was not a "single and local outbreak of crime," "an isolated gang of exceptional criminals." There were other examples, though they did not specify where. The report also hinted that the use of forced labor was not solely a South American phenomenon, saying that as long as there was "an increasing tendency for tropical regions to be developed by absentee and international capital through the use of coloured and native labour," abuses would continue. One would think, the committee argued, that the "economic waste of ill-treating, and perhaps exterminating, the native labour, by which alone such regions can be developed," was illogical, but shortsighted or not, it did not prevent the abuses in the Putumayo, nor, by implication, would it do so in other places.

Therefore, some strengthening of the law was necessary, but which law? The British Companies Acts were not the place to look, because they regulated the machinery of companies and already provided for redress through civil action in case of "gross and culpable negligence of an aggravated kind." But this did not apply apparently to the British directors in the Putumayo. Criminal law, too, was unhelpful, for they had not committed a felony.

The Slave Trade Acts weren't much use at the moment because, according to the report, "the existing law as to slave-dealing and using persons as slaves in Foreign countries (as opposed to within the British Empire) needs to be re-stated, consolidated, and made clear."

The best the committee could do was to state that in cases where British directors could be accused of grave criminal or civil acts, the law as it stood could be applied. But it was not going to be easy to control a concern like the Peruvian Amazon Company, where "a composite board of directors drawn from three nations, sitting in London, nominally professed to direct the operation of rubber production by wild Indians thousands of miles away in the depths of the Amazon forest."

In the end, the committee could not recommend any genuinely effective remedy. The best it could come up with was the suggestion that British companies "employing coloured labour in foreign countries" should notify their intent to the Foreign Office and to the local British consul. But no sooner had the committee members made this recommendation than they realized that it was probably doomed. In what has eerie contemporary resonances, the report added, "but any demand for detailed information which might be resented as inquisitorial, and still more any tax on the companies to provide supervision, would probably defeat their own purpose. The company would simply be registered elsewhere than in London."

Then, as now, governments were loath to regulate where it would discourage investment.

With that, the select committee's work was done, and it was now up to the House of Commons to take the matter further. Perhaps surprisingly, given the amount of publicity the Putumayo had received, there was hardly a murmur out of Parliament. The silence may, however, be explained by the fact that the select committee did not produce recommendations strong enough for parliamentary action.

That was not the view of the Anti-Slavery and Aborigines' Protection Society. It was not going to let the matter drop, and in July, about a month after the publication of the report, the society formed a subcommittee, chaired by Charles Roberts and composed largely of members of the original select committee, to extend its recommendations. It would meet at the House of Commons.

Over the coming months, the subcommittee convened, and toward the end of November 1913 a petition had been drafted for presentation to Herbert Asquith, the prime minister. It was signed by some of the most distinguished members of the political, religious, and commercial community, including four lords who had achieved the highest political offices in the country.

The petition made three specific recommendations. The first was to extend and consolidate the Slave Trade Acts, a recommendation the select committee had already made, but this subcommittee wanted the acts to specify the illegality of British companies, rather than individuals, engaged in slave owning and slave trading. The second recommendation concentrated on the British antislavery treaties with foreign powers and asked the government to revisit and revise these in light of the Putumayo revelations. The final recommendation returned to a point made by the select committee that the Foreign Office should employ specially trained consuls who would visit the "more inaccessible parts of the world" and report back on the conditions of indigenous labor, thereby making a great contribution to "commerce, science and humanity"—a suggestion made by Casement to Roberts nine months earlier.

But again, the sentiments and ideas of the petition, though sanctioned by such distinguished men, fell largely on deaf ears. In March 1914 a bill was introduced into the House of Commons by William Chapple, the Liberal member for Stirlingshire, whose intent to tighten up and extend the Slave Trade Acts to other forms of coerced labor was precisely what the select committee wanted. But the Slavery, Peonage and Forced Labour Bill never got further than its first reading. Then, in July 1914, Lord Lytton—who had taken over the subcommittee's chairmanship from Charles Roberts when Roberts was given the position of undersecretary of state for India—put forth another bill for consideration by Parliament. This bill, titled appropriately the Slavery Bill, like the House of Commons bill, sought radical changes to the Slave Trade Acts but also included the issue of directorial responsibility. It read: "Any director of a British company which deals in slaves shall not be able to plead in defence ignorance of the acts of his agents if it was his business to know of them but for his 'wilful negligence.'" Lytton's bill also wished to widen the term "slave" to include "anyone who is held to service against his free will under an agreement which he was induced to make 'by force, threats, or fraud.'" Lytton fared no better than Chapple before him. The bill was read once, on July 9, but went no further. The issue of directorial responsibility, which Lytton's bill so adventurously addressed, would remain dormant until it was revived after the Second World War, when the mass use of slave labor in German companies was revealed.

By the time of Lytton's bill, Europe was sliding into an abyss. Archduke Franz Ferdinand had been assassinated in Sarajevo less than two weeks before. This was the last time that the Putumayo atrocity appeared in the newspapers; it was shortly to disappear completely from public imagination and memory. On August 4 Britain declared war on Germany, and very soon, Europe would have to deal with its own atrocities.

21

THE DEVIL AND MR. CASEMENT

Julio César Arana was exposed but not finished. On July 9, 1913, he issued a remarkable open letter from Manaus. He claimed that after six years of silently suffering "a campaign of defamation" against his rubber business, he had been forced—by the "foolish attempt" to arrest him in Iquitos and by the public pronouncements of the select committee in London—to defend himself. To this end, he was having published in Barcelona pamphlets by himself and others aiming to show that his accusers were themselves suspect. These publications would show, he stated, that Saldaña Rocca, Hardenburg, Whiffen, the British government, the American government, Michell, and Fuller all had their own motives and agendas and were being influenced by Colombia "to smirch the good name of Peru and to wound the honour of her sons."

Casement's visits to the Putumayo and Iquitos, Arana continued, violated "the most elementary principles of international good faith" and were "subject to a plan made before hand with the triple object of saving the reputation of an officer of the British Army, connected with magnates of his own country; to protect the interests of the review Truth, and to save the amour propre of Mr. Grey."

The letter concluded with the following remark: "The least which is permissible to a man whose honour it has been attempted to wound, whom it has been found possible to damage severely in his finances and who has been dragged to the criminal's dock, is that he shall not keep his silence, unmoved, aloof from all which makes up the reason of his existence and his right to be a conscious human being."

Arana's collection of pamphlets circulated widely. In time they were joined by a number of other publications concerning the Putumayo, which appeared in Barcelona, London, New York, and Lima, penned respectively by Carlos Rey de Castro, Sidney Paternoster, Thomas Whiffen, Norman Thomson—a London-based expert on boundary issues between various South American republics, especially Peru and Colombia—Walter Hardenburg, and Carlos Valcárcel, the judge at the center of the attempts to get the arrest warrants to stick in Iquitos. Even Frederick Bishop, Casement's interpreter and guide on his trip to the Putumayo, got in on the act, giving an exclusive interview recounting his side of the story, in an English-speaking newspaper published in Valparaiso, Chile.

Most of the publications not only used the text to make their case but also carried supporting evidence from photographs. Contrast, for example, the frontispiece of Hardenburg's book—which showed four naked, emaciated, shackled, and chained Indian men—with Arana's, which showed a fully dressed, bountiful Huitoto woman on a shaded veranda, happily working at a sewing machine, the very picture of blissful domesticity.

In the war of words and pictures, however, Arana went one better than anyone else—a sign, perhaps, of his own inventiveness and ambition. He had arranged for Silvino Santos, the photographer who had accompanied Arana and Rey de Castro on the consular visit to the Putumayo the previous year, to spend three months in Paris at the studios of the leading cinema producers Pathé and the Lumière Brothers, learning how to shoot and develop film. Arana's plan was to send Santos to the Putumayo to make a film about the Indians, showing how they lived and how they were benefiting from his presence in the area. Santos, who by now had married Arana's ward, spent two months filming in the Putumayo in the latter part of 1913. Back in Iquitos, he prepared the negatives, but he had to send them to Lima to get positive copies made, in anticipation of a wide showing, particularly in the United States. However, a German U-boat torpedoed the ship containing the negatives, and all but a tiny fragment of this, the first cinematographic record of the Putumayo people, was lost to the sea in 1914.

Roger Casement was back in England by May 10. He had sailed to South Africa to see his brother, unaware that Arana was to be in London, so he had missed confronting Arana in the Palace of Westminster and had also missed meeting Hardenburg. He was now the only one left in London of the three main characters in the story.

Casement was exhausted by the Putumayo, and he assumed Roberts was, too—"I am sure you hate the name of Putumayo." Casement had been thinking of leaving the consular service and was determined not to return to his post in Rio de Janeiro. But what to do and where to go was still in question.

While he considered his future, news was appearing in the Irish press of a terrible outbreak of typhus in the Irish-speaking island communities of Connemara, in the west of Ireland. Casement's first reaction was to refer to the tragedy, where poverty and disease took their appalling toll, as the "Irish Putumayo." Writing about it was one thing, but like the Congo and the Putumayo, there was no substitute for firsthand experience. On June 7 he went to the area from Dublin via Galway and remained there for two days. He was shocked by the deprivation he saw. His reactions were summed up in a note he wrote upon returning to Dublin: "Very wet cold and tired with to-days glimpse of the Irish Putumayo—the 'white Indians' of Ireland are heavier on my heart than all the Indians of the rest of the earth."

What Casement had learned from his experience in the Congo, where Europeans oppressed and exploited Africans, and from the Putumayo, where Peruvians oppressed and exploited Indians, was that one people or race could not be trusted with power over another. "One thing is clear to me," he wrote about the Connemara typhus outbreak. "Only Irishmen and Irishwomen" could be relied on to "clear it up." One set of people, the British, could not be trusted to govern another—the Irish—in an enlightened and civilized way. People with power were all too likely to abuse it. Those over whom they had power were seen as subhuman and disposable, their suffering denied, their rights ignored.

Casement did not need such sights to convert him to the Irish cause. He had told Morel several years earlier that as soon as he was done with the Putumayo, he would put all his energies into freeing Ireland.

On August 1, 1913, Casement formally resigned from the Foreign Office. From then on, he would devote himself to the Irish cause.

He began writing strenuously about Irish affairs and about empire; and he appeared at rallies and gave speeches in which he articulated his vision of a united, independent, and peaceful Ireland. In November he became deeply involved in the formation of the Irish Volunteers, a group organized to counter the unionist movement embodied in the creation of the Ulster Volunteers.

For the next several months, recruiting for and organizing the activities of the Irish Volunteers was Casement's main focus of activity and interest. They remained an unarmed force until the game changed in April 1914, when a shipment of more than twenty thousand German rifles and two million rounds of ammunition was landed to arm the Ulster Volunteers. These arms were brought in from Germany while the British authorities turned a blind eye.

In response, Casement threw himself into the business of arming the Irish Volunteers. This required money and help, and so in July 1914 he traveled to the United States to meet with and drum up support from the powerful and vocal Irish nationalist communities along the country's Eastern Seaboard. By early October, World War I was in its third month. German troops had already swept through Belgium and were poised to launch a major attack in northeastern France. By this time Casement had thoroughly won over his Irish American friends, the members of Clan na Gael. He had also, through the clan, made close contact with representatives of the German government in the United States who were being wooed by clan members—they saw Germany, rather than Britain, as their natural ally.

In meetings held between clan members and German representatives in New York, it was decided that Casement's next move would be to travel to Germany to convince the German imperial government that it should declare that in the case of victory, it would support the Irish cause. On October 15 Casement left from New York bound for Germany via Norway. Two weeks later he was in Berlin.

Casement remained in Germany from the end of October 1914 until April 1916. During these long months, far away from Ireland and with difficult communications both to his homeland and to the United States, he traveled through Germany and its newly occupied territory, meeting high German officials and Irish prisoners of war. What he wanted from Germany was an ironclad declaration that they had no intention of invading and occupying Ireland but would support its struggle for independence from Britain. He also pushed for the formation of an Irish Brigade, made up of Irish prisoners of war, who, with the assistance of the German army and navy, would, at the appropriate time, be landed on Irish shores to spearhead a rebellion for the overthrow of British authority.

Though Casement had, at various times, received assurances from high-ranking German officials—including Arthur Zimmermann, the undersecretary of state for foreign affairs—who were in agreement with his proposals behind the scenes, things were not going well.

Plans were made to send Casement back to Ireland together with the Irish Brigade, and to send a ship, separately, with arms. At the last moment, however, German general staff were not prepared to release Irish prisoners of war as an Irish Brigade with backup from German officers, and Casement left Germany without this support.

Just after midnight on Good Friday, April 21, 1916, the U-boat Casement had boarded in Wilhelmshaven arrived in Tralee Bay, County Kerry, on Ireland's western coast, after a long voyage by way of the Faeroe Islands. The arms ship, *Aud*, which was supposed to rendezvous with Casement, was nowhere to be seen. Unbeknownst to him, the *Aud* had been intercepted by the Royal Navy on the same day, far to the southeast of the submarine's position, nearer to Cork than Tralee.

Later that day, Casement found himself looking at a policeman's revolver, and he was arrested. After his story—that he was an author on a research trip—found no credence, he was taken to the local town of Tralee. His real identity was revealed during his short stay in custody, and he was quickly transferred to Dublin and from there to Holyhead, finally arriving in London on Easter Sunday, April 23, where he was handed over to Special Branch.

He was back in London for the first time in three years, still Sir Roger Casement, but now in circumstances so different from those when he led the Putumayo mission as to be scarcely believable.

Events moved quickly. For three days he was interrogated closely by military intelligence, after which he was taken to the Tower of London and placed in military custody.

On the day of his second interview, Casement learned from his interrogators that a rising against British rule had broken out in Dublin. During the interview Casement tried in vain to convince his inquisitors to get a message on his behalf to the rebels' leaders in Dublin to abort the rebellion. As it was, the rebel leaders went ahead with the rising despite knowing that Casement had been arrested and that the *Aud* had been scuppered by its crew at the entrance to Cork Harbour while under naval escort. With the arms at the bottom of the sea, the rebellion had little chance of success and was soon over.

It was all over, in fact. On May 12, barely two weeks after the failure of the rising, most of the rebel leaders had been summarily executed on British military orders. On May 15 Casement was led from the Tower of London, placed under civil authority, and taken to Bow Street Magistrates' Court, where he was committed for trial at the Old Bailey, scheduled for June 26, and taken to Brixton Prison.

While he was in prison waiting for his trial to begin, Casement saw his remaining friends and relatives. Wednesday, June 14, was not a busy day, and Casement took the opportunity of the unusual calm to write to George Gavan Duffy, his solicitor, complaining about the previous day's meeting with his barrister.

While Casement was putting the finishing touches on the letter, the prison clerk approached the cell. He handed Casement a telegram. This was not the first telegram he had received while in prison. Mostly they were from various parts of Britain and Ireland, and occasionally from the United States, from supporters and well-wishers. But this one was different. It was from Manaus, from Julio César Arana. Casement began to read it.

> On my arrival here am informed you will be tried for High Treason.
> Want of time unables me to write you being obliged to wire you asking
> you to be fully confessing before the human tribunal your guilts only
> known by Divine Justice regarding your dealings in the Putumayo
> business . . . Inventing deeds and influencing Barbadians to confirm
> unconsciously facts never happened, invented by Saldana and thief
> Hardenburg . . . I hold some Barbadians declaration denying all you
> obliged them to declare pressing upon them as English Consul and
> frightening them in the King's name with prison if refusing to sign
> your own work and statements. You influenced the Judges in the Pu-
> tumayo affair who by your ill influence confirmed your own state-
> ments. You tried by all means to be a humanizer in order to obtain
> titles fortune, not caring for the consequences of your calumnies and
> defamation against Peru and myself doing me enormous damage. I
> pardon you, but it is necessary that you should be just and declare
> now fully and truly all the true facts that nobody knows better than
> yourself.

Casement's trial lasted four days and ended with a guilty verdict. Despite the admiration he had received previously from people and governments throughout the world, most of the British public and the state were baying for his blood. Casement knew this, and in his final public utterance—his impassioned, articulate, and now famous speech from the dock—he railed against his accusers and spoke directly to the Irish people, his South American and African experiences layering every phrase.

> Self-government is our right, a thing born in us at birth; a thing no
> more to be doled out to us or withheld from us by another people,
> than the right to life itself—than the right to feel the sun or smell the
> flowers—or to love our kind. It is only from the convict these things
> are withheld for crime committed and proven—and Ireland that has

wronged no man, that has injured no land, that has sought no domin-
ion over others—Ireland is treated today among the nations of the
world as if she was a convicted criminal. If it be treason to fight against
such an unnatural fate as this, then I am proud to be a rebel—and
shall cling to my rebellion with the last drop of my blood. If there be
no right of rebellion against a state of things that no savage tribe would
endure without resistance, then I am sure that it is better for men to
fight and die without right than to live in such a state of right as this.

After the trial Casement was taken to Pentonville Prison and
stripped of his honors. On July 17 and 18 an appeal was heard but
rejected. A whispering campaign, which had been gaining ground
since May, now destroyed most of the support Casement had left.
Only a few, such as George Bernard Shaw, remained steadfast. Rumors had it that Casement had led a secret dual life—a champion of
human rights and a rebel on the one hand, while, as private diaries
found in his trunk at his London flat revealed, he also inhabited another hidden world. He was a man, it was rumored, who had "for years
been addicted to the grossest sodomitical practices."

Homosexuality was a crime and widely regarded as a perversion
and a disgrace. He was finished. At 9:00 a.m. on August 3, 1916,
Roger Casement was hanged, ostensibly for treason. The former hero
was discredited and disgraced, not only as a traitor but also as a sod-
omite. The rumors that were circulated after his conviction no doubt
contributed to the failure of his appeal. Casement himself probably
never knew that his sex life had been exposed and so could not defend
himself (even if he had chosen to do so) against charges of perversions
and unnaturalness. Now that homosexuality is generally legal and acceptable, it is easier to see how irrelevant Casement's sexual orientation was to this story. Of course, if it had come to light earlier in his
career, the impact would have been enormous.

Casement's life ended in tragedy, violently cut short by a rope. It seems
incredible, picturing him tramping through the dense and steamy Amazonian jungle, his senses acute and permanently on guard, notebook

and pencil always at hand, investigating the Putumayo atrocities, that this hero of international humanitarianism was executed for treason by the same state that honored him. Meanwhile, the perpetrators of the crimes he brought to light remained beyond the reach of the law; the British directors of the company feigned ignorance and assumed no responsibility for what had happened; the state could not find any way of punishing them within the laws of the time.

When news of Casement's execution reached him in New York, W.E.B. Du Bois—the great African American man of letters, educator, and tireless campaigner for universal human rights—wrote in the editorial of the September 1916 issue of *The Crisis*, the official magazine of the National Association for the Advancement of Colored People:

> Sir Roger Casement is dead. He has been put to death by the English Government on the charge of treason . . . All the impressionable, vigorous years of [his] manhood . . . were spent in witnessing acts of oppression and lawlessness and in efforts to offset those acts. He became "obsessed" with a horror at the spectacle of the "frightfulness" which those in great places wreak upon those in small . . . Sir Roger Casement—Patriot, Martyr.

Like Du Bois, Casement was a great humanitarian, but unlike most of the others who fought against injustice, he risked his own life by actually going to the scenes of "oppression and lawlessness" and investigating them with a rigor that was new at the time. As a servant of the British state, in his capacity as a consular official Casement brought to the world's attention two of the worst atrocities of the early twentieth century: the one perpetrated in the Congo in Africa, and the other, the subject of this book, in the Putumayo region of South America.

Even after the Congo, Casement was shocked by what he saw in the Putumayo in 1910. He believed that Arana's crime was proportionately greater than Leopold's. Thirty thousand indigenous people, three-quarters of the population in the area, had died for four thousand tons of rubber, which they had been violently forced to provide to a company registered in London. Casement found it hard to capture the horror in words. He tried phrases such as "a carrion—a pestilence," "syndicate of crime," "reign of terror," "piracy and terrorization," and "not merely slavery but extermination," but he preferred a term that has now become all too familiar. It was, he wrote, "a crime against humanity."

At the end of September, two months after Casement's execution, Sir Edward Grey received a letter from George Lepper, Arana's London lawyer, inquiring whether Casement had replied to the telegram. "Mr Arana," Lepper commented, "is suffering from a keen sense of injustice and it would be well to satisfy him upon the point."

Arana continued to extract rubber from his Putumayo estates. The Peruvian Amazon Company had been wound up by March 1914, and Arana now traded under the name of his friend and business partner Cecilio Hernández. During the First World War the price of rubber was maintained, and output returned to levels last seen during the boom years of the previous decade. Arana did very well out of the Putumayo in the war years and continued to do so right through the 1920s. Arana's rubber, as before, went through Iquitos and to Britain, his main market.

Arana also went into national politics and from 1921 to 1925 represented Loreto in Lima. During this time, the controversy between Peru and Colombia over the Amazonian border resurfaced. Under pressure from the United States, the Salomón-Lozano Treaty was drawn up and signed, but not ratified, by both countries in 1922. Under the treaty's terms, Colombia agreed to cede lands between the Napo and the Putumayo rivers to Peru, and in return Peru agreed to cede lands from the Putumayo to the Caquetá River to Colombia, and a parcel of land from the Putumayo south to the Amazon at the port of Leticia now became Colombian. The Putumayo River would become the border between the two countries, and Arana's property would end up being in Colombia.

Arana was vehemently opposed to the treaty and was directly involved in hindering its ratification. He campaigned vigorously from 1925, bombarding the Lima press and political leaders with pamphlets, telegrams, and letters, most of them originating in Loreto. The argument against signing the treaty came down to a matter of Peruvian pride. The patriotic front considered the government of President Augusto Leguía as being too weak in its resolve against Colombia and also too influenced by the American State Department's promise of generous loans should Peru sign. The protests against the treaty delayed the ratification but did not stop it. In December 1927 the treaty came before the National Congress and passed with a large majority. Arana made a final stand when he published a last attack on the treaty as it came up for consideration by the Congress, accusing the government of being unpatriotic in handing over territory to Colombia.

Arana stood to lose most from the treaty, but he had at least ensured that his losses would be compensated. In 1921, the year in which he became a senator, the Peruvian government had granted him legal title to his properties in the Putumayo, and while the treaty was being drafted, he made sure that under its terms he would receive recompense for his losses. Arana was looking for compensation in the region of £2,000,000, but the Colombian government thought the figure preposterous, though they agreed that they and the Peruvians would both respect any land concessions made to private individuals. Arana took no further action in making a claim.

In August 1932 a patriotic junta in Iquitos—initiated by Arana and Enrique Vigil, a wealthy Loretano landowner—whose members included Arana's son and daughter, attempted to retake Leticia by force. Arana provided the rifles. Military responses by both Peru and Colombia led to a four-month war between the two, played out along the length of the Putumayo. A cease-fire, brokered by the United States and Brazil, was agreed to on May 25, 1933, and the status quo of the treaty was reestablished.

Arana's hopes that his properties might remain in Peruvian hands were dashed. By then, however, in the midst of the world's severest depression, rubber prices fell to their lowest level since the beginning of the century, and it took Arana until 1939 to find a buyer for his Colombian claim.

One story has it that he was swindled, another that he simply made a bad mistake, but in any case, he seems to have emerged from the deal penniless. He left Iquitos and the Amazon forever and went to live in a small, dark house in Magdalena del Mar, a coastal suburb of Lima. A photograph of him from that time shows an elderly man slumped in a chair in front of a wooden hut, a far cry from his once glamorous life in London, Geneva, and Biarritz.

In September 1952 Julio César Arana died at age eighty-eight, his passing virtually unnoticed by the public. His grave is in a cemetery reserved for the poor, where he has a simple tombstone made of cement.

A CRIME AGAINST HUMANITY

In February 1913 the United States Congress published *Slavery in Peru*. This 440-page volume was the result of a resolution passed by the House of Representatives in August 1912 to make publicly available the correspondence and reports that the State Department had received over the years about the Putumayo. The volume contained correspondence between London and Washington and reprinted all the major investigations, both of Eberhardt's reports (now judiciously edited to exclude the comment about the genocide of the North American Indian), Paredes's report, Casement's Blue Book, and Stuart Fuller's report. The strong title seemed to promise further governmental involvement or even intervention. However, in only a matter of weeks following publication, the State Department, in a message to Cecil Spring Rice, the newly instated British ambassador in Washington, effectively withdrew its concern for conditions in the Putumayo and clearly expected Britain to do the same. "In view of the vigorous policy," the note began,

> apparently animating the present administration in Peru, the remoteness of the district, and the attendant obstacles in the way of effective

reform, I am of the opinion that any further action on the part of His Majesty's Government or of the American Government would appear inopportune, at least at the time being, inasmuch as it might be instrumental in stirring up public sentiment in Peru to such an extent as to hinder whatever real desire now exists there for bettering the conditions under which the Indians labor.

The State Department was as good as its word. In September 1913 the consulate in Iquitos was closed, and Stuart Fuller was transferred to Durban, South Africa.

The British consulate in Iquitos continued to function, but as far as the Putumayo was concerned, the Foreign Office followed the State Department's advice to leave the rest to Peru, and it took no further interest in the region. With Casement "turned traitor," Ernest Rennie, the first minister at the British legation in Lima, advised that "the intervention of His Majesty's Government in the further investigation of charges that were originally formulated by a man whose name is now the subject of universal reprobation" would be wholly unwelcome. He counseled that the Putumayo should no longer be mentioned in diplomatic encounters.

Casement would have been gratified to know that a week after his execution, a group of Indians who had been working for the Atenas rubber station turned on their "employers"—who had force marched them for three days to cut rubber without providing adequate food— and killed nine of them. The Indians wanted to "clear the region of the whites." Father Leo Sambrook, an Irish missionary and head of the four-man Franciscan mission at La Chorrera that had been sent to the area in November 1912 following the papal encyclical of the same year, reported to the British consul in Iquitos that there was a force of some nine hundred Indians, mostly Bora, intent on making the whites "reap a little of what they have sown." Though "the shootings, tortures and all the villainy Casement exposed" seemed to have abated, the Indians, Sambrook observed, continued to be beaten, and the resentment they felt now exploded. He wondered why it had not happened before.

"Really they have had provocation enough, poor devils," remarked Sambrook, "and I am afraid that if the whites come out on top, the natives will pay a fearful price for what they have done." He was right. As soon as word got to Iquitos that some of Arana's employees had been killed, the authorities responded immediately by dispatching thirty troops to the area, some of them armed with machine guns. One month later Sambrook wrote that the uprising was over; the Atenas rubber station had been recaptured, the Indians' homes had been burned to the ground, and the Peruvian troops were rounding up those rebels who remained alive.

The Huitoto, Andoke, and Bora Indians did not encounter white men until the last decade of the nineteenth century; there was only one generation between their first encounter with the *caucheros* and the publication of the Blue Book that so shocked the civilized world. The white's lust for latex had devastated the Indians in a dreadfully short time. There was nowhere for them to turn, nowhere for them to hide or escape to. Their homeland was virtually sealed off from the rest of the world—their only contact with it via the launches of the Peruvian Amazon Company.

Even after the demise of the Peruvian Amazon Company, Arana continued to export rubber from the Putumayo to Britain, and Britons as well as Arana continued to profit from the rubber trade. The slave labor of the Indians went on profiting their exploiters. From 1924 until 1930, during the years he was trying to stall the ratification of the Salomón-Lozano Treaty, Arana, realizing the inevitability of losing his territory to Colombia, forcibly moved more than six thousand Huitoto, Andoke, and Bora men, women, and children from their homes around the Caraparaná and Igaraparaná rivers to the south bank of the Putumayo River, into what was to be Peruvian territory. Hardly any were left behind. Casement's words echo: "The whites . . . did not give a damn where the trees were, all they troubled about is where the Indians were." The Indians were still at Arana's mercy.

Nothing and no one seemed to help the Indians. It took a papal intervention to establish the Franciscan mission in La Chorrera in 1912, but it lasted less than five years. The mission's work was limited by the Indians' fear of whites. It was only in 1933, when the

Barcelona-based Capuchin missionaries settled in the area, that some of the Indians who had been forcibly relocated were able to return to their homeland. The Capuchins had been invited into the area by the Colombian government to Christianize the Indians. A school was built, and the plots, in which the Indians used to grow food, were again cultivated.

The numbers of Huitoto, Andoke, and Bora Indians had been severely depleted by Arana's brutal system. With the failure of armed resistance, and escape virtually impossible, the Indians were now taking matters into their own hands by using herbal abortifacients to limit the number of children they produced. According to Felix Ryan, one of Sambrook's colleagues, the Indians would sooner die out than live as slaves.

In the event, the Indians hung on, their numbers hardly changing over the decades. An estimate in 1940 put the number of Huitoto, Andoke, and Bora living in their homelands within the Putumayo and Caquetá rivers at five thousand. Recent estimates put the number of those speaking these indigenous languages at around six thousand.

Ironically, what really saved the Indians from extinction was the fact that on the other side of the world, one million tons of plantation rubber were being produced annually in British, Dutch, and French colonies in Malaya, India, Indonesia, and Indochina. A process of domestication of the rubber tree begun in the 1890s—using *Hevea brasiliensis* seeds stolen from Brazil—resulted in cheap, abundant, and reliable plantation rubber. Wild rubber was no longer so important to the international market. Arana's thirty years of terror and exploitation had ended. That particular nightmare was over for the Indians, but a new one was around the corner.

Unfortunately, synthetic rubber, which came to surpass plantation rubber by 1960, is derived from petroleum. The Texaco Petroleum Company (now Chevron) "invaded" the Upper Putumayo in 1963. The peaceful Indian village of Orito, Colombia, was transformed into a booming oil town. This time the outsiders did not require Indian labor; they helicoptered in their own personnel, but they took the Indians' land and their women and polluted their rivers. Although Texaco had moved on by the 1970s, the pollution remained, ruining the rivers as sources of food and water. The Indians are still victims of pollution, deforestation, and the drug trade. Caught in the cross fire between government troops, guerrilla groups, drug barons, and loggers, they are still struggling to maintain their lives and their culture.

DRAMATIS PERSONAE AND CHRONOLOGY

THE DEVIL—JULIO CÉSAR ARANA

1864   born in Rioja, northern Peru, on April 12

1887   marries childhood sweetheart, Eleanora Zumaeta

1889   establishes partnership with his brothers-in-law in the rubber trade in Iquitos

1903   creates J. C. Arana y Hermanos, concentrating on the rubber industry in the Putumayo region

1906   J. C. Arana y Hermanos becomes the largest rubber exporter in Peru

1908   Arana creates the Peruvian Amazon Company, registered in London with a capital of £1,000,000, successor to J. C. Arana y Hermanos

1911   the Peruvian Amazon Company goes into liquidation

1913   compulsory wind-up order for Peruvian Amazon Company

1921   Arana becomes senator for Loreto in Lima

1927   Arana publishes a pamphlet vehemently criticizing his government for signing the Salomón-Lozano Treaty, giving Colombia jurisdiction over the entire Putumayo region

1932   Arana initiates an armed junta to take the Amazonian town of Leticia by force and return it to Peru, leading to four-month war between Peru and Colombia

1933   peace declared between Peru and Colombia, and the Salomón-Lozano Treaty comes into force, making the Putumayo River the border between the two countries

1939   Arana cuts all ties with the Putumayo
1952   Arana dies in Lima, age eighty-eight

MR. CASEMENT—ROGER CASEMENT

1864   born in Dublin on September 1
1883   travels to West Africa as purser on Liverpool-based ship
1884   decides to remain in Africa
1895   becomes British consul for Portuguese East Africa
1900   becomes British consul for Congo Free State and the French Congo
1904   Foreign Office publishes Casement's report on the administration of the Congo Free State
1905   Casement awarded the Companion of Saint Michael and Saint George for his Congo work
1906   appointed British consul in Santos, Brazil
1907   appointed British consul in Pará, Brazil
1909   appointed British consul general in Rio de Janeiro
1910   arrives in Iquitos to investigate conditions in the Putumayo
1911   knighthood conferred for his work in Peru
1912   Blue Book, containing Casement's report on the Putumayo, published
1913   resigns from the Foreign Office
1914   travels to the United States and then Germany, where he remains until 1916
1916   arrested on west coast of Ireland on Good Friday and committed for trial on charge of high treason in London on June 26
1916   hanged on August 3, age fifty-one

NOTES ON SOURCES

In referring to the material I have used in researching this book, I have adopted the following system.

For manuscript sources, I have abbreviated the name of the depository (an archive or library) and continued the citation following the depository's own system. I have also abbreviated the title of government reports. A full list of these abbreviations can be found below.

For published material, I have used shortened titles (often the first one or two words). The full bibliographical citation for each of these titles can be found in the bibliography.

ABBREVIATIONS FOR PRIMARY MATERIAL

ACH	Archivo Central Histórico, Ministerio de Relaciones Exteriores, Lima
AGN	Archivo General de la Nación, Bogotá
AHL	Archivo Histórico de Límites, Ministerio de Relaciones Exteriores, Lima
AR	Archives Robuchon, privately held
ASG	Archives de la Société de Géographie
BL	British Library, London
BLCASRH	Bodleian Library of Commonwealth and African Studies at Rhodes House, University of Oxford, Oxford
BLPES	British Library of Political and Economic Science, London School of Economics, London

BM   British Museum, London

BN   Bibliothèque Nationale, Paris

BodL   Bodleian Library, University of Oxford, Oxford

BPP   British Parliamentary Papers

CBCSP   *Correspondence Respecting the Treatment of British Colonial Subjects and Native Indians Employed in the Collection of Rubber in the Putumayo District*, British Parliamentary Papers,1912–13 [Cd.6266] LXVIII.819

ETH   Ethnography

FDHAC   *Fuentes documentales para la historia de la amazonia colombiana. Volumen VI. Documentos relativos a las violaciones del territorio colombiano en el Putumayo. 1903–1910.* Universidad Nacional de Colombia. Augusto Javier Gómez López & Cindy Katherine Avendaño Castañeda. Coautores (in preparation).

HLHU   Houghton Library, Harvard University, Cambridge, Massachusetts

LRO   Liverpool Record Office, Liverpool

MCIHP   Maloney Collection of Irish Historical Papers

NARA   National Archives and Record Administration, College Park, Maryland

NLI   National Library of Ireland, Dublin

NYPL   New York Public Library, New York

PD   Parliamentary Debates (Official Report)

RBG   Royal Botanic Gardens, London (Kew)

RSRSC   *Report and Special Report from the Select Committee on Putumayo Together with the Proceedings of the Committee, Minutes of Evidence and Appendices*, British Parliamentary Papers, 1913 (148) xiv.1

SP   *Slavery in Peru: Message from the President of the United States Transmitting Report of the Secretary of the Department of State, with Accompanying Papers, Concerning the Alleged Existence of Slavery in Peru*, United States House of Representatives, Document no. 1366 (62nd Congress, 3rd Session), (Washington, D.C., 1913)

TNA   The National Archives, London (Kew)

WHP   Walter Hardenburg Papers, privately held

INTRODUCTION: *LA SELVA* COMES TO LONDON

The parliamentary questions and answers are from PD.

For the history of *Truth*, I have relied on the following sources: Hirshfield, "Truth"; Weber, "Henry Labouchere"; and Hampton, "Rethinking." The quotation about the anxious moments felt by some as they opened their copy of *Truth* is from Joseph Hatton, the British novelist and journalist and contemporary of Henry Du Pre Labouchere, as cited in Weber, "Henry Labouchere," p. 41.

I have used a number of sources for the rubber regime of the Congo Free State. These include Harms, "The End"; Louis, "Roger Casement"; Grant, *A Civilised*; Hochschild, *King Leopold's*; and Stengers, "King Leopold's."

I have used a number of sources to reconstruct Casement's life and the contexts in which it evolved until his return from the Congo. These are Mitchell, *Casement*; Reid, *The Lives*; Inglis, *Roger Casement*; Daly, *Roger Casement*; Ó Síocháin and O'Sullivan, *The Eyes*; Ó Síocháin, *Roger Casement*; Osborne, "Wilfred G. Thesiger"; Burroughs, "Britain's Travelling"; Louis, "Roger Casement"; Cline, "E. D. Morel"; Cline, *E. D. Morel*; Louis and Stengers, *E. D. Morel's*; Stengers, "Leopold II"; Gann, "The Berlin Conference"; Miers, "Humanitarianism"; Hochschild, *King Leopold's*; Grant, *A Civilised*; and Mitchell, "Roger Casement."

The resolution passed by the House of Commons in 1903 is referred to in Ó Síocháin and O'Sullivan, *The Eyes*, p.11; Casement's letter to Bigelow can be found in Ó Síocháin and O'Sullivan, *The Eyes*, p. 13.

Casement's dispatches to the Foreign Office from the Congo during the months from June to October 1903 are in TNA, FO 10/805, FO 10/806, and FO 403/338. The draft report is in TNA, FO 10/806; and the published version is in BPP, (1904), LXII.

CHAPTER 1: ACROSS THE ANDES

Hardenburg's and Perkins's experiences in the Putumayo are told in several places. In 1912 Hardenburg published a book, *The Putumayo*, telling the story. Hardenburg's unedited manuscript is in BLCASRH, Mss Brit. Emp., s.22, G325 and G329. I have used it rather than the book. There is very little in the published book about the pair getting from Buenaventura to the Putumayo. Perkins also wrote about his experiences mostly at the hands of the Peruvians in a series of correspondence he had with State Department officials. This material is in NARA, RG59, M862, Roll 860 (file 13,889). Perkins also provided the Anti-Slavery and Aborigines' Protection Society with a short description of the trip. This can be found in BLCASRH, Mss Brit. Emp., s.22, G338. The quotation about the purchase of half of Serrano's property is in a letter Perkins wrote to the State Department dated May 22, 1908, and is also in this file.

The full list of provisions Hardenburg and Perkins bought before setting out on the Putumayo is given by Hardenburg as

half a dozen felt hats, a dozen red shirts, seven machetes, ten pounds of assorted beads, two dozen small mirrors, nine butcher-knives, a dozen harmonicas. All these articles were for the Indians, while for our own use we got a shot-gun with plenty of powder, shot and percussion caps, a rifle, a machete, an *arroba* (25 pounds) of salt, another of rice, and a quantity of enameled iron crockery. In the afternoon we ordered the fabrication of two mosquito-bars, gloves and veils as a protection against the *moscos* (egg-laying gnats), also six pairs of trousers for presents to the Indian chiefs. In addition to this, we gave orders for the preparation of ten pounds of chocolate, half an *arroba* of cracked wheat and an equal quantity of *aco*—a specially prepared flour . . . composed of wheat, cinnamon, sugar and several other ingredients. The next afternoon we continued our purchases among which may be mentioned six dozen red handkerchiefs, an enormous quantity of fishhooks, several rolls of brightly-colored woolen yarn, some forty yards of muslin and a large assortment of needles and thread for the Indians, while for ourselves we bought a small stock of medicines, notably quinine and salts, several pairs of *alpargatas* (hemp sandals), a lot of rope and twine. The next day we finished our shopping by the purchase of a big ham, an outfit of knives, forks and spoons and most important of all a good lantern and a broiler.

Further information about the Colombian Pacific Railroad is in Rippy, "Dawn," and Ortega, *Ferrocarriles*. The Madeira-Mamoré Railway is the subject of Werner, "All Aboard," and Gauld, *The Last*.

For background to the border problems between Colombia and Peru, and their partial solutions, including the modus vivendi, I have consulted the following sources: Ireland, *Boundaries*; Olarte Camacho, *Los convenios*; Thomson, *The Putumayo*; Bákula, *La política*; and Wagner de Reyna, *Historia diplomática*.

For information on the early rubber trade in the Putumayo, I have relied on Reyes, *Memorias*; Stanfield, *Red Rubber*; Dominguez and Gómez, *La economía extractiva*; and Santos-Granero and Barclay, *Tamed Frontiers*.

Hardenburg's letter to Miranda (and also one to his old boss in Buenaventura venting a similar outrage against the Peruvians) is in FDHAC (originals in AGN, Archivo diplomático y consular, Ministerio de relaciones exteriores, Sección República, Caja 600, "Documentos relativos a las violaciones del territorio colombiano en el Putumayo, 1903–1910").

CHAPTER 2: IQUITOS AND RUBBER

For the history of Iquitos, including the Jesuit period, I have used a number of sources including Grohs, *Los indios*; Negro and Marzal, *Un reino*; García, *Historia*; Mörner, "The Expulsion"; Reeve, "Regional Interaction"; Santos-Granero and Barclay, *Tamed Frontiers*; Stanfield, *Red Rubber*; John, *A Liverpool*; Haring, *Boomtown*; and Romero, *Iquitos*.

The quote from Lucien Jerome, dated January 20, 1908, is in TNA, FO 369/161.

I have used a number of sources to tell the story of the early history of the rubber business, as well as the history of bicycles, cars, and tires. These include Drabble, *Rubber*; Bardou et al., *The Automobile Revolution*; Foreman-Peck, "Multinational Companies"; Ribeill, "From Pneumatics"; Herlihy, *Bicycle*; Ritchie, *King*; and Loadman, *Tears*.

For information about the rubber boom along the Amazon and down its many tributaries, I have consulted Drabble, *Rubber*; Weinstein, *The Amazon*; Barham and Coomes, "Wild Rubber"; Burns, "Manaus"; Frank and Musacchio, "Brazil"; Resor, "Rubber"; Fifer, "The Empire Builders"; Pennano, *La economía*; Bonilla, "Estructura"; De la Flor Fernández, "La economía"; Dominguez and Gómez, *La economía extractiva*; and Gómez, Lesmes, and Rocha, *Caucherías*.

NOTES ON SOURCES

The description of tapping trees and preparing rubber in the Putumayo is taken from TNA, FO 371/1202.

CHAPTER 3: ARANA'S WORLD

The details of Perkins's enforced stay in El Encanto are recorded in a series of letters to the State Department held in NARA, RG59, M862, Roll 860 (file 13,889), and RG 59, 423.11P41.

I have relied on a number of sources to tell the story of Arana's life until 1908. They include Stanfield, *Red Rubber*; Lagos, *Arana*; Collier, *The River*; Karno, "Julio César Arana"; Santos-Granero and Barclay, *Tamed Frontiers*; and De la Flor Fernández, "La economía." For conditions in the Ceará in the 1880s, I have benefited from Greenfield, *The Realities*. Arana's own version of the events leading up to his controlling the entire rubber trade in the Putumayo can be found in his affidavit in TNA, J13/6373. The same statement was published in Spanish as Arana, *Las cuestiones*. The information about setting up the Peruvian Amazon Rubber Company and dropping the word "rubber" from the name is taken from TNA, BT 31/18205/94839, and TNA, BT 31/18220/95023.

On the subject of debt peonage, I have relied on Knight, "Debt," and Dore, "Debt."

For information about Barbadians on the move in the early twentieth century, I have found the following sources very useful: Johnson, "Barbadian"; Greenfield, "Barbadians"; Thomas-Hope, "The Establishment"; Roberts, "Emigration"; and Newton, *The Silver Men*.

The argument about the change in Arana's labor system is made convincingly in Santos-Granero and Barclay, *Tamed*, pp. 48–49.

The events and ramifications of the 1907 bank panic are covered in Moen and Tallman, "The Bank Panic"; Jeanne, "Monetary Policy"; and Bruner, *The Panic*.

CHAPTER 4: SALDAÑA ROCCA'S WORLD

The description of Perkins meeting Arana on the Amazon is in a series of letters to the State Department held in NARA, RG59, M862, Roll 860 (file 13,889), and RG 59, 423.11P41. This source also includes the actual letter of the offer of sale. Perkins repeated the details in an affidavit he sent to the Anti-Slavery and Aborigines' Protection Society, which can be found in BLCASRH, Mss Brit. Emp., s.22, G338.

Hardenburg's dreams of seeing the Amazon are referred to in letters he wrote to his mother from Panama, Colombia, and Iquitos. They are in WHP.

The story about Miguel Galvez is taken from Collier, *The River*.

I have used the English version of Saldaña Rocca's indictment that is printed in BLCASRH, Mss Brit. Emp., s.22, G335. The Spanish original, which was printed in *La Sancion* in five installments in October 1907, was also reproduced in the book by Olarte Camacho, *Las crueldades*. The translation of Rocca's mission statement in the first issue of *La Sancion* is my own.

An almost full run of both *La Felpa* and *La Sancion* is in the Bodleian Library, University of Oxford. These were the issues that Walter Hardenburg brought with him from Iquitos. One issue of *La Felpa* and a few cartoons, all of which are missing from the Bodleian collection, can be found in AGN, Archivo diplomático y consular, Ministerio de relaciones exteriores, Sección República, Caja 600. When these collections are put together, they make a full and complete run of *La Felpa*.

The depositions Hardenburg collected in Iquitos are in BLCASRH, Mss Brit. Emp., s.22, G823. How he collected these depositions in Iquitos is explained in RSRSC.

CHAPTER 5: OVER TO THE FOREIGN OFFICE

I have used a number of sources for the history of the British and Foreign Anti-Slavery Society and the Aborigines' Protection Society. These include the following: Grant, *A Civilised*; Grant, "Christian"; Louis, "Roger Casement"; Porter, "Sir Roger Casement"; Swaisland, "The Aborigines"; and Nworah, "The Aborigines."

John Harris's recollection of first meeting Walter Hardenburg is in RSRSC.

The major source for the government's reactions and actions taken to the revelations in *Truth* is TNA, FO 371/722.

Charles Eberhardt's dispatches to the State Department are in NARA, RG59 Microfilm M862, Rolls 481, 736, 757, 775, and 1207. One of these, Roll 757, "Indians of Peru," was subsequently published with the same title by the Smithsonian Institution in *Smithsonian Miscellaneous Collections* 52 (1910): 181–94. The published version, however, omitted much of what Eberhardt had observed about the enslavement of the Indians. A good overview of the fear expressed in anthropology about the extinction of races is in Brantlinger, *Dark Vanishings*.

The report "General Conditions in the Putumayo River District of Peru" is in NARA, RG59 Microfilm M862, Roll 775.

CHAPTER 6: AN OFFICER AND A GENTLEMAN

For biographical information and Whiffen's military record, I have used Cadbury's "Imagining" and TNA, WO 374/73501.

Whiffen's report to Ambrose Pogson is in TNA, FO 369/198, and a subsequent dispatch to the French government, informing it of Whiffen's conclusions regarding Robuchon's disappearance, is in TNA, FO 146/4102.

Whiffen's own account of his search for Robuchon was published as Whiffen, *The North-West Amazons*.

The details of Eugène Robuchon's life and his two trips to the Putumayo, most of which have never been made public, are taken from material in AR; BN, ASG/colis 11bis; and BN, ASG/colis 37bis. Robuchon's copy of the journal he compiled during his first trip to the Putumayo is in BM, ETH/Doc 1347. A copy of a fragment of his second journal is in AGN, Archivo diplomático y consular, Ministerio de relaciones exteriores, Sección República, año 1911, Caja 743, carpeta 331, fol. 91–103 (I thank Juan Alvaro Echeverri for this reference).

Robuchon's artifacts make up a substantial part of the British Museum's Upper Amazon collection. Correspondence about this collection can be found in BM, Keeper's Letters, 1904 and 1905. Details about Jules Robuchon's photography, and therefore the background to Eugène Robuchon's own education in this field, can be found in Ribemont, *Jules Robuchon*.

The instructions for Robuchon's ill-fated final trip to the Putumayo are in the contract published in Robuchon, *En el Putumayo*, pp. xi–xiii.

Arana's letters to Hortensia and the photograph showing an Indian being flogged are in AR. Hardenburg's comment on the rumors surrounding Robuchon's death is in Hardenburg, *The Putumayo*, p. 218, while Hispano's is in Hispano, *De París*, pp. 272–73.

Whiffen's report to the Foreign Office is in TNA, FO 371/722.

James Bryce's communication with the Foreign Office is to be found in TNA, FO 115/1548.

CHAPTER 7: OUR MAN IN THE PUTUMAYO

This chapter is based, for the most part, on documents in the following sources: TNA, FO 371/277, FO 371/967, FO 371/968, FO 115/1548; and BLCASRH, Mss Brit. Emp., s.22, G342.

For the background to U.S. policy toward Latin America, I have found the following sources most helpful: Veeser, "Inventing"; Gilderhus, "The Monroe"; Ricard, "The Roosevelt"; Scholes and Scholes, "The United States"; Healy, *Drive*; and Gilderhus, *The Second Century*.

Sir Edward Grey's comment on the United States in Latin America comes from Salisbury, "Great Britain," pp. 393–94.

Both the Foreign Office and the Colonial Office had files dating back to 1905 about the ill-treatment of Barbadians. It came about that in June 1905, two Barbadian women, Helen Sealy and Rebecca Harvey, wrote to the governor of Barbados, Sir Gilbert Carter, in Bridgetown, about their respective sons, Stanley Sealy and Samuel Harvey. The two mothers had not heard from their sons since they had left the island for Peru earlier that year but had heard from a returning Barbadian that conditions there were dangerous. The two mothers feared the worst: that Stanley, age nineteen, and Samuel, age twenty, were dead. Carter got in touch with Cazes in Iquitos, and he informed the Colonial Office that the source of the Barbadians' problems in the Putumayo was an employee of Arana's called Ramon Sanchez. Cazes took the matter up with Arana, who, Cazes reported, not only listened to the complaints but promptly dismissed Sanchez. These files are in TNA, CO 28/264, CO 28/265, FO 177/326, FO 177/330, FO 177/327, and FO 177/331.

The Ecuador-Peru border dispute is discussed in detail in Zook, "The Spanish Arbitration," and Wood, *Aggression*.

Arana's letter to Cazes of July 25, 1910, is in TNA, FO 371/968.

CHAPTER 8: EYES OF ANOTHER RACE

Casement's letter to Edward Clarke is in Reid, *The Lives*, p. 72.

The direct quotes in the chapter are from the following sources: Morel's description of meeting Casement for the first time is in Louis and Stengers, *E. D. Morel's*, pp. 158–62; Stephen Gwynn's description of Casement is in Gwynn, *Experiences*, p. 260; Herbert Ward also made a point of commenting on Casement's voice— Ward, *A Voice*, p. 237; his voice resembling a purr comes from Hambloch, *British Consul*, p. 71.

Casement's correspondence with Foreign Office personnel while he was working in Pará is in TNA, FO 128/324 and FO 169/123. His correspondence with Morel from Rio de Janeiro is in BLPES, Morel Papers, F8/23. Other correspondence with Morel used in this chapter is in BLPES, Morel Papers, F8/24.

Material for the section of the chapter dealing with the selection of Casement as the Foreign Office investigator in the Putumayo comes from the following sources: TNA, FO 371/967; BLCASRH, Mss Brit. Emp., s.19, D3/1; BLCASRH, Mss Brit. Emp., s.22, G322; and Dudgeon, *Roger Casement*.

Casement's meeting with Arana on the *Clement* is reconstructed from a letter Casement wrote on board RMS *Anselm* (for which I have to thank Brendan Callaghan for a copy); LRO, BOO3/10; NLI, Collection List 103 (Casement to Francis Cowper, March 18, 1908); *A Provincia do Pará*, issue of February 22, 1908; and RSRSC, Question 399.

Casement's dispatch about the Peruvian assault on Colombian properties in the Putumayo is in TNA, FO 128/324. His recollection about Williamson visiting him in the Pará consulate is in RSRSC, Question 399.

I have reconstructed the voyage to Iquitos through the use of the following sources: Sawyer, *Roger Casement's Diaries*; Sawyer, *Casement*; Reid, *The Lives*; Mitchell, *Casement*; and especially Mitchell, *The Amazon Journal*.

Carlos Rey de Castro edited and translated Robuchon's journal of his first trip to the Putumayo for publication. Although Arana later stated that the publication was also available in a French and an English translation, there is no record that these were ever published. There was a copy of Robuchon's journal in the offices of the Peruvian Amazon Company in London, but this copy seems to have disappeared. However, Robuchon did send a copy of this journal to the keeper of the British Museum, Charles Read, in 1905 in the hope that he might find a publisher for it. Unfortunately, Read didn't think it was worthy of publication, but he kept the copy. It can be found in the British Museum as BM, ETH/Doc 1347.

Casement kept notes of his conversation with Grey during their private meeting on July 13. These are in NLI, MS 13,080 (6/iii).

The quotation from Casement's letter to Gertrude Bannister at the start of the chapter is from Reid, *The Lives*, p. 75.

Casement's letter to Alice Stopford Green is in NLI, MS 10,464 (3).

CHAPTER 9: THE UTTERMOST PARTS OF THE EARTH

This chapter draws on a wide range of archival material. The sources are TNA, HO 161/3, FO 177/356, FO 371/968, and FO 371/1200; NLI, MS 13,087 (8).

The manuscript of Roger Casement's Putumayo journal, covering the period from September 23 to December 6, 1910, is in NLI, MS 13,087, but I have used the superbly annotated version in Mitchell, *The Amazon Journal*. In addition to the journal itself, Mitchell's documentation takes the reader from August 2, 1909, when Casement was on his way to Pará, until January 7, 1911, a few days after he returned to London.

The quotation about India rubber comes from Mitchell, *The Amazon Journal*, p. 85.

The Barbadian statements are printed in CBCSP. Casement's drafts and notes from the interviews he conducted are in NLI, MS 13,087 (27); and TNA, FO 371/1200.

CHAPTER 10: LA CHORRERA

Casement recorded his experiences of this trip to the Putumayo region in a number of places. His personal papers, which are in the National Library of Ireland, in Dublin, contain two significant collections: a scattered bunch of notes and parts of more sustained writings, and the journal covering the period from his arrival in La Chorrera on September 23, 1910, until his departure from Iquitos on December 6, 1910. This journal exists in two manuscript versions, one handwritten and the other typed. They are not identical in the sense that the typed version takes certain liberties with the handwritten version. The journal has been published in two forms: an abridged version, published by Roger Sawyer, as one part of the book *Roger Casement's Diaries*; and Angus Mitchell's, *The Amazon Journal*, an accurate and total transliteration, annotated expertly. Casement also wrote down his daily activities in two other places: the so-called Black Diaries, which are in TNA, HO 161/3-5 (and have been published in various forms—see Singleton-Gates and Girodias, *The Black Diaries*; Dudgeon, *Roger Casement*; and Sawyer, *Roger Casement's Diaries*); and a green notebook, which is frequently referred to by Casement himself but has, unfortunately, not yet surfaced.

This chapter draws on all this manuscript material, namely: NLI, MS 13,087; and TNA, HO 161/3; plus TNA, FO 371/968, FO 371/1200; BLCASRH, Mss Brit. Emp., s.19, D3/1; Mitchell, *The Amazon Journal*; and CBCSP. This latter official publication contains all the Barbadian depositions. The originals are in NLI, and copies of them are in TNA.

NOTES ON SOURCES

CHAPTER 11: GODFORSAKEN HELL-HAUNTED WILDS

This chapter draws on much of the same material as the previous chapter, namely: NLI, MS 13,087; and TNA, HO 161/3, plus FO 177/286, FO 371/968, and FO 371/1200. All quotes from Casement's journal are taken from Mitchell, *The Amazon Journal*.

A copy of Enrique Deschamps's letter and José Cavero's response, both of which were printed in *El Comercio*, can be found in TNA, FO 371/968.

Casement's admission that he went well beyond his instructions is contained in a letter to Charles Roberts MP, which can be found in BLCASRH, Mss Brit. Emp., s.22, G344c. The letter from Arana to Cazes can be found in TNA, FO 371/968 (in English and Spanish), and a printed copy (in English) is in BLCASRH, Mss Brit. Emp., s.22, G335.

CHAPTER 12: A SYSTEM OF ARMED EXTORTION

This chapter draws on material from the following sources: NLI, MS 13,087; TNA, FO 371/1200; and BLCASRH, Mss Brit. Emp., s.22, G335.

Many of the documents have been transcribed, annotated, and published in Mitchell, *Sir Roger Casement's*.

Arana's letters to Casement are in BLCASRH, Mss Brit. Emp., s.22, G344a.

CHAPTER 13: DEUS EX MACHINA

This chapter draws on material from the following sources: NLI, MS 13,087 (for letters to Roger Casement from the Peruvian Amazon Company Commission members); TNA, FO 371/1200, 1201, and 1202 (for all Foreign Office correspondence, including internal memos, and the final report of the commission as it was delivered to the board of the company); and BLCASRH, Mss Brit. Emp., s.22, G344a and G335 (for the minutes of the meetings of the Peruvian Amazon Company and for Roger Casement's notes during the time he was present).

Many of the documents, with the exception of the internal Foreign Office memos, have been transcribed, annotated, and published in Mitchell, *Sir Roger Casement's*.

The letter from Walter Fox to the director of the Royal Botanic Gardens is in RBG, DC217, dated November 13, 1910. It is also printed in Schultes, "Lacticiferous."

Details on the financial situation of the Peruvian Amazon Company are drawn from RSRSC.

The newspaper interview with Arédomi and Omarino took place in William Rothenstein's London studio. It is discussed in correspondence between Casement and Rothenstein. Casement's letters to Rothenstein are in HLHU, BMS ENG 1148(234). Rothenstein's letters to Casement are in NLI, MS 13,073 (37).

CHAPTER 14: THE VEIL OVER THE PUTUMAYO MYSTERY

The following sources have provided the material for this chapter: NLI, MS 13,073, MS 13,087, and MS 17,443; TNA, CO 28/279, FO 128/361, FO 369/400, FO 371/1200, 1201, 1202, 1203, 1450, and FO 369/400, HO 161/4, and HO 161/5; *New York Times* November 12, 1948, p. 7; and BLCASRH, Mss Brit. Emp., s.22, G334a, G344c, and G335.

Many of the documents in the sources above, especially letters written to and from Casement, have been transcribed, annotated, and published in Mitchell, *Sir Roger Casement's*.

Casement's letters to Rothenstein are in HLHU, BMS ENG 1148(234). Rothenstein's letters to Casement are in NLI, MS 13,073 (37).

Herbert Dickey's recollections of his time with Casement appear in Dickey, *The Misadventures*, in NLI, MS 17,443; NYPL; and MCIHP, 7IHP-116.

Judge Valcárcel's version of events is in Valcárcel, *El proceso*. A copy of Rómulo Paredes's typewritten version (1,350 pages) of the handwritten 3,000-page dossier of depositions and evidence he collected while visiting the rubber stations of the Peruvian Amazon Company is in AHL, LEK 13-11. A copy of the full report that Casement read in Iquitos is in AHL, LEK 13-13.

A copy of Paredes's report was forwarded to the Foreign Office in late March 1912. It was the same report that Casement had read, except that one section, Chapter 3, had been omitted. The Foreign Office copy is in TNA, FO 177/373. Another copy was sent to the State Department in Washington, again without Chapter 3. It is in NARA, Central Decimal File 823.5048. It was translated into English and was published in SP, pp. 144–72.

On August 16, 1912, *El Diario*, a Lima newspaper, published an interview with Paredes in which he amplified on a number of points in his report (there is a copy of the article in TNA, FO 371/1453). It, too, was translated into English and published in SP, pp. 187–99. The manuscript original is in AHL, LEK 13-12.

Paredes's interview and his full report (including chapter 3) are being republished by CAAAP (Centro Amazónico de Antropología y Aplicacíon Práctica), Lima, Peru, and edited by Alberto Chirif.

CHAPTER 15: PUBLISH AND BE DAMNED

This chapter draws on material from the following sources: NLI, MS 13,073 and 13,087; TNA, FO 115/1642 and 1698, FO 128/361, FO 371/1450, 1451, and 1452; NARA, M973, roll 176, and Central Decimal Files, 823.5048; BodL, MSS. Bryce, 48; BLCASRH, Mss Brit. Emp., s.19, D2/3, D4/1, Mss Brit. Emp., s.22, G334a and G335; ACH, 5-17, Año 1912; and PD. Also of value were Karno, "Julio César Arana," and Karno, "Augusto B. Leguía."

The quotation from George Young is taken from Fisher, *James Bryce*, vol. 2, p. 24.

The final quotation comes from a letter Casement wrote to his cousin, Gertrude Bannister, on July 25, 1912, and is kept in NLI, MS 13,074.

Paredes paraded his pro-Peruvian, anti-British sentiments in an interview that was published on July 26, 1912, in the *New York Herald*. He repeated these views in a longer piece in September, published in the magazine *American Review of Reviews*. (See bibliography under Paredes, "Peruvian.")

Further information about the papal encyclical can be found in Turvasi, *Giovanni*, and García Jordán, "En el corazón."

CHAPTER 16: AN INTERNATIONAL SCANDAL

This chapter draws on material in the following sources: NLI, MS 13,073 and 13,087; TNA, FO 115/1642 and 1698, FO 128/361, FO 371/1450, 1451, and 1452; NARA, M973, roll 176, and Central Decimal Files, 823.5048; BodL, MSS. Bryce, 48; BLCASRH, Mss Brit. Emp., s.19, D2/3, D4/1, Mss Brit. Emp., s.22, G334a and G335; ACH, 5-17, Año 1912; and PD.

The Blue Book was published as CBCSP.

Casement's report to Grey dated November 24, 1911, is in TNA, FO 128/361.

CHAPTER 17: THE OLD GANG

This chapter draws on material from the following sources: NLI, MS 13,073, 13,081, and 13,087; TNA, CO 28/278 and 279, FO 115/1642 and 1698, FO 128/361, FO 371/1452, 1453, 1454, and 1455, and FO 371/1732; NARA, M973, roll 176, and Central Decimal Files, 823.5048; BLCASRH, Mss Brit. Emp., s.22, G334a, G344b, G344c, and G335; ACH, 5-17, Año 1912. Also of use were Stanfield, *Red Rubber*; Martínez Riaza, "Política regional"; and Quiroz, "Redes."

Consul Stuart Fuller's unpublished report is in NARA, Central Decimal Files, 823.5048, and was published in SP (pp. 9–70). Consul George Michell's unpublished report is in TNA, FO 369/495, and was published in BPP, 1913 [Cd.6678] li. 791.

Casement translated Alarco's interview in *El Comercio* for the Foreign Office; Charles des Graz, the British chargé d'affaires in Lima, translated the article in *La Prensa* referring to Saldaña Rocca and to Robuchon; and George Michell translated the newspaper article that reported the banquet in Iquitos.

CHAPTER 18: THE CANON AND THE BOARD

I have used the respective issues of the *Manchester Guardian* and *The Times* to tell the story of Henson and the directors of the Peruvian Amazon Company. Henson recounted the event in his memoirs, *Retrospect*. For biographical information about Henson, I have relied on Chadwick, *Hensley Henson*. The original letters to and from Henson are in BLCASRH, Mss Brit. Emp., s.19, D4/2a.

NOTES ON SOURCES

This chapter draws on material in TNA, FO 371/1452 and 1454, and in PD.

The cabinet minute authorizing the appointment of a select committee to inquire into the connection between the Peruvian Amazon Company and the Putumayo atrocities is in TNA, CAB 41/33. The description of Roberts was published in the April 9, 1913, issue of *Truth*.

CHAPTER 19: *LA SELVA* RETURNS TO PARLIAMENT

This chapter draws on background material in TNA, FO 371/1452 and 1454.

The correspondence between Roberts and Casement is in two places. The National Library of Ireland has one set, which includes letters both ways—NLI, MS 13,073/36(i-iii). The other set, which includes letters from Casement to Roberts only, is in BLCASRH, Mss Brit. Emp., s.22, G344c.

More on Casement's health problems during the hearings of the select committee can be found in Ó Síocháin, *Roger Casement*, pp. 346–48.

The verbatim proceedings of the select committee are to be found in RSRSC.

I have also used respective issues of the *Manchester Guardian* and *The Times*.

CHAPTER 20: THE PERUVIAN, THE AMERICAN, AND THE SELECT COMMITTEE

This chapter draws on material that can be found in TNA, FO 177/286, FO 371/1454, 1455, 1732, and 1733, FO 128/373, J13/6373; BLCASRH, Mss Brit. Emp., s.22, G344c; RSRSC; NARA, Central Decimal Files, 823.5048; and *The Anti-Slavery Reporter* (1914).

My discussion of the winding-up of the Peruvian Amazon Company is based on material in BLCASRH, Mss Brit. Emp., s.22, G322 and G345. These files also contain correspondence with Roberts. Buxton's and Harris's correspondence with Hardenburg leading to his arrival in Liverpool can be found in BLCASRH, Mss Brit. Emp., s.19, D1/12, D2/4, and D3/8 and in Mss Brit. Emp., s.22, G343. Perkins's affidavit is in BLCASRH, Mss Brit. Emp., s.22, G338, and Hardenburg's letter to Bennett at the offices of *Truth* is in BLCASRH, Mss Brit. Emp., s.22, G323.

The proceedings of the select committee are to be found in RSRSC.

John Harris's review of Hardenburg's book appeared in the *Manchester Guardian*, December 11, 1912.

I have also used respective issues of the newspapers and periodicals mentioned in the text. There is a scrapbook containing some of the principal articles in BLCASRH, Mss Brit. Emp., s.22, J28.

For information on the continuing struggle against slavery and its historical background in the twentieth century, I have relied on the following sources: Miers, *Slavery*; Bales, *Ending*; Bales, *New*; and Bales, *Understanding*.

The question of directorial responsibility at the Nuremberg trials after the Second World War is taken up in Ramasastry, "Corporate Complicity," while McCartney and Arnold's "A Vast Aggregate" looks at an earlier case.

CHAPTER 21: THE DEVIL AND MR. CASEMENT

The original and the English translation of Arana's open letter from Manaus are in TNA, FO 177/386. The pamphlets he referred to are listed in the bibliography under the appropriate author's name—Arana, Larrabure y Correa, and Zumaeta.

The publications concerning the Putumayo mentioned in the chapter can be found in the bibliography using the authors' surname.

The story about Santos is told in Vale da Costa, *Eldorado*; Vale da Costa and Lobo, *No rastro*; and Souza, *Silvino Santos*. The nature of French cinematography, especially the dominant role of Pathé, is told in Abel, *The Ciné*, and Abel, *The Red Rooster*. Santos had better luck with his next Amazonian film, *Huitoto Indians of the Putumayo River*, once again financed by Arana and shown, for the first time, in Manaus in June 1916. Santos's reputation as a filmmaker, particularly on ethnographic subjects, led him to be invited in 1924 to accompany the American explorer Alexander Hamilton Rice and the German anthropologist Theodor Koch-Grünberg to the region near the frontier of Brazil and Venezuela. This story is covered in Martins, "Illusions."

Information about Casement's life after the Putumayo until his execution, as well as the Irish political context, come from the following: Mitchell, "An Irish"; Mitchell, "John Bull's"; Mitchell, *Casement*; Townshend, *Easter 1916*; Ó Síocháin, *Roger Casement*; Bowman, *Carson's*; Doerries, *Prelude*; Doerries, "Hopeless"; Roth, "The German"; and Clayton, *Aud*.

In recent years the National Archives in Kew have released new documents concerning Casement's years in Germany and the time between his arrest and execution. These can be found in TNA, HO 144/1636, HO 144/1637, and KV 2/6–10.

The diaries in question are referred to in the notes accompanying Chapter 10 of this book.

Readers interested in pursuing the controversies surrounding Casement's afterlife will find the following sources helpful: Daly, *Roger Casement*; McCormack, *Roger Casement*; McDiarmid, *The Irish*; Ó Síocháin, *Roger Casement*; and Grant, "Bones."

Correspondence between Arthur Conan Doyle and Clement Shorter, the journalist and magazine editor, concerning the attempt to get Casement reprieved, together with the signed petitions, are in BL, Add. 63596. George Bernard Shaw's papers relating to Casement are in BL, Add. 50678.

W.E.B. Du Bois's obituary of Casement appeared in the September 1916 issue of *The Crisis*, pp. 215–16.

The phrase "crime/crimes against humanity" is widely used today, but it is probably just over a century old. One of the first, if not the first use of it can be traced back to a letter George Washington Williams, a black American journalist, wrote to James Blaine, the U.S. secretary of state, on September 15, 1890, concerning what he had seen in the Congo. The key sentence in Williams's letter is as follows: "The State of Congo is in no sense deserving of your confidence or support. It is actively engaged in the slave trade and is guilty of many crimes against humanity." This letter is reproduced in Bontinck, *Aux Origines*, pp. 448–49. Another, and later, appearance of the phrase was on May 24, 1915, in a joint communiqué from Britain, France, and Russia, charging the Ottoman Empire with a "crime against humanity" in its treatment of the Armenian people.

That Casement should have used the same phrase between, at one end, a comment on the Congo and, at the other, a state-sponsored genocide is telling. Casement spoke of a "crime against humanity" in his journal on October 5, 1910, while in the Putumayo—NLI, MS 13,087. It can also be found in Mitchell, *The Amazon Journal*, p. 178. By this phrase he meant precisely how it has come to be defined: the systematic practice of inhumane acts—murder, enslavement, extermination, torture, and so on—committed against any civilian population.

There is a large literature examining genocides and other crimes against humanity. I have found the following sources useful for thinking about this problem: Palmer, "Colonial"; Stone, "The Historiography"; Dadrian, "Patterns"; and Bartov, "Defining."

A copy of Arana's telegram to Casement as well as the letter from George Lepper to Sir Edward Grey are in TNA, FO 371/2798.

I have drawn on the following sources for Arana's life after he returned to Peru in 1913: Stanfield, *Red Rubber*; De la Flor Fernández, "La economía"; Karno, "Julio César Arana"; Bákula, *La política*; Lagos, *Arana*; Ireland, *Boundaries*; García Jordán, "En el corazón"; and Arana, *American*.

Arana's attack on the legitimacy of the Salomón-Lozano Treaty was published as Arana, *El protocolo*.

EPILOGUE: A CRIME AGAINST HUMANITY

Ernest Rennie's dispatch, dated May 8, 1916, is in TNA, FO 371/2739.

Leo Sambrook's and Felix Ryan's reports are in TNA, FO 371/2990. An account of the first year of the mission can be found in Gridilla, *Un año*. The uprising may be the same as the one that is known in local oral culture as the Yarocamena Rebellion, though no one has been able to establish from the stories told about it precisely when it took place. However, the fact that the Yarocamena uprising began at Atenas suggests that it might be the same as the one reported by Sambrook. For the oral tradition of the uprising, see Yepez and Pineda Camacho, "La rabia."

The deportation of Indians to the Peruvian side of the Putumayo is told in San Román, *Perfiles*, and also in Pineda Camacho, *Holocausto*. Population figures for 1940 are from Steward, "The Witotoan," pp. 750–51. Recent estimates are from www .ethnologue.com. Forced labor is still a problem in Amazonia. See the pamphlet Sharma, *Contemporary*, for further information. A chilling reminder that debt peonage enforced by the rifle has not disappeared from Amazonia can be found in an article published in *The Guardian*, January 3, 2009, p. 25.

Rubber output figures come from Barker, *Rubber*. The story about the domestication of *Hevea brasiliensis* has been told in many places. The best account is Dean, *Brazil*. There is also a biography of Henry Wickham, the man who smuggled the seeds out of Brazil, which also tells the story—Jackson, *The Thief*.

NOTES ON SOURCES

Information about oil exploration and exploitation in the Upper Amazon is from Hvalkof, "Outrage." Other information can be found on websites, two examples of which are: www.sacbee.com/static/live/news/projects/denial/c1_1.html and www.texacotoxico.org/eng/node/1. The legal case against Chevron is the subject of a recent documentary, *Crude* (U.S.A., 2009), directed by Joe Berlinger.

NOTES ON ILLUSTRATIONS

As I mention in the final chapter of this book, toward the end of the Putumayo story as I have recounted it, a war of words and images broke out on both sides of the Atlantic. While we now take the use of images in cases of atrocities for granted, at the time of the Putumayo story, this was a novel practice. Thus we see Walter Hardenburg using a photograph of chained Indians to make his point, while Carlos Rey de Castro uses the photograph of a Europeanized, domesticated Indian to make his. Both of these photographs are reproduced in the book's inset of illustrations.

When images were first used in this way is not clear, but the practice most likely originated in the Congo atrocity, where the photographs of mutilations were used to great effect by the Congo Reform Association in public lectures throughout Britain in the early years of the twentieth century. Kevin Grant in *A Civilised Savagery* and Sharon Sliwinski in "The Childhood of Human Rights" cover the use of photographs in publicizing the Congo atrocity.

The photographic record of the Putumayo atrocities is extensive. It began in 1903 with Eugène Robuchon and ended in 1916 with Silvino Santos. In the intervening years, Henry Gielgud, Thomas Whiffen, Roger Casement, and Stuart Fuller contributed substantially to the record. There is no doubt that what has survived from those years is but a fraction of the total number of photographs taken. In addition, and for the most part, only a very small number have been published.

I list below the major collections of Putumayo photographs known to me:

NOTES ON ILLUSTRATIONS

Eugène Robuchon: photographs at the Bibliothèque Nationale, Paris, but the bulk are in private hands in France.

Henry Gielgud: photographs in the World Museum Liverpool.

Thomas Whiffen: photographs in the Museum of Archaeology and Anthropology at the University of Cambridge. Copies of many of the images are widely scattered. There is one collection at the Royal Anthropological Society in London, another at the Bibliothèque Nationale in Paris, and a third at the Philipps-Universität Marburg.

Roger Casement: photographs at the National Photographic Archive, Dublin. Copies of many of these are in the National Archives and Record Administration, College Park, Maryland.

Stuart Fuller: photographs at the National Archives and Record Administration, College Park, Maryland.

Silvino Santos: photographs in the Museu Amazônico, Manaus, Brazil, and in private collections in Brazil.

There is also a small set of postcards, many of them made from Robuchon's photographs, in the Pitt Rivers Museum, University of Oxford.

The best account of the Putumayo photographs is given in Maria del Rosario Flores Paz, "The Visual Making."

BIBLIOGRAPHY

This bibliography contains full citations for all the published material referred to in the notes on chapters. Additionally, I include here published material I found particularly useful in working through the book's main themes.

Abel, Richard. *The Ciné Goes to Town: French Cinema, 1896–1914*. Berkeley: University of California Press, 1998.
_____. *The Red Rooster Scare: Making Cinema American, 1900–1910*. Berkeley: University of California Press, 1999.
Alvaro Echeverri, Juan. "The Colombo-Peruvian Border Conflict of 1932–1933 and the Magic of Nation and Border Common Sense." Unpublished paper, 2007.
_____. "La suerte de Robuchon." Unpublished paper, 2007.
Alzate Angel, Beatriz. *Viajeros y cronistas en la Amazonia colombiana: catálogo colectivo*. Bogotá: Corporación Araracuara, 1987.
Ans, André-Marcel d'. *L'Amazonie péruvienne: anthropolgie écologique, ethno-histoire, perspectives contemporaines*. Paris: Payot, 1982.
Anstey, Roger. "The Congo Rubber Atrocities—A Case Study." *African Historical Studies* 4 (1971): 59–76.
Arana, Julio C. *Las cuestiones del Putumayo*. Barcelona: Imp. Vinda de L. Tasso, 1913.
_____. *El protocolo Salomón-Lozano, o el pacto de límites con Colombia: al Congreso Nacional*. Lima: La Tradición, 1927.
Arana, Marie. *American Chica: Two Worlds, One Childhood*. New York: Random House, 2001.

Bákula, Juan Miguel. *La política internacional entre el Perú y Colombia*. Bogotá: Editorial Temis, 1988.

Bales, Kevin. *Ending Slavery: How We Free Today's Slaves*. Berkeley: University of California Press, 2007.

_____. *New Slavery*. Oxford, UK: ABC-CLIO, 2001.

_____. *Understanding Global Slavery: A Reader*. Berkeley: University of California Press, 2005.

Barclay Rey de Castro, Frederica. "Olvido de una historia: reflexiones acerca de la historiografía andino-amazónica." *Revista de Indias* 61 (2001): 493–511.

Bardou, Jean-Pierre, Jean-Jacques Chanaron, Patrick Fridenson, and James M. Laux. *The Automobile Revolution: The Impact of an Industry*. Chapel Hill: University of North Carlionia Press, 1982.

Barham, Bradford L., and Oliver T. Coomes. "Wild Rubber: Industrial Organisation and the Microeconomics of Extraction During the Amazon Rubber Boom (1860–1920)." *Journal of Latin American Studies* 26 (1994): 37–72.

Barker, Preston W. *Rubber Statistics, 1900–1937*. Washington, D.C.: GPO, 1938.

Bartov, Omer. "Defining Enemies, Making Victims: Germans, Jews, and the Holocaust." *American Historical Review* 103 (1998): 771–86.

Blanchard, Peter. "The Recruitment of Workers in the Peruvian Sierra at the Turn of the Century: The Enganche System." *Inter-American Economic Affairs* 33 (1979): 63–85.

Block, David. *Mission Culture on the Upper Amazon: Native Tradition, Jesuit Enterprise, & Secular Policy in Moxos, 1660–1880*. Lincoln: University of Nebraska Press, 1994.

Bonilla, Heraclio. "El caucho y la economía del oriente peruano." *Historia y Cultura* 8 (1974): 69–80.

_____. "Estructura y eslabonamientos de la explotación cauchera en Colombia, Perú, Bolivia y Brasil." *DATA: Revista del Instituto de Estudios Andinos y Amazónicos* 4 (1993): 9–22.

Bonilla, Victor Daniel. *Servants of God or Masters of Men? The Story of a Capuchin Mission in Amazonia*. Harmondsworth, UK: Penguin, 1972.

Bontinck, François. *Aux Origines de l'État Indépendent du Congo*. Louvain, Belgium: Nauwelaerter, 1966.

Bowman, Timothy. *Carson's Army: The Ulster Volunteer Force, 1910–22*. Manchester, UK: Manchester University Press, 2007.

Brantlinger, Patrick. *Dark Vanishings: Discourse on the Extinction of Primitive Races, 1800–1930*. Ithaca: Cornell University Press, 2003.

Bruner, Robert F. *The Panic of 1907: Lessons Learned from the Market's Perfect Storm*. Hoboken: Wiley, 2007.

Burns, E. Bradford. "Manaus 1910: Portrait of a Boom Town." *Journal of Inter-American Studies* 7 (1965): 400–21.

Burroughs, Robert M. "Britain's Travelling Eyewitnesses: Narratives of the New Slaveries, 1884–1916." Ph.D. thesis, Nottingham Trent University, UK, 2006.

Cadbury, Tabitha. "Imagining the Amazon: The Whiffen Collection at Cambridge." *Journal of Museum Ethnography* 16 (2004): 85–100.

Carey, James C. *Peru and the United States, 1900–1962*. Notre Dame: University of Notre Dame Press, 1964.

Casa Aguilar, Justo. *Evangelio y colonización: una aproximación a la historia del Putumayo desde la época prehispánica a la colonización agropecuaria*. Bogotá: ECOE Ediciones, 1999.

Casement, Roger. "The Putumayo Indians." *Contemporary Review* 102 (1912): 317–28.

Chadwick, Owen. *Hensley Henson: A Study in the Friction Between Church and State*. Oxford, UK: Clarendon Press, 1983.

Chirif, Alberto, ed. *La defensa de los caucheros*. Iquitos: CETA, 2005.

_____. "Introducción." In Alberto Chirif, ed. *Carlos A. Valcárcel: El proceso del Putumayo y sus secretos ineditos*. Iquitos: CETA, 2004. Pp. 15–77.

_____. "Presentación." In Alberto Chirif, ed. *La defensa de los caucheros*. Iquitos: CETA, 2005. Pp. 51–72.

Clayton, Lawrence A. *Peru and the United States: The Condor and the Eagle*. Athens: University of Georgia Press, 1999.

Clayton, Xander. *Aud*. Privately published, 2007.

Cline, Catherine Ann. "E. D. Morel and the Crusade Against the Foreign Office." *Journal of Modern History* 3 (1968): 126–37.

_____. *E. D. Morel, 1873–1924: The Strategies of Protest*. Belfast: Blackstaff, 1980.

Collier, Richard. *The River That God Forgot*. London: Collins, 1968.

Corp, Edward T. "Sir William Tyrrell: The *Éminence Grise* of the British Foreign Office." *Historical Journal* 25 (1982): 697–708.

Dadrian, Vahakn. "Patterns of Twentieth Century Genocides: The Armenian, Jewish, and Rwandan Cases." *Journal of Genocidal Research* 6 (2004): 487–522.

Daly, Mary E., ed. *Roger Casement in Irish and World History*. Dublin: Royal Irish Academy, 2005.

Davies, Thomas M. *Indian Integration in Peru: A Half Century of Experience, 1900–1948*. Lincoln: University of Nebraska Press, 1974.

Davis, Wade. *One River: Explorations and Discoveries in the Amazon Rain Forest*. New York: Simon and Schuster, 1996.

Dean, Warren. *Brazil and the Struggle for Rubber: A Study in Environmental History*. Cambridge, UK: Cambridge University Press, 1987.

Deas, Malcolm. *Del poder y la gramática*. Bogotá: Tercer Mundo Editores, 1993.

De la Flor Fernández, Alejandro Juan. "La economía de exportación en la Amazonía peruana (1898–1930): el caso de las gomas." Thesis, Pontificia Universidad Católica del Perú, Lima, 1989.

De La Pedraja, René. *Wars of Latin America, 1899–1941*. London: McFarland and Co., 2006.

De Osa, Verónica. *The Troubled Waters of the Amazon: The Plight of the Colombian Indians in Amazonia*. London: Hale, 1990.

Dickey, Herbert Spencer. *The Misadventures of a Tropical Medico*. London: John Lane and the Bodley Head, 1929.

Doerries, Reinhard R. "Hopeless Mission: Sir Roger Casement in Imperial Germany." *Journal of Intelligence History* 6 (2006): 25–39.

_____. *Prelude to the Easter Rising: Sir Roger Casement in Imperial Germany*. London: Cass, 2000.

Domínguez, Camilo, and Augusto Gómez. *La economía extractiva en la Amazonia colombiana, 1850–1930*. Bogotá: Tropenbos, 1990.

Dore, Elizabeth. "Debt Peonage in Granada, Nicaragua, 1870–1930: Labor in a Non-capitalist Transition." *Hispanic American Historical Review* 83 (2003): 521–59.

Drabble, John H. *Rubber in Malaya, 1876–1922: The Genesis of an Industry*. Kuala Lumpur: Oxford University Press, 1973.

Drinot, Paulo. "Peru, 1884–1930: A Beggar Sitting on a Bench of Gold?" In Enrique Cárdenas, José Antonio Ocampo, and Rosemary Thorp, eds. *An Economic History of Twentieth-Century Latin America, Volume 1*. Basingstoke, UK: Palgrave, 2000. Pp. 152–87.

Dudgeon, Jeffrey. *Roger Casement: The Black Diaries*. Belfast: Belfast Press, 2002.

Fifer, J. Valerie. "The Empire Builders: A History of the Bolivian Rubber Boom and the Rise of the House of Suarez." *Journal of Latin American Studies* 2 (1970): 113–46.

Fisher, H.A.L. *James Bryce*. London: Macmillan, 1927.

Flores Paz, Maria del Rosario. "The Visual Making of a Regional Society: Photography and Amazonian History." Ph.D. thesis, Birkbeck College, University of London, 2008.

Foreman-Peck, James. "Multinational Companies and the International Transfer of Technology in the Motor Industry to 1939." In Lennart Jörberg and Nathan Rosenberg, eds. *Technical Change, Employment and Investment*. Lund: Department of Economic History, University of Lund, 1982. Pp. 95–110.

Franco, Roberto. *Los carijonas de Chiribiquete*. Bogotá: Fundación Puerto Rastrojo, 2002.

Frank, Zephyr, and Aldo Musacchio. "Brazil in the International Rubber Trade, 1870–1930." In Steven Topik, Carlos Marichal, and Zephyr Frank, eds. *From Silver to Cocaine: Latin American Commodity Chains and the Building of the World Economy, 1500–2000*. Durham, NC: Duke University Press, 2006. Pp. 271–99.

Furneaux, Robin. *The Amazon: The Story of a Great River*. London: Hamilton, 1969.

Gann, Lewis H. "The Berlin Conference and the Humanitarian Conscience." In Stig Förster, Wolfgang J. Mommsen, and Ronald Robinson, eds. *Bismarck, Europe, and Africa: The Berlin Africa Conference, 1884–1885 and the Onset of Partition*. Oxford, UK: Oxford University Press, 1988. Pp. 321–31.

García, P. Lorenzo. *Historia de las misiones en la Amazonía ecuatoriana*. Quito: Ediciones Abya-Yala, 1985.

García, Victor Manuel. "Colombian and Peruvian Rubber Industry: A Regional Approach to the Putumayo Scandal 1850–1925." M.A. thesis, University of Texas at Austin, 2000.

García Calderon, V. *The White Llama*. London: Golden Cockerel Press, 1938.

BIBLIOGRAPHY

García Jordán, Pilar, ed. *La construcción de la Amazonía andina, siglos XIX–XX: procesos de ocupación y transformación de la Amazonía peruana y ecuatoriana entre 1820 y 1960*. Quito: Ediciones Abya-Yala, 1995.

_____. "En el corazón de las tiembras . . . del Putumayo, 1890–1932: fronteras, caucho, mano de obra indígena y misiones católicas en la nacionalización de la Amazonía." *Revista de Indias* 61 (2001): 591–617.

_____, ed. *Fronteras, colonización y mano de obra indígena Amazonía andina (siglos XIX–XX): la construcción del espacio socio-económico amazónico en Ecuador, Perú y Bolivia (1792–1948)*. Lima: Pontificia Universidad Católica del Perú, Fondo Editorial, 1998.

_____. "El infierno verde. Caucho e indios, terror y muerte: reflexiones en torno al escándolo del Putumayo." *Anuario del IEHS* 8 (1993): 73–85.

Gasché, Jürg. "La ocupación territorial de los nativos Huitoto en el Perú y Colombia en los siglos 19 y 20." *Amazonía Indígena* 4/7 (1983): 2–19.

Gauld, Charles A. *The Last Titan, Percival Farquhar: American Entrepreneur in Latin America*. Palo Alto: Institute of Hispanic and American and Luso-Brazilian Studies, Stanford University, 1964.

Gilderhus, Mark. "The Monroe Doctrine: Meaning and Implications." *Presidential Studies Quarterly* 36 (2006): 5–16.

_____. *The Second Century: U.S.–Latin American Relations Since 1889*. Wilmington, DE: Scholarly Resources, 2000.

Gómez, Augusto. "Amazonía colombiana: formas de acceso y de control de la fuerza de trabajo indígena, 1870–1930." *DATA: Revista del Instituto de Estudios Andinos y Amazónicos* 4 (1993): 99–122.

Gómez, Augusto, Ana Christina Lesmes, and Claudia Rocha. *Caucherías y conflicto colombo-peruano: testimonios 1904–1934*. Bogotá: Disloque Editores, 1995.

Gómez Valderrama, Pedro. "Los infiernos de Jerarca Brown." *Revista de la Universidad de los Andes* 10 (1960): 3–27.

_____. *Los infiernos de Jerarca Brown y otros textos*. Bogotá: Fundación Simón y Lola Guberck, 1984.

Grant, Kevin. "Bones of Contention: The Repatriation of the Remains of Roger Casement." *Journal of British Studies* 41 (2002): 329–53.

_____. "Christian Critics of Empire: Missionaries, Lantern Lectures, and the Congo Reform Campaign in Britain." *Journal of Imperial and Commonwealth History* 29 (2001): 27–58.

_____. *A Civilised Savagery: Britain and the New Slaveries in Africa, 1884–1926*. London: Routledge, 2005.

Gray, Andrew. "Las atrocidades del Putumayo reexaminadas." In Alberto Chirif, ed. *La defensa de los caucheros*. Iquitos: CETA, 2005. Pp. 15–50. English original, "The Putumayo Atrocities Re-Examined." Unpublished paper, 1990.

Greenfield, Gerald M. *The Realities of Images: Imperial Brazil and the Great Drought*. Philadelphia: American Philosophical Society, 2001.

Greenfield, Sidney M. "Barbadians in the Brazilian Amazon." *Luso-Brazilian Review* 20 (1983): 44–64.

Gridilla, Alberto. *Un año en el Putumayo*. Lima, 1943.

Grohs, Waltraud. *Los indios del Alto Amazonas del siglo XVI al siglo XVIII: poblaciones y migraciones en la antigua provincia de Maynas*. Bonn: Seminar für Völkerkunde der Universität Bonn, 1974.

Guyot, Mireille. "Le récit d'O'ioi." In Robert Jaulin, ed. *De l'ethnocide*. Paris: Berger-Levrault, 1972. Pp. 137–57.

———. "El relato de O'ioi." *Amazonía Indígena* 3/6 (1983): 3–10.

———. "Le travail du caoutchouc chez les Indiens Bora et Miraña (Amazonie colombienne)." In Georges Balandier et al., eds. *L'Autre et l'ailleurs: hommages à Roger Bastide*. Paris: Berger-Levrault, 1976. Pp. 380–92.

Gwynn, Stephen. *Experiences of a Literary Man*. London: Thornton Butterworth, 1926.

Hambloch, Ernest. *British Consul: Memories of Thirty Years' Service in Europe and Brazil*. London: G. G. Harrap and Co., 1938.

Hampton, Mark. "Rethinking the 'New Journalism,' 1850s–1930s." *Journal of British Studies* 43 (2004): 278–90.

Hardenburg, Walter E. "Los Huitotos de la Chorrera en 1930." *Mirador Amazónico* 8 (1961): 38–40.

———. "The Indians of the Putumayo, Upper Amazon." *Man* 10 (1910): 134–38.

———. *The Putumayo: The Devil's Paradise*. London: T. Fisher Unwin, 1912.

———. "Story of the Putumayo Atrocities." *The New Review* (in seven consecutive installments, July–December 1913 and January 1914).

———. "Travel and Colonisation." *The Field* 114 (September 25, 1909): 550.

———. "The White Man's Burden." *The New Review* (May 1913): 495–501.

Haring, Rita. *Boomtown aan de Amazone: een Historisch-Sociologische Studie over de Peruaanse Amazoneregio en de Stad Iquitos, met Nadruk op de Periode 1880–1980*. Utrecht, Netherlands: Instituut voor Culturele Antropologie, Rijksuniversiteit Utrecht, 1986.

Harms, Robert. "The End of Red Rubber: A Reassessment." *Journal of African History* 16 (1975): 73–88.

Harris, John. *The Peruvian Rubber Crime*. London: Anti-Slavery and Aborigines' Protection Society, 1912.

Harris, Peter James. "From the Putumayo to Connemara: Roger Casement's Amazon Voyage of Discovery." *ABEI Journal* 4 (2002): 131–38.

Healy, David Frank. *Drive to Hegemony: The United States in the Caribbean, 1898–1917*. Madison: University of Wisconsin Press, 1988.

Henson, Herbert Hensley. *Retrospect of an Unimportant Life*, volume 1. Oxford, UK: Oxford University Press, 1942.

Herlihy, David. *Bicycle: The History*. New Haven: Yale University Press, 2004.

Hirshfield, Claire. "Truth." In Alvin Sullivan, ed. *British Literary Magazines: The Victorian and Edwardian Age, 1837–1913*. London: Greenwood, 1984. Pp. 423–32.

Hispano, Cornelio. *De París al Amazonas: las fieras del Putumayo*. Paris: Libreria Paul Ollendorff, 1914.

Hochschild, Adam. *King Leopold's Ghost: A Story of Greed, Terror, and Heroism in Colonial Africa*. New York: Houghton Mifflin, 1998.

Hvalkof, Søren. "Outrage in Rubber and Oil: Extractivism, Indigenous Peoples, and Justice in the Upper Amazon." In Charles Zerner, ed. *People, Plants, and Justice: The Politics of Nature Conservancy*. New York: Columbia University Press, 2000. Pp. 83–116.

Inglis, Brian. *Roger Casement*. London: Hodder and Stoughton, 1973.

Ireland, Gordon. *Boundaries, Possessions, and Conflicts in South America*. Cambridge: Harvard University Press, 1938.

Jackson, Joe. *The Thief at the End of the World: Rubber, Power, and the Seeds of Empire*. London: Duckworth, 2008.

Jarrell, Jan. "'A Tremendous Fascination': Medicine and Exploration in the South American Travel Narratives of Herbert Spencer Dickey, 1900–1925." Unpublished paper, 2001.

Jeanne, Olivier. "Monetary Policy in England 1893–1914: A Structural VAR Analysis." *Explorations in Economic History* 32 (1995): 302–26.

John, Arthur H. *A Liverpool Merchant House*. London: Allen and Unwin, 1959.

Johnson, Howard. "Barbadian Migrants in the Putumayo District of the Amazon, 1904–11." In Mary Chamberlain, ed. *Caribbean Migration: Globalised Identities*. London: Routledge, 1998. Pp. 177–87.

Karno, Howard L. "Augusto B. Leguía: The Oligarchy and the Modernization of Peru, 1870–1930." Ph.D. thesis, University of California, Los Angeles, 1970.

_____. "Julio César Arana, Frontier Cacique in Peru." In Robert Kern, ed. *The Caciques: Oligarchical Politics and the System of Caciquismo in the Luso-Hispanic World*. Albuquerque: University of New Mexico Press, 1973. Pp. 89–98.

Kiernan, Ben. *Blood and Soil: A World History of Genocide and Extermination from Sparta to Darfur*. New Haven: Yale University Press, 2007.

Klarén, Peter F. "The Origins of Modern Peru, 1880–1930." In Leslie Bethell, ed. *The Cambridge History of Latin America, Volume V c.1870 to 1930*. Cambridge, UK: Cambridge University Press, 1986. Pp. 587–640.

Knight, Allan. "Debt Bondage in Latin America." In Léonie J. Archer, ed. *Slavery and Other Forms of Unfree Labour*. London: Routledge, 1988. Pp. 102–17.

Lagos, Ovidio. *Arana, rey del caucho*. Buenos Aires: Emecé, 2005.

Landaburu, Jon, and Roberto Pineda Camacho. *Tradiciones de la gente del hacha: mitología de los indios andoques del Amazonas*. Bogotá: Instituto Caro y Cuevo, UNESCO, 1984.

Larrabure y Correa, Carlos. *Perú y Colombia en el Putumayo*. Barcelona: Imp. Vinda de L. Tasso, 1913.

Lawrence, James Cooper. *The World's Struggle with Rubber 1905–1931*. New York: Harper and Brothers, 1931.

Loadman, John. *Tears of the Tree: The Story of Rubber*. Oxford, UK: Oxford University Press, 2005.

Louis, William Roger. "Roger Casement and the Congo." *Journal of African History* 5 (1964): 99–120.

Louis, William Roger, and Jean Stengers, eds. *E. D. Morel's History of the Congo Reform Movement*. Oxford, UK: Clarendon Press, 1968.

McCartney, Sean, and A. J. Arnold. "'A Vast Aggregate of Avaricious and Flagitious Jobbing'? George Hudson and the Evolution of Early Notions of Directorial Responsibility." *Accounting, Business & Financial History* 11 (2001): 117–43.

McConnell, Anita. "La Condamine's Scientific Journey Down the River Amazon, 1743–1744." *Annals of Science* 48 (1991): 1–19.

McCormack, W. J. *Roger Casement in Death or Haunting the Free State*. Dublin: University College Dublin Press, 2002.

McDiarmid, Lucy. *The Irish Art of Controversy*. Ithaca: Cornell University Press, 2005.

McEvoy, Carmen. *La utopía republicana: ideales y realidades en la formación de la cultura política peruana, 1871–1919*. Lima: Pontificia Universidad Católica del Perú, Fondo Editorial, 1997.

McKenna, Terence. *True Hallucinations: Being an Account of the Author's Extraordinary Adventures in the Devil's Paradise*. London: Rider, 1994.

Martínez Riaza, Ascensión. "Política regional y gobierno de la Amazonía peruana." *Histórica* 23 (1999): 393–462.

Martins, Luciana. "Illusions of Power: Vision, Technology and the Geographical Exploration of the Amazon, 1924–1925." *Journal of Latin American Cultural Studies* 16 (2007): 285–307.

Miers, Suzanne. "Humanitarianism at Berlin: Myth or Reality?" In Stig Förster, Wolfgang J. Mommsen, and Ronald Robinson, eds. *Bismarck, Europe, and Africa: The Berlin Africa Conference, 1884–1885 and the Onset of Partition*. Oxford, UK: Oxford University Press, 1988. Pp. 333–45.

———. *Slavery and Antislavery in the Twentieth Century*. Oxford, UK: Rowman and Littlefield, 2002.

———. "Slavery and the Slave Trade as International Issues 1890–1939." *Slavery & Abolition* 19 (1998): 16–37.

Miller, Rory. "British Business in Peru: From the Pacific War to the Great Depression." In Nikolaus Böttcher and Bernd Hausberger, eds. *Dinero y negocios en la historia de América Latina*. Frankfurt am Main: Vervuert, 2000. Pp. 379–412.

———. "British Free-Standing Companies on the West Coast of South America." In Mira Wilkins and Harm Schröter. *The Free-Standing Company in the World Economy, 1830–1996*. Oxford, UK: Oxford University Press, 1998. Pp. 218–52.

Mitcham, Roderick Ellis. "The Geographies of Global Humanitarianism: The Anti-Slavery Society and Aborigines' Protection Society, 1884–1933." Ph.D. thesis, University of London, 2002.

Mitchell, Angus, ed. *The Amazon Journal of Roger Casement*. London: Anaconda, 1997.

———. *Casement*. London: Haus Publishing, 2003.

BIBLIOGRAPHY

_____. "'An Irish Putumayo': Roger Casement's Humanitarian Relief Campaign Among the Connemara Islanders 1913–14." *Irish Economic and Social History* 31 (2004): 41–60.

_____. "John Bull's Other Empire: Roger Casement and the Press, 1898–1916." In Simon J. Potter, ed. *Newspapers and Empire in Ireland and Britain, c.1857–1921.* Dublin: Irish Manuscripts Commission, 2004. Pp. 217–33.

_____. "New Light on the 'Heart of Darkness.'" *History Today* 49 (1999): 20–27.

_____. "Roger Casement in Africa: An Archaeology of Resistance to the Acts of Berlin and Brussels & the Origins of the Congo Reform Association 1884–1904." Ph.D. thesis, University of Limerick, 2004.

_____. *Sir Roger Casement's Heart of Darkness: The 1911 Documents.* Dublin: Irish Manuscripts Commission, 2003.

Moen, Jon, and Ellis Tallman. "The Bank Panic of 1907: The Role of the Trust Companies." *Journal of Economic History* 52 (1992): 611–30.

Mörner, Magnus. "The Expulsion of the Jesuits from Spain and Spanish America in 1767 in Light of Eighteenth-Century Regalism." *The Americas* 23 (1996): 156–64.

Morrison, Tony, Ann Brown, and Anne Rose, eds. *Lizzie: A Victorian Lady's Amazon Adventure.* London: British Broadcasting Corporation, 1985.

Mullen, Patrick. "Roger Casement's Global English: From Human Rights to the Homoerotic." *Public Culture* 15 (2003): 559–78.

Negro, Sandra, and Manuel M. Marzal, eds. *Un reino en la frontera: las misiones jesuitas en la América colonial.* Lima: Pontificia Universidad Católica del Perú, Fondo Editorial, 1999.

Neilson, Keith. "'Control the Whirlwind': Sir Edward Grey as Foreign Secretary, 1906–16." In T. G. Otte. *The Makers of British Foreign Policy: From Pitt to Thatcher.* Basingstoke, UK: Palgrave, 2002. Pp. 128–49.

Newton, Velma. *The Silver Men: West Indian Labour Migration to Panama, 1850–1914.* Kingston, Jamaica: Institute of Social and Economic Research, University of the West Indies, 1984.

Nworah, Kenneth D. "The Aborigines' Protection Society, 1889–1909: A Pressure-Group in Colonial Policy." *Canadian Journal of African Studies* 5 (1971): 79–91.

O' Callaghan, Margaret. "'With the Eyes of Another Race, Of a People Once Hunted Themselves': Casement, Colonialism and a Remembered Past." In D. George Boyce and Alan O'Day, eds. *Ireland in Transition, 1867–1921.* London: Routledge, 2004. Pp. 159–75.

Olarte Camacho, Vicente. *Los convenios con el Perú.* Bogotá: Imp. Eléctrica, 1911.

_____. *Las crueldades en el Putumayo en el Caquetá,* 1st edition. Bogotá: Imp. Eléctrica, 1910.

Ortega Díaz, Alfredo. *Ferrocarriles colombianos.* Bogotá: Imp. Nacional, 1920–49.

Orton, James. *The Andes and the Amazon or, Across the Continent of South America.* New York: Harper, 1876.

Osborne, Emily Lynn. "'Rubber Fever,' Commerce and French Colonial Rule in Upper Guinée, 1890–1913." *Journal of African History* 45 (2004): 445–65.

Osborne, John B. "Wilfred G. Thesiger, Sir Edward Grey, and the British Campaign to Reform the Congo, 1905–9." *Journal of Imperial and Commonwealth History* 27 (1999): 59–80.

Ó Síocháin, Séamas. "Roger Casement, Ethnography, and the Putumayo." *Eire* 29 (1994): 29–41.

_____. *Roger Casement: Imperialist, Rebel, Revolutionary*. Dublin: Lilliput Press, 2008.

Ó Síocháin, Séamas, and Michael O'Sullivan. *The Eyes of Another Race: Roger Casement's Congo Report and 1903 Diary*. Dublin: University College Dublin Press, 2003.

Palmer, Alison. "Colonial and Modern Genocide: Explanations and Categories." *Ethnic and Racial Studies* 21 (1998): 89–115.

Paredes, Rómulo. "Peruvian Rubber and International Politics." *American Review of Reviews* 46 (September 1912): 325–28.

Paternoster, G. Sidney. *The Lords of the Devil's Paradise*. London: S. Paul and Co., 1913.

Pennano, Guido. *La economía del caucho*. Iquitos: Centro de Estudios Teológicos de la Amazonía, 1988.

Philip, Kavita. "Imperial Science Rescues a Tree: Global Botanic Networks, Local Knowledge and the Transcontinental Transplantation of Cinchona." *Environment and History* 1 (1995): 173–200.

Pineda Camacho, Roberto. "El Comercio infame: el Parlamento Británico y la Casa Cauchera Peruana (Casa Arana)." *Boletín de Historia y Antigüedades* 89 (2002): 379–99.

_____. "Historia oral de una maloca sitiada en el Amazonas—aspectos de la rebelión de Yarocamena contra la Casa Arana." *Anuario Colombiano de Historia Social y de la Cultura* 16–17 (1988): 163–82.

_____. *Holocausto en el Amazonas: una historia social de la Casa Arana*. Bogotá: Planeta Colombiana Editorial, 2000.

_____. "Novelistas y etnógrafos en el infierno de la Casa Arana." *Boletín de Historia y Antigüedades* 91 (2004): 485–522.

_____. "Les orphelins de *La Vorágine*: mémoire, holocauste cauchero et reconstruction culturelle indigène dans le moyen Caquetá (Amazonie colombienne)." Ph.D. thesis, Université de la Sorbonne Nouvelle Paris III, 2006.

Porter, Andrew. "Sir Roger Casement and the International Humanitarian Movement." *Journal of Imperial and Commonwealth History* 29 (2001): 59–74.

Quiroz, Alfonso W. "Redes de alta corrupción en el Perú: poder y venalidad desde el Virrey Amat a Montesinos." *Revista de Indias* 66 (2006): 237–48.

Ramasastry, Anita. "Corporate Complicity: From Nuremberg to Rangoon. An Examination of Forced Labor Cases and Their Impact on the Liability of Multinational Companies." *Berkeley Journal of International Law* 20 (2002): 91–159.

Reeve, Mary-Elizabeth. "Regional Interaction in the Western Amazon: The Early Colonial Encounter and the Jesuit Years: 1538–1767. *Ethnohistory* 41 (1993): 106–38.

Reid, B. L. *The Lives of Roger Casement*. New Haven: Yale University Press, 1976.

Resor, Randolph R. "Rubber in Brazil: Dominance and Collapse, 1876–1945." *Business History Review* 51 (1977): 341–66.

BIBLIOGRAPHY

Rey de Castro, Carlos. *Los escándalos del Putumayo: carta abierta dirigida a Mr. Geo B. Michell consul de S.M.B.* Barcelona: Imp. Vinda de L. Tasso, 1913.

_____. *Los escándalos del Putumayo: carta al director del* Daily News & Leader, *de Londres.* Barcelona: Imp. Vinda de L. Tasso, 1913.

_____. *Los pobladores del Putumayo.* Barcelona: Imp. Vinda de L. Tasso, 1914.

Reyes, Rafael. *Memorias, 1850–1885.* Bogotá: Fondo Cultural Cafetero, 1986.

Ribeill, George. "From Pneumatics to Highway Logistics: André Michelin, Instigator of the 'Automobile Revolution.' " *History and Technology* 8 (1992): 193–216.

Ribemont, Francis, ed. *Jules Robuchon 1840–1922: imagier de la Vendée et du Poitou.* Bordeaux: Horizon Chimérique, 1999.

Ricard, Serge. "The Roosevelt Corollary." *Presidential Studies Quarterly* 36 (2006): 17–26.

Rippy, J. Fred. "Dawn of the Railway Era in Colombia." *Hispanic American Historical Review* 22 (1943): 650–63.

Ritchie, Andrew. *King of the Road.* London: Wildwood House, 1975.

Rivera, José Eustasio. *The Vortex.* Translated by Earle K. James. Bogotá: Panamericana Editorial, 2001.

Roberts, G. W. "Emigration from the Island of Barbados." *Social and Economic Studies* 4 (1955): 245–88.

Robuchon, Eugenio. *En el Putumayo y sus afluentes.* Lima: Imp. La Industria, 1907.

Romero, Fernando. *Iquitos y la fuerza naval de la Amazonía (1830–1933).* Lima: Dirección General de Intereses Marítimos, Ministerio de Marina, 1983.

Rosenberg, Emily S. *Financial Missionaries to the World: The Politics and Culture of Dollar Diplomacy, 1900–1930.* Cambridge: Harvard University Press, 1999.

Rosenzweig, Alfredo. "Judíos en la Amazonía peruana, 1870–1949." *Maj'Shavot* 12 (1967): 19–30.

Roth, Andreas. " 'The German Soldier Is Not Tactful': Sir Roger Casement and the Irish Brigade in Germany during the First World War." *Irish Sword* 19 (1995): 313–32.

Roux, Jean-Claude. *L'Amazonie péruvienne: un eldorado dévoré par la forêt 1821–1910.* Paris: L'Harmattan, 1994.

Ruiz, Jean L. "Civilized People in Uncivilized Places: Rubber, Race, and Civilization during the Amazonian Rubber Boom." M.A. thesis, University of Saskatchewan, 2006.

Salisbury, Richard V. "Great Britain, the United States, and the 1909–1910 Nicaraguan Crisis." *The Americas* 53 (1997): 379–94.

San Román, Jesús Victor. *Perfiles históricos de la Amazonía peruana.* Lima: Ediciones Paulinas, 1975.

Santos-Granero, Fernando, and Frederica Barclay. *Tamed Frontiers: Economy, Society, and Civil Rights in Upper Amazonia.* Oxford, UK: Westview, 2000.

Satre, Jowell Joseph. *Chocolate on Trial: Slavery, Politics, and the Ethics of Business.* Athens: Ohio University Press, 2005.

Sawyer, Roger. *Casement: The Flawed Hero.* London: Routledge and Kegan Paul, 1984.

————. *Roger Casement's Diaries 1910: The Black and the White*. London: Pimlico, 1997.

Scholes, Walter V., and Marie V. Scholes. "The United States and Ecuador, 1909–1913." *The Americas* 19 (1963): 276–90.

Schultes, Richard Evans. "Lacticiferous Plants of the Karaparaná-Igaraparaná Region of Colombia." *Acta Botanica Neerlandica* 15 (1966): 178–89.

Segal, Ariel. *Jews of the Amazon: Self-Exile in Paradise*. Philadelphia: Jewish Publication Society, 1999.

Serier, Jean-Baptiste. *Les Barons du caoutchouc*. Paris: Karthala, 2000.

Sharma, Bhavna. *Contemporary Forms of Slavery in Peru*. London: Anti-Slavery International, 2006.

Simson, Alfred. *Travels in the Wilds of Ecuador: and the Exploration of the Putumayo River*. London: Sampson Low, Marston, Searle, and Rivington, 1886.

Singleton-Gates, Peter, and Maurice Girodais. *The Black Diaries: An Account of Roger Casement's Life and Times with a Collection of his Diaries and Public Writings*. Paris: Olympia Press, 1959.

Sliwinski, Sharon. "The Childhood of Human Rights: The Kodak on the Congo." *Journal of Visual Culture* 5 (2006): 333–63.

Smith, Anthony. *Explorers of the Amazon*. London: Viking, 1990.

Souza, Márcio. *Silvino Santos: o cineasta do ciclo do borracha*. Rio de Janeiro: FUNARTE, 1999.

Stanfield, Michael Edward. *Red Rubber, Bleeding Trees: Violence, Slavery and Empire in Northwest Amazonia, 1850–1933*. Albuquerque: University of New Mexico Press, 1998.

Steiner, Zara. *The Foreign Office and Foreign Policy, 1898–1914*. Cambridge, UK: Cambridge University Press, 1969.

Stengers, Jean. "King Leopold's Congo, 1886–1908." In Roland Oliver and G. N. Sanderson, eds. *The Cambridge History of Africa*, volume 6. Cambridge, UK: Cambridge University Press, 1985. Pp. 315–58.

————. "Leopold II and the *Association Internationale du Congo*." In Stig Förster, Wolfgang J. Mommsen, and Ronald Robinson, eds. *Bismarck, Europe, and Africa: The Berlin Africa Conference, 1884–1885 and the Onset of Partition*. Oxford, UK: Oxford University Press, 1988. Pp. 229–44.

Steward, Julian H. "The Witotoan Tribes." In Julian H. Steward, ed. *Handbook of South American Indians*, volume 3. Washington, D.C.: GPO, 1948. Pp. 749–62.

Stone, Dan. "The Historiography of Genocide: Beyond 'Uniqueness' and Ethnic Competition." *Rethinking History* 8 (2004): 127–42.

Swaisland, Charles. "The Aborigines Protection Society, 1837–1909." *Slavery & Abolition* 21 (2000): 265–80.

Taussig, Michael. "Culture of Terror—Space of Death: Roger Casement's Putumayo Report and the Explanation of Torture." *Comparative Studies in Society and History* 26 (1984): 467–97.

_____. *Shamanism, Colonialism, and the Wild Man*. Chicago: University of Chicago Press, 1987.

Thomas-Hope, Elizabeth M. "The Establishment of a Migration Tradition: British West Indian Movements to the Hispanic Caribbean in the Century After Emancipation." In Colin G. Clarke, ed. *Caribbean Social Relations*. Liverpool: Centre for Latin-American Studies, University of Liverpool, 1978. Pp. 66–81.

Thompson, Andrew S. "The Language of Imperialism and the Meanings of Empire: Imperial Discourse in British Politics, 1895–1914." *Journal of British Studies* 36 (1997): 147–77.

Thomson, Norman. *The Putumayo Red Book*. London: N. Thomson and Co., 1914.

Townshend, Charles. *Easter 1916: The Irish Rebellion*. London: Allen Lane, 2005.

Triana, Miguel. *Por el sur de Colombia*. Bogotá: Ministerio de Educación Nacional, 1950.

Turner, John Kenneth. *Barbarous Mexico*. Chicago: Charles H. Kerr and Co., 1911.

Turvasi, Francesco. *Giovanni Genocchi and the Indians of South America, 1911–1913*. Rome: Editrice Pontificia Universitá Gregoriana, 1988.

Ure, John. *Trespassers on the Amazon*. London: Constable, 1986.

Valcárcel, Carlos A. *El proceso del Putumayo y sus secretos inauditos*. Lima: Impr. Comercial de Horacio La Rosa, 1915.

Vale da Costa, Selda. *Eldorado das ilusões. Cinema & sociedade: Manaus (1897/1935)*. Manaus, Brazil: Editora da Universidade do Amazonas, 1996.

Vale da Costa, Selda, and Narcisco Júlio Freire Lobo. *No rastro de Silvino Santos*. Manaus, Brazil: SCA/Edições Governo do Estado, 1987.

Veeser, Cyrus. "Inventing Dollar Diplomacy: The Gilded-Age Origins of the Roosevelt Corollary to the Monroe Doctrine." *Diplomatic History* 27 (2003): 301–26.

Wagner De Reyna, Alberto. *Historia diplomática del Perú, 1900–1945*. Lima: Ediciones Peruanas, 1964.

Ward, Herbert. *A Voice from the Congo*. London: William Heinemann, 1910.

Weber, Gary. "Henry Labouchere, *Truth* and the New Journalism of Late Victorian Britain." *Victorian Periodicals Review* 26 (1993): 36–43.

Weinstein, Barbara. *The Amazon Rubber Boom, 1850–1920*. Palo Alto: Stanford University Press, 1983.

Weisbord, Robert G. "The King, the Cardinal and the Pope: Leopold II's Genocide in the Congo and the Vatican." *Journal of Genocide Research* 5 (2003): 35–45.

Werner, Louis. "All Aboard to Nowhere: The Mad Mary," *Américas* 42 (1990): 6–17.

Whiffen, Thomas. *The North-West Amazons: Notes of Some Months Spent Among Cannibal Tribes*. London: Constable and Co., 1915.

_____. "A Short Account of the Indians of the Issa-Japura District (South America)." *Folklore* 24 (1913): 41–62.

Wolf, Howard, and Ralph Wolf. *Rubber: A Story of Glory and Greed*. New York: Covici, Friede, 1936.

Wood, Bryce. *Aggression and History: The Case of Ecuador and Peru*. Ann Arbor: University Microfilms International, 1978.

Woodroffe, Joseph F. *The Rubber Industry of the Amazon and How Its Supremacy Can Be Maintained*. London: Unwin, 1915.

———. *The Upper Reaches of the Amazon*. London: Methuen and Co. Ltd., 1914.

Wylie, Lesley L. "Colonial Tropes and Post-Colonial Tricks: Rewriting the Tropics in the *Novella de la Selva*." Ph.D. thesis, University of Cambridge, 2007.

Yepez, Benjamín, and Roberto Pineda Camacho. "La rabia de Yarocamena." *Tolima* 2 (1985): 29–59.

Yungjohann, John C. *White Gold: The Diary of a Rubber Cutter in the Amazon 1906–1916*. Oracle, AZ: Synergetic Press, 1989.

Zook, David H., Jr. "The Spanish Arbitration of the Ecuador-Peru Dispute." *The Americas* 20 (1964): 359–75.

Zumaeta, Pablo. *Las cuestiones del Putumayo*. Barcelona: Imp. Vinda de L. Tasso, 1913.

ACKNOWLEDGMENTS

In researching and writing this book, I have benefited enormously from the generous support and assistance of many people and institutions. I would now like to thank them, each and every one.

In the United Kingdom: Cordelia Sealy, Eric Hirsch, Alan Knight, Steve Nugent, Rosario Flores, Tabitha Cadbury, Luciana Martins, Roger Sawyer, Lesley Wylie, Rob Burroughs, Rory Miller, Ruth Bloom, Ben Buchan, John Loadman, Stephen Hugh-Jones, and Frank Dobson MP. In Ireland: Anthony McElligott and Séamas Ó Síocháin. In the United States: Vaughan Stanley, Larry Youngman, César Cornejo, Henry Lovejoy, Adam Hochschild, Michael Stanfield, Steve Topik, Michael Dove, David Hebb, Brad Barham, Zephyr Frank, Jan Jarrell, Robert Brandt, Marie Arana, Wade Davis, Miguel Pinedo-Vasquez, Miranda Mollendorf, Glenn Penny, and Janet Browne. In Canada: Paul Lovejoy and Oliver Coomes. In France: Matthias Dörries, Arouna Ouedraogo, Jorge Gasché, and Francis Ribemont. In Germany: Michael Kraus and Paul Hempel. In Panama: Fernando Santos-Granero. In Venezuela: Ariel Segal. In Colombia: Augusto Gómez, Jaime Arocha, Juan Alvaro Echeverri, and Cindy Katherine Avendaño. In Peru: Alberto Chirif, Flica Barclay, and Pepe Barletti. In Brazil: Márcio Souza, Selda Vale da Costa, Carlos Rojas, Aurelio Michiles, Andreas Valentin, and William Cajueiro.

The staffs of the libraries and archives I consulted were exemplary, and I would like to thank them for their support and valuable time. In the United Kingdom: University College London Library (particularly Interlending and Document Supply services); the National Archives, Kew; the Bodleian Library of Commonwealth and African

ACKNOWLEDGMENTS

Studies at Rhodes House, Oxford (particularly Lucy McCann); the British Library of Economics and Political Science, London; the British Library, London; the Royal Botanic Gardens, Kew; the British Museum, London; the Liverpool Record Office; the World Museum Liverpool (especially Joanna Ostapkowicz); the Royal Anthropological Institute, London; the Pitt Rivers Museum, Oxford; and the Public Record Office of Northern Ireland, Belfast. In Ireland: the National Library of Ireland and Birr Castle Archives, Birr (especially the Earl of Rosse). In the United States: the National Archives and Records Administration, College Park, Maryland; the Houghton Library, Harvard University; the New York Public Library; and the National Anthropological Archives, Smithsonian Institution, Washington (especially Vyrtis Thomas). In France: Bibliothèque Nationale, Paris; Archives des Affaires Étrangères, Paris; and Centre des Archives Diplomatiques de Nantes. In Germany: the Philipps-Universität Marburg. In Portugal: Arquivo Regional de Madeira, Funchal (especially Maria da Cunha Paredes), and Serviço de Arquivo Histórico Diplomático, Ministerio dos Negócios Estrangeiros, Lisbon (especially Maria Isabel Fevereiro). In Colombia: Archivo General de la Nación, Bogotá. In Peru: Archivo Central Histórico, Ministerio de Relaciones Exteriores, Lima; Archivo Histórico de Límites, Ministerio de Relaciones Exteriores, Lima; and Biblioteca Amazonica, Iquitos. In Brazil: Museu Amazônico, Manaus.

Early in the preparation for this book I was fortunate in making contact (initially through Larry Youngman) with Mary Bressi. With great kindness she put me in touch with her mother-in-law, Deborah MacClosky, Walter Hardenburg's daughter, who generously invited me into her home, made me welcome as a member of the family, and shared her father's correspondence with me. I thank her so much. In France I was equally thrilled when Jean-Pierre Remaud of the Conservation Départementale des Musées de la Vendée in La Roche-sur-Yon introduced me to M. Georges Rondeau and his daughter, Mme Françoise Degois, who provided me with copies of Eugène Robuchon's correspondence and showed me their albums of the photographs he took while he was in Iquitos and the Putumayo. I thank them for their generosity to me.

When, in 2005, I first began weighing up the possibilities of this book, my friend Tony McElligott put me in touch with Angus Mitchell, who had done a great deal of work on Roger Casement, focusing especially on his time in the Congo and the Putumayo. Out of this came a series of articles and books, all of which I fully acknowledge in the bibliography. Without this material I would have found the research for this book much more difficult. For this I thank Angus, but also for much more than that, since he has been a constant source of support, inspiration, and friendship over the years.

Will Francis, my agent, deserves a special mention not only because he believed in this book from the very beginning and found a home for it at Verso, but also because he has read and reread several drafts, thereby, in the process, making the book much better than it would have been otherwise. Thanks, too, to Anna Stein for her support and encouragement and for getting this book to Farrar, Straus and Giroux.

Tom Penn, my editor at Verso, and Gena Hamshaw, my editor at Farrar, Straus and Giroux, guaranteed by their careful and creative reading of the manuscript that it could only become better. I hope they feel that their efforts were rewarded. Staff at both publishers have done brilliantly in getting this book into its final shape.

The Society of Authors generously supported the costs of a research trip to the United States and South America.

My final and biggest thanks goes to my partner, Dallas Sealy, who has lived through and contributed so very much to this book, all the while with wonderful love and support. No one can ask for more than that.

INDEX